A
Challenge
for the Actor

Uta Hagen

A Robert Stewart Book
SCRIBNER

SCRIBNER
1230 Avenue of the Americas
New York, NY 10020

Copyright © 1991 by Uta Hagen.

All rights reserved,
including the right of reproduction
in whole or in part in any form.

SCRIBNER and design are trademarks of Macmillan Library Reference USA, Inc.,
used under license by Simon & Schuster, the publisher of this work.

Manufactured in the United States of America

20 19 18 17 16

Library of Congress Cataloging-in-Publication Data

Hagen, Uta.
    A challenge for the actor / Uta Hagen.
        p. cm.
    Includes index.
    ISBN 0-684-19040-0
    1. Acting.   I. Title.
PN2061.H27 1991
792'.028—dc20   91-15782
                                                            CIP

In memory of Herbert,
my inspiritor

CONTENTS

Part Three: The Exercises

Part Four: The Role

ACKNOWLEDGMENTS,
AN APOLOGY,
AND A LITTLE ADVICE

I've always thought that acknowledgments belong at the end because it is only after I have enjoyed a book very much that I am interested in knowing who helped bring it about. However, I will adhere to convention and offer my thanks at the beginning.

In my earlier book, *Respect for Acting,* whenever doubts arose about the scientific validity of my explanations or pronouncements about human motivation and its psychological causes, I consulted Dr. Jacques Palaci. At the time, he assured me that most of my theories (which were based solely on intuition and personal life experience) were sound. The clarifications he provided in other areas are still credited to him in this book. In *A Challenge for the Actor* I have deepened and expanded my explorations of human behavior and, since Dr. Palaci has long since moved to Paris, I was fortunate to become acquainted with the noted New York psychologist and psychiatrist, Dr. Harvey White. I want to thank him for his invaluable help and enlightenment. Although we were not always in total agreement, he said he was eventually "comfortable" with my conclusions.

Without the back-breaking efforts of my student Jane Flanagan, this book would probably have taken six years to write instead of four. Late into the nights, after her other job, she retyped each messy page I handed her, correctly interpreting my scribbled notes and additions in the margins and in between the lines. I was then able to read her cleaned-up version and test its content on my classes. I am also grateful to the students who listened to each new chapter. By their questions, expressions of edification, and delight, they assured me that I was on the right path. Their puzzlement or confusion resulted in many fruitful revisions. These same students became willing guinea pigs when trying out the new exercises, thereby giving substance to their validity.

When I was finally able to present a completed, spanking-clean script to my editor, Robert Stewart, he brilliantly messed it up again with his many suggestions, for which I am deeply grateful. At this stage, my close friend, the playwright and computer whiz Jesse I. Feiler, stepped in to save me from the mountainous task of typing another fresh manuscript. He had it "scanned" by one computer, producing a disk which he then used in his own computer to enter the endless corrections. The result was something so beautiful that even Robert Stewart marveled. Jesse gets big hugs for this.

I now had my first personal experience with copy editors, those creatures who, on my previous books, were mainly responsible for correcting punctuation marks, grammar, syntax, paragraphing, repetitions, and the like. The thoroughness and nature of the work done by Carole McCurdy and Linda Epstein astounded me. I never met Ms. Epstein but I sat elbow to elbow for several days with Carole McCurdy as she explained their markings and revisions. Rearrangements and rewritten sentences were always better than mine. I thank them with all my heart, particularly for finally accepting my use of capitalizations and bold type as a means of emphasizing all the things I usually need to repeat ten times to actors in class, of stressing the content that I believe is at the heart of acting and the actor's problems— something that in the reading might otherwise be skimmed over.

My apologies to feminists who may take offense at continual references to members of the profession as "the actor" and "he." They must understand how tedious it would be if I always had to mention both sexes—"he or she," "the actor or actress." I call myself an actor, rarely an actress, and think of myself as a member of mankind—not of personkind. Ladies are definitely included.

The content of this book is meant to be put into practice. It will be of best service to those actors who patiently test its proposals step by step over a period of years. It cannot be assimilated or absorbed in a gulp. And theorizing without action is most often burdensome or confusing, leading to unsubstantiated opinions.

PROLOGUE:
WHAT DOES IT TAKE?

It takes talent. TALENT is defined in the dictionary as "the natural endowment of a person with special or creative aptitudes." In an actor, I believe, these endowments consist of high sensitivity and responsiveness to sight, sound, touch, taste, and smell, of exceptional sensitivity to others, of being easily moved by beauty and pain, and of having a soaring imagination without losing control of reality. Once one is blessed with these endowments, it takes AN UNSHAKABLE DESIRE TO BE AN ACTOR together with A NEED TO EXPRESS what one has sensed and felt in the concrete terms of the characters with whom one will identify on stage. The need to express should not be confused with vanity or a kind of "Look at me, here I am!" egotism, which is so prevalent in the theatre. Nor should sensitivity be confused with neuroses or their personal display.

Theoretically, the actor ought to be more sound in mind and body than other people, since he learns to understand the psychological problems of human beings when putting his own passions, his loves, fears, and rages to work in the service of the characters he plays. He will learn to face himself, to hide nothing from himself—and to do so takes AN INSATIABLE CURIOSITY ABOUT THE HUMAN CONDITION.

It takes A SOUND BODY, as well developed and cared for as that of an athlete. It takes A TRAINED VOICE, as flexible as that of a singer, and FINE STANDARD SPEECH which must be developed for use in all the dramatic literature that makes greater demands on him than the regional speech with which he began his life.

When a God-given or genetically inherited talent exists, the would-be actor must face the fact that it is of little use without the TENACITY AND DISCIPLINE it takes to make something of the talent.

To be more than an adequate or serviceable actor, it takes A BROAD EDUCATION in the liberal arts. If this has not been provided for, remember that once you can read, you can educate yourself in the understanding of human beings and the social conditions under which man has struggled throughout history by reading not just dramatic literature, but also masters of the novel and the endless biographies that substantiate faith in the realities of the past. Your feet can take you to museums, galleries, libraries, theatres, concerts, and dance performances. Your need for enlightenment will increase as you realize the ways in which these sources stimulate your own creative drives.

I wrote a memoir, *Sources,* for my granddaughter in response to her curiosity about what had made me an actress. I also clarified for myself the things that had been essential to my work. The advantages of my heritage, for which I can take no credit, my parents' influence on my first seventeen years, the development of a work ethic, the values I assimilated—all the things which were important to my artistic growth and still sustain me today—were extraordinary, and I'm aware that not everyone has been as lucky. Nevertheless, a little information about these "sources" may be of value to you.

I was born after World War I in Göttingen, one of the oldest university towns in Germany. Its cobbled streets and medieval architecture made it easy to identify with the realities of life in the Middle Ages. Our tall brick house with "my" beautiful garden in back stood near the meadows, woods, and streams, the hills and valleys rolling at the outskirts of the town. Almost daily roamings through them yielded discoveries that rivaled those made in the garden and at the seashore where we spent the summers. The recall of the visions, sounds, smells, and textures of my childhood serves my acting to this day. My mother was always near enough to be shown a newfound shell or pebble or flower, to answer questions, and to urge me on to other explorations.

In our home art and creativity were the religion, and God existed only insofar as He might be responsible for them. History was explored to lead to an understanding of man's struggle to overcome the problems of society. It was up to us to learn to appreciate and grasp the miracle of the artist producing for his community, how he left an imprint on each successive epoch while rebelling against the status quo, to learn from the artist's attempt to enlighten and offer food for man's soul.

My Welsh-German father, the son of a violinist, had been an actor in his teens, a composer and musicologist in his twenties, and eventually he became a professor of art history.

During the First World War, as a result of illness that kept him out of the army and a lack of students because so many had to serve, my father was left with much free time. So he unearthed the scores of Handel's operas, which hadn't been performed since the composer's death, edited them, and translated them into German. After the war, he produced and conducted them, founding the soon to be renowned Göttingen Handel Festivals. My Danish mother was a soprano and sang such roles as Rhodelinde, Cleopatra, and Teofane at these festivals. I remember attending a dress rehearsal at the age of three, seated in someone's lap in a loge. I *still* shiver with pleasure whenever I sit in a loge today. I'm also told that I toddled around humming and singing Handel's melodies before I could speak in sentences.

In the mid-1920s, Germany was caught in inflation, unemployment, and dire social unrest, so my father gladly accepted the offer to come to the United States to chair the art history department at the University of Wisconsin in Madison. I was six years old when I experienced my first pain at leave-taking from friends, relatives, familiar rooms, and landscapes, and from my garden. I cried because the grown-ups cried and shared their foreboding of something forever lost. Nevertheless, my heart pounded as each new adventure confronted me. I must have begun role-playing at this time; I remember the ride to the boat train in my aunt's Mercedes-Benz, an open car in which even the leather seats smelled of luxury. As we drove through the villages, I "acted" to the manner born, waving to passersby as though I were a princess.

I was rarely consciously unhappy in Madison, but deep down I felt uprooted and alienated by the differences between the values of our family and those of the others in this community of the Middle West. I had no problem with the new language, which I seem to have absorbed rather than learned, but among my schoolmates I was always considered "odd"—from the time I arrived until I left Madison for good at seventeen. Even my parents seemed strange to my peers because they didn't belong to the country club, play bridge or golf, or otherwise involve themselves in the typical social life of the town. They managed to make friends among some of the faculty who shared their interests, but I had only one real friend in grammar school and another in high school with whom I felt a close affinity. I'm sure that many artists share this sense of estrangement as children, which turns them to the life of their imagination as fed by literature, music, painting, and the performing arts.

Reading was considered as important as eating in our house. Lively and impassioned debates took place, usually around the dinner table, about the merits of William Faulkner, Virginia Woolf, Willa Cather, Ernest Hemingway, Thomas Mann, etc. Disagreement was encouraged because it led to the forming of one's own opinions. My father sometimes gave seminars to his students in our home and by eavesdropping I learned a great deal, even about the evaluation of a work of art—not to accept it simply because it was famous. I was never barred from adult discussions provided I didn't create a disturbance. If things were over my head or I grew restless, I simply went about my own business.

After my determination to become an actress set in (which took place upon seeing a performance of Elizabeth Bergner's Saint Joan when I was nine), I read as many actors' biographies as I could lay my hands on: Duse, Bernhardt, Bergner, Basserman, Kean, Booth, Barrymore, etc. My parents plied me with a history of the theatre and with plays. By the time I was fifteen I had read, if not grasped, most of the classics by Goethe, Molière, Schiller, Shakespeare, Shaw, Lessing, Hauptmann, O'Neill, Ibsen, Strindberg, Chekhov, etc. I remember being given a fancy makeup box and a book of illustrations, how I made up for hours on end as an Oriental, a clown, a ballerina, a Russian peasant. I remember the pleasure with which I confronted my transformed face in the mirror. Very important to my theatrical education were the years I spent in learning modern dance. My mother had been a student of Dalcroze at Hellerau and a fan of Mary Wigman, so she steered me to the fine dance department at the university, where I also worked with visiting teachers like Harald Kreutzberg and Hanya Holm. The kinetic agility and bodily freedom achieved in this art form is of value to every young (or old) actor.

xvi

Thus I was blessed with a home life crammed with more than eating, sleeping, studying, and doing chores. My brother played the fiddle, my mother taught singing and prepared for the lieder recitals she gave. My father composed, when he wasn't working on a new book, and I practiced the piano for hours each day. The Pro-Arte String Quartet used the good acoustics in our living room to practice chamber music, and I became familiar with their repertoire without leaving my house.

Then came the trips to Europe. My father had an arrangement with the university whereby he took six months' leave to do research for his books every three years in place of the customary sabbatical at the end of seven. During these trips we traveled together through Scandinavia, Belgium, Holland, Switzerland, Germany, France, and England. I had tutors and attended schools whenever we settled down in one place for a few months. My real lessons lay in the variety of cultures in which I partook. My role-playing developed and increased. Each palace was fuel for my imagination as I wandered through the rooms and gardens pretending to be queen, princess, lady-in-waiting, servant, mistress—whatever suited my fancy in making believe I lived at that place in a distant time. In cloisters, churches, cathedrals, I was a penitent, a martyr, a heretic, a member of the choir, a nun, a recluse. I was always stimulated by my father's vivid descriptions of the life of a painter, sculptor, architect, or artisan who had created the places we visited. (One discovered small obscene sculptures, for example, carved into the pillar of a church by an artist protesting the serfdom imposed on him by the ruling clergy or nobles who had commissioned his work.) I grasped in my very bones that people really *lived* in these buildings, allowing me to believe later on in the noncontemporary characters I played. I actually lived for a week in a castle on the Rhine belonging to a friend of the family. It was complete with moat, drawbridge, great stone halls, even a dungeon. Playing at knights and robbers became more than a game. My fantasies of living at a different time and place have never abated. Recently in Paris, at a visit to the Conciergerie, standing in Marie Antoinette's cell, I had an almost mystic sense of being there with her.

I admit that sometimes I had to be dragged through museums and galleries, preferring to be outside playing in an amusement park like the Tivoli Gardens in Copenhagen. But today I am as grateful for these experiences as I am for the hours I was made to practice the piano until it became a pleasure to play. Every extra penny was spent on theatre, ballets, operas, and concerts, and I heard and saw many of the great artists of that time. Some of them became my role models, and I was continually reminded by my parents that their achievements were based on dedication and discipline as intense as those required to become a priest or a nun. My developing work ethic sent me rushing from a piano lesson to a modern dance class, back home to read a play, downstairs to hear an opera on the radio, back upstairs to practice making up, finally plopping into bed with satisfied feelings of accomplishment. Or conversely, going to bed with a slightly sick feeling, if I had goofed off or wasted a day and missed a chance to learn or achieve something.

The examples given me by great artists and a growing awareness of the requirements and necessary dedication to one's field also introduced nagging doubts about my ability to fulfill these enormous responsibilities. Did I *really* have the strength or even the *desire* to be "like a nun," with the same kind of devotion to my calling? I had a great appetite for living, and the example of a happy family life in my own home did not let me exclude it from my dreams for the future. My mother encouraged my doubts, urging me to examine them fully. But every time I got a crush on someone or fell in love and dreamt of children and marriage, with the innocence of youth, I convinced myself that I could have it all. Periods of doubt never left me entirely, and conflicts arising between my personal and professional life made for a struggle lasting into my forties.

My last trip to Europe under my parents' wing occurred after my graduation from high school when I was sixteen. I attended the Royal Academy of Dramatic Art in London and felt more and more like an adult with my own room in a boarding house, coming and going as I chose between classes and my discoveries of the city. The parks and palaces, the Tower, Parliament, Windsor Castle, Westminster Abbey made the Elizabethans leap from the page. And I loved the notion of studying for my profession with classmates who shared my dreams even though the actual training was poor. At best it was academic, stressing the training of voice, speech, and movement, but I knew there was something wrong with being lined up against the barre to recite the speeches of Rosalind or Gertrude in unison with twenty others, with the same gestures and inflections.

As a consequence of this burst of freedom, of feeling on my own in the pursuit of a life in the theatre, it was extremely difficult to fulfill the promise to my parents to complete my education at the university in Madison. From February till June of 1937, while attending school, I balked, complained, and cried that I wanted to *act*, not to pursue science and mathematics, until they relented and with faith and encouragement let me try my wings in the East. My first "professional" audition resulted in my earning the role of Ophelia in Eva Le Gallienne's production of *Hamlet*, which rehearsed all summer in Westport, Connecticut, and was performed at Dennis, Massachusetts, on Cape Cod in late August.

It was a terrifying yet euphoric experience: terrifying because of the responsibility of having been entrusted with such a role, and euphoric because I was in a professional company in a great play under the tutelage of a person who shared my parents' ideals of theatre as an art form, as opposed to its being simply a commodity for entertainment or diversion. When the successful production was over, I returned with the other actors of the company to Westport to rehearse a series of plays for a proposed future repertory company. This venture collapsed after several months, and with a heavy heart I turned to New York City to look for work. In January 1938 I auditioned for Alfred Lunt and Lynn Fontanne and won the magnificent role of Nina in *The Sea Gull*, and so my Broadway career was launched.

Of course I was lucky, but what did I bring with me that made me (almost) ready for these roles? The background which my parents had given me, my education, a well-trained body, a sense of historic faith which let me wear the *clothes* of my characters rather than their costumes, a fairly decent voice, standard speech, and the *talent* of the amateur who still *believes* in the given circumstances of the play before this faith is short-circuited by the awareness of external professional skills. My tenacity saw me through the challenges presented by rehearsals and performances with the Lunts, although their discipline far exceeded mine. They ate, slept, and breathed the play and their roles. The attention to detail of even a few split seconds on stage was never-ending. You were expected at a rehearsal half an hour before it was scheduled and to be in your dressing room hours before the performance, every hairpin in place, every line on your eyebrow perfect. (As Miss Fontanne said, "You don't make up for someone with opera glasses in the balcony but for someone with opera glasses in the front row.") And your mind and spirit had to be sharply tuned in to the adventure of making each performance alive for that wonderful audience who had come to share the experience.

I think of the next nine years from the summer of 1938 until the spring of 1947 as the transitional years of my career, during which time I sadly became a Broadway "pro," a slick hack, during which I lost my way and a love of acting until I finally regained it to begin a true life in the theatre. During each of those years I played six to ten weeks of summer stock, even managing to butcher a few beautiful Shaw plays with only one week of rehearsal. I played in seven Broadway productions with actors like Paul Muni, José Ferrer (whom I shortly married), Paul Robeson, Alfred Drake, etc. I worked with directors such as Guthrie McClintic, Margaret Webster, and Marc Connelly. I toured extensively. In 1939, through the prodding of my agent, I almost gave in to the lure of Hollywood. Film stars were then still the victims of the large studios, which referred to them as members of their "stable." Actors were truly considered to be pieces of merchandise and had no voice in the choice of films in which they were contracted to play or the roles assigned to them, all of which was too much for my need to determine my own destiny. (Years later when John Houseman once chided me for not becoming a member of his "stable" of actors at Stratford, Connecticut, I assured him that I was not a horse.)

At twenty-one, I had a child and a house in the country. It wasn't just the pull between a career and motherhood that confused me, but rather the state of my acting. I had been strongly influenced by the Broadway scene, the "lingo," and the work habits that surrounded me. Once I had left the Lunts, I became enmeshed in a professionalism that is based on external shapes and styles, tricks used to shape a performance almost at the first rehearsal. This resulted in the kind of acceptable clichés I had already rejected when I saw them on stage as a child. It was deemed "professional" to be able to tell a joke in the wings just before making an entrance in a serious scene, never to seem to take the whole thing too seriously, to falsely accelerate tempos, to carefully place your laugh lines, to push for a theatrical energy, or to hush your voice for effective audience attention, to throw back your head on an exit to guarantee applause, to glide across the stage in a costume, to drape yourself charmingly across the arm of a sofa instead of sitting in it. I was always a good mimic and picked up such externals with ease. I wondered if I had learned all there was to learn. I got great reviews, I was "starred" on the marquee, and still I was left with an empty, hollow feeling of being only egotistically effective in a display of pyrotechnics. The approval, applause, and good reviews were not enough of a reward. I actually began to dislike going to work. In 1946 my marriage came to an end. I was on my own again and continued to work, but almost solely out of financial necessity.

In 1947 my luck changed—twice. First, Harold Clurman cast me for a Broadway play. I had never worked with such a director. In the early stages of rehearsal I felt as though he had pulled the rug out from under me so that I had to learn to walk and talk all over again. He never allowed the setting of line readings, mechanizing of stage positions or pieces of "business," exploring instead the existence of the characters and their behavior as they came into conflict with each other in the action of the play. I was asked to work subjectively, to give birth to the new person I was to become rather than to present a preconceived, theatrical illustration of her on the stage. My love, my "amateur's" faith in the work, was revived. I must admit that as the externals which had given me security in the past years were stripped from me, I needed the assurance of those whose opinion I respected that my new way of work was communicating. Without it I would not have fully trusted this way of working.

The second stroke of luck occurred when the leading actor in Clurman's production had to leave the company and was replaced by Herbert Berghof. A renowned European actor with a total understanding of contemporary acting, he helped me almost at once in the understanding and development of the new techniques I was testing, which I still apply, which are never-ending in terms of their discoveries. They constitute a craft as challenging, perhaps more so, than that of any of the other performing arts. I was now ready to begin the battle to be a real artist, as well as my own battle with the commercial theatre which continues to this day.

Herbert and I fell in love, and, as our lives became ever more closely linked, he invited me to join him in teaching at his studio. I was stunned. What did I know about teaching? He reminded me that as an actress who had worked continuously for almost ten years, having achieved a certain skill and the awareness of many errors as well, I should be willing to share this experience with less knowledgeable colleagues. The concept of sharing appealed to my desire to be of service to others, which was, in fact, a prime motivation for my having wanted to be a part of the theatre in the first place. While teaching, I soon learned that anything I was unable to verbalize or explain usually related to areas of confusion or muddiness in my own techniques. So the teaching of others forced me into clarifications of my personal work. It raised my standards. In upholding honesty in the work of others, denying their right to be superficial or to take shortcuts, one can't allow oneself to cheat. I'm far more nervous when students are in the audience than when the critics are there, because the students know more about the craft than the critics do. I simply want to emphasize that although I have become recognized as a teacher and feel that I am a good one, it is because I am, first and foremost, an *actress* and I teach what I am continually learning. I would like to disagree with George Bernard Shaw's statement that "He who *can*, does. He who *cannot*, teaches" to express my personal belief that "Only he who *can* should teach!"

Part One:
The Actor

1

The Actor's World

SINCE the time of the ancient Greeks a democracy has depended on its philosophers and creative artists. It can only flourish by continuous probing, prodding, and questioning of the social conditions under which man exists and tries to better himself. One of the first moves of a dictatorship is to stifle the artists and thinkers who have the ability to stir up dissent from any prescribed dogma which might enslave them. Because the artist can arouse the curiosity and conscience of his community, he becomes a threat to those who have taken power. We have countless examples in recent history: Hitler's ban, not only of the contemporary artists who challenged his regime, but even of some of the works of German classicists like Schiller and Goethe who defended freedom of thought and condemned anti-Semitism. He forbade performances of Beethoven's opera *Fidelio* because it espoused the cause of those imprisoned for their political beliefs. Contemporary artists who have dissented from dictatorships, from racism in South Africa, from military oppression in Latin America, and from our own bout with McCarthyism are legion. They have set an example as to the power of art.

As actors we must not consider ourselves immune from the need to learn about our world, our country, and our immediate community. We must arrive at the formation of a point of view. The aftermath of the "me generation" is producing many young people with reawakened concerns about their society; but it is often accompanied by a sense of futility in the belief that individual action won't make any

3

difference. I know that if I cast my one vote I can be sure that thousands of others are doing the same, that if I give only one dollar for famine relief, environmental protection, or civil liberties, thousands of others are giving, too. I also know that if I give or do nothing, many, many others will be as remiss.

Once we begin to learn about some of the world's problems and come to an understanding of our country's relationship to them, we can tackle the problems of our immediate surroundings. "My country, right or wrong!" is often taken out of context and used in an *un*patriotic, even dangerous sense. In any country, as in the individual, there is always room for improvement. The struggle to make changes for the better, to be of service in this quest, is the obligation of responsible citizenship. It is true that a by-product of being a performer is to jump on the bandwagon of a good cause. We have an intuitive compassion for our fellow man so we give freely of our time and talent to aid the hungry, the ill, and the homeless, and to protest against nuclear proliferation, unjust wars, and oppression, *once these things have been brought to our attention.* However, an educated grasp of false national values and the exploitative practices in our own society is glaringly lacking. We are lax in making changes in existing conditions, even within our own profession. To plead ignorance or to play the ostrich, to assume that individual actions don't count, can only result in further enslavement.

By going back to the origins of theatre art, in briefly tracing the history of its development, I want you to discover how and why it reached high peaks and why it so often sank into a shambles, why in America it has been dubbed "The Fabulous Invalid," and why it should be viewed as an invalid at all, fabulous or otherwise.

The ancient theatre of the Greeks, with its enormous arenas providing intellectual enlightenment as well as an emotional catharsis for the populace, spread to the Romans, where, under dictatorship and in its increasing attempts merely to entertain, it gradually declined into a state of soulless spectacle. It died out and the arenas fell into ruin. (How many such spectacles fill our arenas today—sometimes on roller skates? How many of our theatres have been allowed to fall to ruin or demolition?) Centuries later, in the Dark Ages, as people

4

reached for light, the theatre reemerged in the form of religious "miracle" and "passion" plays. Finally, it spilled into the streets and marketplaces as troupes of strolling players mocked and mimed and improvised their views of local political problems as well as the eternally fascinating problems of love and sex and family life. (How many churches, garages, or basements are we occupying today in our search for an audience, in our attempts to be heard?)

A flowering rebirth of the theatre began with the Elizabethans and continued in the epochs that followed with the great poet-dramatists of Germany and France. The recognition by heads of state that fine theatre reflected glory on their communities led them to increase their patronage and support. Abroad this support is still traditional, even though many of the theatres are grappling with the invasion of bureaucratic merchandising that threatens genuine artistic contribution to a nation. Throughout Europe we have examples of theatres subsidized by both the state and the municipality. (In Germany theatre is additionally subsidized by industry *and* labor.) Through continuous and *affordable* offerings, the audiences have also developed a tradition of theatre*going*. It has become a part of their lives. (While standing in line for tickets at Vienna's Burgtheater, I overheard a young woman chatting with a friend about her problems as a salesgirl. Then, casually, she asked her opinion about a recent film. "I haven't seen it. Why should I go to a movie when I can see a play?" was the reply.) These subsidized playhouses, which are the backbone of the countries' theatres, exist happily side by side with commercial playhouses, experimental theatres, and political cabarets. They provide enormous variety, not just for the public but also for actors deciding what kind of theatre they long to be a part of. (In Germany and Austria, in the state theatres, the actors are employed for life with paid vacations and retirement pensions equaling their salaries.)

In stressing the importance of subsidized theatre, I don't mean to imply that it is necessarily ideal for solving the artists' problems, but rather to emphasize that when this kind of support is given, it is an *acknowledgment* of the cultural benefits, the value that theatre can have for its community, on a par with its orchestras, operas, dance companies, museums, and libraries. It implies respect for the theatre artists. In the United States we have yet to *earn* this respect and support. We will need to do so if we are to get out of the swamp of commercialization in which we seem to be stuck at the present. How did we get into this predicament?

Whenever I despair about the condition of the present American theatre, I remind myself how very young our country is, and I take courage in the awareness of its speed of growth from wilderness to civilization. Our first hundred years left little time for anything but clearing the wilds, breaking ground to provide shelter and arable land, gradually providing schoolrooms, churches, and town halls. The creation of a viable government, communication between settlements, a pursuit of higher education, and the arts had to wait their turn.

When we began to establish ourselves economically through the mining of our natural resources, through trading in furs, lumber, and cotton, we were deemed worthy of exploitation. There was renewed oppression from the colonial bosses abroad, which made revolt almost inevitable. Our Founding Fathers, making use of Greek philosophers, promised liberty and justice for all, even the right to a pursuit of happiness. The fight to fulfill these promises has not been won. It took us a long time to accept the very idea of what justice and liberty "for all" means, and that meaning is being sorely tested in the present. I believe that the right of the individual to pursue happiness is continually bent and perverted into something sought at the expense of others. "Free enterprise" has come to mean the right to exercise control over others, even to undo them. Corporate mergers are made, not to be of service to others, but for personal enrichment and self-aggrandizement. Our theatre is an integral part of this society.

The theatre's evolution is not only fascinating but totally relevant to our present dilemma.* From the Puritans we inherited the notion that all forms of theatre were immoral, that all performers were vagabonds, harlots, and charlatans (as indeed some of them were and some still are). As settlement of the colonies grew, laws forbidding any kind of performance were enforced in all but Maryland and Virginia. These laws were only lifted about 150 years after the Rev-

---

* Read Garff B. Wilson's *Three Hundred Years of American Theatre and Drama* (Englewood Cliffs, N.J.: Prentice-Hall, 1973).

olution, although laws forbidding actors burial in consecrated ground were not officially rescinded until the twentieth century. (In the late nineteenth century, New York's "Little Church Around the Corner" became the first to sanction burials, as well as church weddings, for actors—which is why I selected it for my first marriage!) Nevertheless, there were always actors willing to buck these obstacles, ready to slake the people's thirst for entertainment, ready to provide solace for their troubled lives, even if only on a primitive level.

Although French and Spanish settlers founded a few acting companies, it was the British immigrant actors who made a lasting impact. At first they performed on makeshift platforms in town halls and taverns, calling their performances lectures or "moral dialogues" in order to circumvent the law. The number of companies increased, and in 1752 the first real playhouse was built by merchants in Williamsburg, Virginia, for the troupe of Walter Murray and Thomas Kean. These companies were often family affairs in which man, wife, and children performed with the help of other actors. They all shared in the proceeds, scrounging for a living as most actors still do today. They played their English repertoires of Shakespeare and playwrights of the Restoration, and translations of German and French morality plays, usually in very abridged versions for reasons of time, budget, and the provision of more popular fare. They traveled extensively, particularly between the more sophisticated townships of Charlotte, North Carolina; Philadelphia; New York; and, after the Revolution, Boston. The trips were hazardous, roads and means of transportation were miserable, but even when our frontiers moved westward, the actors moved with them.

As native-born actors began to join the ranks of the British companies, they developed an inferiority complex, which seems to have intensified with the years. Charlotte Cushman and Edwin Forrest, in the early 1800s, were the first American-born actors to establish themselves, with great difficulty, as performers of importance. All during the nineteenth century, with the continuing arrival of prominent visiting English players, this sense of colonial inferiority continued and has not been entirely shaken off to this day. It is still fostered by some of our English colleagues and, certainly, by our own lack of a sense of self-worth.

William Dunlap, born in 1766, was our first American playwright;

he developed a type of morality play acceptable even to the Puritans. From it sprang the melodramas which became popular for everyone, including the most unschooled audiences. As a reflection of the social problems of poverty, drink, bossism, and slavery, they gave righteous answers in which villains got their due and victims were saved or went to heaven. (*Uncle Tom's Cabin* and *The Drunkard* became American classics.) Playgoers found a release from their daily troubles through their tears and cheers, their boos and hisses. The form of melodrama, gradually more skillfully conceived, gained in sophistication and continued as a mainstay of the theatre for many years, being played by the various companies along with the standbys in their repertoire. Melodrama faded at the end of the nineteenth century with the discovery on our shores of the new social realists, Ibsen, Chekhov, and Shaw, who not only made other demands on the actors but also deeply influenced our young playwrights—Eugene O'Neill among them.

I was always fascinated by the sense of heritage I felt when reading about nineteenth-century American theatre. But it came vividly alive for me when I first delved into a biography of Edwin Booth, who was certainly one of our greatest actors. I was suddenly able to identify with those times, to participate in the daily activities of the actors, to imagine their working conditions and draw conclusions from their struggles.

Edwin Booth was born in 1833, the second son of the British-born actor Junius Brutus Booth. He served his apprenticeship in his father's company, and, even before his father's death when he was nineteen, seems to have opted for a simple, realistically human kind of acting rather than the bombastic, emotionally histrionic style of his father. He strove throughout his career to deepen his skills. He traveled extensively with other companies. (I was amazed to learn that once when Booth was acting an abridged version of a Shakespearean play in a mining camp out west, the miners, many of whom were Welsh and English, interrupted the actors, shouting back the lines that had been cut—so well did they know the text.) For a few years in the latter half of the century Booth became one of the famous actor-managers who had their own companies and who made up what was called the Golden Age of the Actor. Eventually, Booth returned to being a guest player in other companies. He traveled abroad, pitting his talents against the greatest actors of England and Germany. He suffered through the terrible time of his actor-brother John Wilkes Booth's assassination of Abraham Lincoln, which not only damaged his own career, but also reflected badly on the entire profession. Performers were once again looked upon as scoundrels, now even as murderers. It is a tribute to Edwin Booth's greatness that he recovered from this stigma and was mourned at his death in 1893 as "The Prince of Players."

Today, with permission of the Players' Club in Gramercy Park in New York City, you can still visit his home, the upper floors of which are maintained as a museum. You will get goose pimples, as I did, when walking into his bedroom to see his slippers placed at the side of his bed, imagining that he will come in at any moment. You can see his costumes, props, books, and scripts, which are beautifully displayed there. All this will, hopefully, whet your appetite for other biographies of the period.

Read about the young American, born in New York City in 1807, who fell in love with the theatre while attending performances sitting at the rear of the balcony and, realizing he would not be allowed to perform in fine plays in the United States, reversed the trend by going to England to make a career. He became one of the greatest tragedians of his generation and was eventually decorated by all the crowned heads of Europe for his portrayals of characters like Lear, Shylock, and Othello. In 1867 he died on tour in Lodz, Poland, where he was buried as an honored artist. His name was Ira Aldridge—and he was black.

Each actor-manager of the Golden Age had a home base with a theatre of his own and a company and repertoire of his own choosing. Everything was under his control: acting, directing, sometimes even the writing of the plays. These actors played melodramas, classics, and translations of new European plays. They took their plays on the road, often undermining the stability of the resident stock companies that had established themselves throughout the country. They vied with each other for supremacy. Their growing renown attracted prominent players from abroad who sometimes came without their own companies, as guest players. As the visiting actors began to bring in large profits, the "star system" took hold and, because these guest stars demanded that the resident actors bow to their own style of performing, the quality of the local companies deteriorated. (Does this sound familiar?) Soon the actor-manager relinquished his responsibility for the company and also played as a "guest star." The supporting actors became convenient, necessary props. These circumstances helped to spawn a new creature: the nonperforming producer.

In the latter part of the century men like Augustin Daly and David Belasco started to take the reins away from the remaining actor-managers, hiring companies that they directed, for which they sometimes wrote plays, and for whom they devised more and more spectacular and scenically realistic productions. They took pride in developing new stars over whom they ruled like kings, treating them, as well as the other actors, like children to be taken care of. Actors lost control, not only over their choice of plays, roles, and the nature of their interpretations, but over their personal lives as well, as they were guided into fulfilling a salable public image contrived for them by their managers. (This type of star-making was later adopted by the Hollywood studios, which also made short shrift of any performer who dared to rebel.) P. T. Barnum, a showman if there ever was one, was not only establishing the circus in America but producing plays, importing performers, and building theatres for them. He once said, "Show business has *all* phases of dignity, from the exhibition of a monkey to the exposition of that highest art in music and drama." The terms *legitimate theatre* and *legitimate actor* derived from this period to differentiate them from the more popular forms of *show business* (which included the ever-growing entrenchment of minstrel shows, circus, vaudeville, and burlesque). But *legitimate* or not, they were still a part of the *business*.

By this time, civic orchestras and opera companies existed in most of our major cities, having been recognized as a cultural boon by the leading citizenry and consequently receiving their sponsorship. Theatre was considered a commercial, less reputable stepchild unworthy of civic support, and the leading actors did not fight to cast off this mantle of second-class artists. They satisfied themselves with the personal glory and accolades heaped on them while the supporting players dreamed of attaining the same status. Also, they no longer shared in the take but received a fixed salary at the discretion of the management, and this salary lasted no longer than the run of the play. They were now "for hire."

Producers like Daly and Belasco at least had their roots in the theatre. They had spent their lives serving as apprentice actors, stage managers, and writers and were passionately involved in all aspects of production no matter how dictatorial they may have been. But toward the end of the century, the real villains of the theatre emerged in the form of the nonartists—the businessmen and entrepreneurs— and in each succeeding generation they have managed to exert a stranglehold over the artists who had higher aspirations than those of buying and selling merchandise. Sensing that enormous profits could be made, Charles and Daniel Frohman and half a dozen others formed the Theatrical Syndicate in 1896. (I don't know which word makes me shudder more, "syndicate" or "entrepreneur," with their connotations of racketeering, exploitation, and enslavement.) The Frohmans were already established businessmen-managers when they created this Theatrical Syndicate, which reigned for more than ten years as a prosperous but highly destructive monopoly. They bought or leased *all* major playhouses in the country, thereby forcing everyone to perform under their aegis, dictating who could play and what would be played. Since their prime purpose was to make money, to pack their houses, they pandered to the largest numbers and the shabbiest taste. Raising the awareness of the public, providing them with masterpieces, which had been a cause for some of the actor-managers, was deliberately ignored. Any actor or producer who rebelled was shut out and had to resort to inferior theatres or, once again, to makeshift platforms. A few fought back: Belasco, some prominent actors like Minnie Maddern Fiske, Joseph Jefferson, and, interestingly, James O'Neill, the father of Eugene. But they didn't make much of a dent. The syndicate began to lose some of its power only with the arrival in 1905 of *another* monopoly: the Shubert brothers, whose legacy remains with us today. And their real estate cartel was further weakened by others, some of whom are still firmly entrenched on Broadway.

The transition between the nineteenth and twentieth centuries produced many notable actors about whom it is wonderful to read: Julia Marlowe, Helena Modjeska, Ada Rehan, Maude Adams, Richard

Mansfield, Otis Skinner, E. H. Sothern, the Drews, and the Barrymores, among many others. But it is Minnie Maddern Fiske who stands out as an example for us all, a courageous, pioneering artist, incorruptible in her stand against the shutout of the businessmen-managers, playing in dilapidated or improvised theatres, maintaining her Manhattan Theatre Company, introducing the works of Ibsen as well as a "new" kind of acting, which was described over and over again as incredibly "lifelike" and "unstudied."

A superb black actor of the transition was Charles S. Gilpin, whom Eugene O'Neill later considered to be "the only actor who carried out every notion of a character I had in mind," when referring to Gilpin's portrayal of Brutus Jones in *The Emperor Jones*. Gilpin was also producer of the nation's only black stock company, at the Lafayette Theatre in New York.

Of course many young players of importance were putting down their roots at this time: Pauline Lord, Alice Brady, Helen Hayes, Laurette Taylor (the greatest actress in my memory), Alfred Lunt and Lynn Fontanne.* But in the early 1900s "show business" in the large cities and on the road continued to burst with activity—and predominantly trashy plays.

The first outside move to counter these conditions was made by a group of men already known for their philanthropic contributions to the other arts: J. P. Morgan, Andrew Carnegie, John Jacob Astor, and Otto Kahn. Inspired by the recent international success of the Moscow Art Theatre, they built the New Theatre with modern technical facilities and a revolving stage. They engaged the idealistic director, Winthrop Ames, and a "permanent company" aiming for a repertory of classics and exceptional new plays. However, the productions seem to have been administered by the star system, and, perhaps for other reasons, the venture collapsed after a few years. But an artists' rebellion against the broad reign of second-rate popular entertainment was inevitable.

In most generations grumblings and rumblings can be heard among

---

* Read *The Fabulous Lunts* by Jared Brown (New York: Atheneum, 1986). It will paint a lively picture of much of the theatrical scene from the end of the last century right up to the 1960s, in addition to providing inspiration for a dedicated, single-minded pursuit of your goals.

people with visions of theatre as an art form. Within the same year, 1915, independent of each other, *three* ventures were born which had a long-lasting influence on the future of our theatre. Alice and Irene Lewisohn began The Neighborhood Playhouse as part of the Henry Street Settlement on the Lower East Side of New York. They served that community with challenging plays and performances for fifteen years, branching out to found The Neighborhood Playhouse School of the Theatre, which is still one of the finest of its kind. In the arts colony on Cape Cod the Provincetown Players started as a writers' theatre headed by the brilliant Susan Glaspell and her husband, George Cram Cook. They were joined by Edna St. Vincent Millay and the young playwright Eugene O'Neill, among others, and their works were played by such talented actors as Jasper Deeter and Walter Huston (John Huston's father). They moved to MacDougal Street in Greenwich Village for the winter season, where they continued until the stock market crash of 1929. (Who says Off-Broadway is a recent movement?) The third group called themselves the Washington Square Players. Dedicating themselves to performances of meaningful plays under the guidance of Edward Goodman, they functioned with young performers like Katharine Cornell and Roland Young, with designers like Lee Simonson and Robert Edmond Jones, and writers like Zoë Akins and Philip Moeller. But, more importantly, after three years they joined with a handful of others to lay the foundations of the famous Theatre Guild.

The Guild, founded in 1919, was the longest successful venture of its kind in our history, spanning almost forty years, functioning within the commercial system of paying for itself with the support of backers plus the use of subscription tickets as had become customary for concerts. Another new concept was to operate under the management of a board, comprised not just of an attorney and a business manager, but of actors, designers, directors, and playwrights. In their glory days they played a modified version of repertory with a company of some of the finest character actors of that time and young players like the Lunts. They launched great designers like Robert Edmond Jones, Jo Mielziner, Donald Oenslager, and Lee Simonson and writers like O'Neill, Sidney Howard, Elmer Rice, S. N. Behrman, Robert Sherwood, Maxwell Anderson, and many European playwrights, among them George Bernard Shaw.

13

(Allow me to stray from the subject to tell one of my favorite stories about an encounter between Shaw and the Guild. When they sent a cable asking him to make cuts in the play they were previewing because the curtain came down too late for commuters to catch their trains, Shaw cabled back, "Run later trains!")

Inevitably, the board of the Guild experienced a good deal of infighting and the artists began to relinquish their voice in decision making. Many of them also left the company for more lucrative offers elsewhere. Even the Lunts went out on their own, feeling they were being misused, but returned when they were allowed to be at the helm of their productions. Gradually, the Guild declined in quality and its influence over Broadway. In its last years, when the nonartist was once more in control, it became almost a booking agent for other productions.*

As an offshoot of the Guild, another noble experiment was attempted by artists in search of control over their own work: the Playwrights Company. It spanned the years from 1938 to 1960.† Disillusioned by the economic and artistic dictatorship of commerce, by theatre owners such as the Shuberts, by producers, even by the Theatre Guild, Robert Sherwood, Sidney Howard, Elmer Rice, Maxwell Anderson, and S. N. Behrman banded together to eliminate the nonartist producer by becoming their own producers. They were all established, Pulitzer Prize–winning authors and true liberals who believed that theatre should have social meaning providing moral enlightenment. They had many successful productions and were joined in the passing years by other prominent playwrights. But as they, too, were operating under the system of profit and loss, in economic competition with the rest of Broadway, their path was strewn with all the problems of the commercial scene which finally engulfed them, spiritually as well as economically.‡ When they disbanded they stressed, optimistically, that a similar attempt should be

---

* Between 1938 and 1952 I was in three of their productions: *The Sea Gull* with the Lunts, *Othello* with Paul Robeson and José Ferrer, and Shaw's *Saint Joan* with John Buckmaster.

† Read John Wharton's *Life Among the Playwrights* (New York: Quadrangle Publications, 1974).

‡ Under their aegis, I appeared opposite Paul Muni in Maxwell Anderson's *Key Largo*.

made again, but that its successes would depend on *the respect that the artists must have for each other and particularly their loyalty to a shared ideal!* But let me go back to the twenties for the proper sequence of our evolution.

In her teens Eva Le Gallienne had become a Broadway star in two of Ferenc Molnár's plays, *The Swan* and *Liliom*. Fired by her admiration of European actors and their traditions, she founded the Civic Repertory on Fourteenth Street. With unbelievable skill and tenacity, she enlisted philanthropic support for the productions of classical and neoclassical plays performed in repertory by a standing company with the occasional addition of guest players. From 1926 to 1932 the theatre was able to operate at prices that allowed real theatregoers (few of whom are rich) as well as young people to attend with regularity. The Civic is remembered by many with love and nostalgia and for the fact that a professional repertory had actually once existed in America.* In 1937, when I was yearning to be in the profession, it was to Eva Le Gallienne that I wrote for an audition. I *knew* of the Civic's reputation and believed that it was the only kind of theatre I wanted to dedicate myself to. I *didn't* know that it had been out of existence for five years, and that Le Gallienne was then battling to reestablish herself in independent productions while valiantly dreaming of a new Civic.

Inevitably, the economic collapse of 1929 and the ensuing depression of the 1930s had its effect on the entire theatre community. Social consciousness was almost *forced* on members of all the arts—and it developed to a high degree. Many actors' "labs" and workshops arose, based on political activism. But the Group Theatre was conceived as a theatre not only of social ideas but one with high artistic ideals. Strongly influenced by the principles of Stanislavsky and the precepts under which the Moscow Art Theatre had been built, it arose under the leadership of Harold Clurman. It began as a summer colony in Connecticut in 1931. Most of the twenty-eight actors and the three directors, Clurman, Lee Strasberg and Cheryl

---

* For a fuller understanding of Le Gallienne's vision and her struggles, read her two autobiographies: *At Thirty-Three* (New York, Toronto: Longmans Green, 1934) and *With a Quiet Heart* (New York: Viking Press, 1953).

Crawford, had worked together at the Guild, the Provincetown, and the Neighborhood Playhouse. They shared a disgust for commercialism and hotly debated everything from a lack of artistic integrity to inadequacies in acting and directing. They longed for an ensemble of merit with a shared language and ever-improving acting skills to perform plays of social significance. (As *always* in art, the inception of a fruitful collaboration is made possible by shared passions, by the airing of passionate disagreements, as well as by a search for answers. Nothing comes of the superficial social intercourse so commonly practiced by would-be artists.) In the summer of 1931, with the encouragement and some financial assistance of the Theatre Guild, Clurman was able to persuade the others to join in the experiment in Connecticut with only a promise of room and board. Among the actors were Sanford Meisner, Stella Adler, Elia Kazan, Franchot Tone, Morris Carnovsky, J. Edward Bromberg, and Clifford Odets. Later they were joined by John Garfield, Luther Adler, Lee J. Cobb, Irwin Shaw, William Saroyan, Frances Farmer, Sidney Kingsley, Robert (Bobby) Lewis, and Margaret Barker. The roster is testimony to the impact the Group made on our theatre. For ten years they were a major force in New York, making for change in directing, ensemble acting, and the kind of plays that attracted a new audience as well as the old.*

At the height of the depression, when the bottom fell out of commercial productions in New York and on the road, the thousands of actors *usually* unemployed were joined by thousands of others. Even worse, the jobs on which most actors subsist while waiting for roles in the theatre had also disappeared: waiting on tables, working in restaurant kitchens, doing office work, running errands, or being domestics. They were truly on the street. Young Henry Fonda joined the ranks of those selling apples on Times Square.

One of Franklin Delano Roosevelt's innovative ideas to pull us out of the muck was the Works Progress Administration (WPA), which included the Federal Theatre. This was the only time in our history

---

* For a full comprehension of their turbulent times, read *The Fervent Years* by Harold Clurman (New York: Knopf, 1945). In it there are many lessons to be learned from their successes and perhaps *even more* from their failures.

when we had a national theatre supported by the government. There was even an initial promise of no government interference or censorship. The project was so vast, so ambitious, it's a miracle that it ever got on its feet, but it survived from 1935 to 1939. Its defeat was entirely due to red-baiting congressional committees, which, in any event, wanted it off the federal payroll.

The statistics make my head spin. In four years, more than 1,200 projects were produced including everything from circuses, puppet shows, and musicals to operettas, new plays, and classics. In the first year alone, more than 12,000 theatre workers were employed in thirty-one cities; their work reached an audience numbering in the millions. Playwrights, impressed by these efforts, contributed their work without asking for royalties. Some of the productions were highly successful; others were innovative. Although the caliber of work was often poor, it never seems to have lacked in the enthusiasm of the performers.

Among the plays produced were fourteen by O'Neill, nine by Shaw, T. S. Eliot's *Murder in the Cathedral,* an all-black *Macbeth,* and Marlowe's *Doctor Faustus* (under the aegis of Orson Welles and John Houseman, who collaborated soon afterward in the creation of the exciting though short-lived Mercury Theatre). Marc Blitzstein's *The Cradle Will Rock* was considered so "subversive" as to be partially responsible for the act of Congress that ended the Federal Theatre in June of 1939. One congressman asked if Christopher Marlowe was a communist. Others found Shakespeare too subversive. (Note the parallel in recent Congressional attempts to eliminate the National Endowment for the Arts or those of the Moral Majority to try to have *Romeo and Juliet* taken from the shelves, claiming that it encourages teenage suicide and drug use.) The central figure in charge of the Federal Theatre was the phenomenal Hallie Flanagan.*

The first half of the forties were, ironically, a time of economic recovery due to World War II. The commercial theatre rebounded with escapist plays, foolish wartime comedies (two of which I was

---

* To gain a complete picture of this woman and her unique achievements in spite of seemingly insurmountable obstacles, read the biography *Hallie Flanagan: A Life in the American Theatre* by Joanne Bentley (New York: Knopf, 1988).

guilty of participating in: *The Admiral Had a Wife* and *Vicki*, both with José Ferrer), and a few serious productions like *There Shall Be No Night* and *Othello*. Little was stirring of a noncommercial nature except for the ventures begun by European refugees like the theatre department at the New School for Social Research headed by Erwin Piscator, the opening of the Max Reinhardt Seminar in California, and, in 1945, in New York, the founding of the HB Studio by Herbert Berghof. Berghof wanted to create a space and a home in which he and his colleagues could experiment and study to improve their skills instead of hanging around drugstores and cafés like vagrants, complaining about their inability to find a creative outlet. In 1947 the Actors' Studio, of which Herbert Berghof was a charter member, was founded, on the same principle. Meanwhile, with the arrival of new playwrights like Tennessee Williams, Horton Foote, and Arthur Miller, and productions of the established Playwrights Company, plus important new forms of the American musical, the forties ended with a sense of hope and started off the fifties with a bang.*

I have the ad of a theatrical ticket agency from the end of December 1950 presenting a choice of the entertainment one could see *on Broadway* within the same week. It included three plays by George Bernard Shaw, one Shakespeare, a Pinero, an Anouilh, a Van Druten, the musicals *Guys and Dolls, Pal Joey, The King and I, South Pacific,* and *Call Me Madam,* with performers like Judy Garland, Gertrude Lawrence, Yul Brynner, Ethel Merman, Bert Lahr, Phil Silvers, Audrey Hepburn, Richard Burton, Julie Harris, David Niven, Jessica Tandy, Hume Cronyn, Charles Laughton, Charles Boyer, Vivien Leigh, Laurence Olivier, Henry Fonda, Cedric Hardwicke, and yours truly. As the decade drew on, productions declined in quality and popular commercial fare prevailed, but even when things seemed rosier many of us were unhappy with the lack of continuity and the conditions of marketing that always accompanied our efforts. As a

---

* For a brilliant overview of all aspects of theatre in America and Europe in the early 1950s, read Eric Bentley's *In Search of Theatre* (New York: Knopf, 1953).

direct consequence of this unrest, young artists rebelled. Off-Broadway stirred again with notable efforts by the Phoenix Theatre*, The Circle in the Square, and the Cherry Lane Theatre, among others. Many young performers making their mark—Geraldine Page, Jason Robards, Maureen Stapleton, to mention only a few—were training at the HB Studio. Samuel Beckett was being recognized as a great force, Edward Albee was making them sit up with *The Zoo Story, The Sandbox,* and *The American Dream.*

But the curtain of McCarthyism had descended over the nation and for most of the "fabulous fifties" its influence on the established theatre community of writers, directors, and actors made for an atmosphere of fear and the occasion for betrayals, sellouts, and suicides, or simply the stifling of voices. Unless you're already familiar with this black period when personal beliefs and convictions were challenged, when being left of center was considered a crime, when people of note were made the dupes of congressional committees in order to intimidate lesser-known citizens into submission, you can read about it in the many available political assessments or in the biographies of the victims and the perpetrators of these crimes. It's important if you want to guard against the recurrence of such shameful times. I still have difficulty in dealing with my memory of those days, so deeply was I wounded. I would like to reprint a statement I was allowed to make by Edward R. Murrow, the courageous journalist who took a stand against Senator Joseph McCarthy, who was responsible for some of the anti-Communist witch-hunting of the period. For a while, one of the features of Murrow's radio program was a segment called "This I Believe . . ." in which he gave McCarthy's victims a few minutes to air their credos. More than a hundred of their statements were eventually gathered in a little book.† Mine begins with a quotation:

> "I know that in an accidental sort of way, struggling through the unreal part of my life, I haven't always been able to live up to my ideal.

* For whom I played Turgenev's *A Month in the Country* and Brecht's *The Good Woman of Setzuan.*
† *This I Believe,* Vol. 2, ed. Raymond Swing (New York: Simon & Schuster, 1954).

But in my own real world I've never done anything wrong, never denied my faith, never been untrue to myself. I've been threatened and blackmailed and insulted and starved. But I've played the game. I've fought the good fight. And now it's all over, there's an indescribable peace. I believe in Michelangelo, Velásquez, and Rembrandt; in the might of design, the mystery of color, the redemption of all things by Beauty everlasting, and the message of Art that has made these hands blessed. Amen. Amen." These words were given to the dying painter, Louis Dubedat, in George Bernard Shaw's *The Doctor's Dilemma*. It is the credo of an artist, a specific human being, and only part of the author's credo, whose beliefs are summed up in the entirety of his work. Not being a writer, a prophet, or a philosopher, but an actress, I will again employ the help of a playwright to paraphrase my faith: I believe in the ancient Greeks who initiated our theatre 2,500 years ago, in the miracle of Eleonora Duse's gifts, in the might of truth, the mystery of emotions, the redemption of all things by imagination everlasting, and the message of Art that should make the untiring work and striving, the inspiration and creation of all actors blessed. Amen. Amen.

In the other part of my life I feel "guilty" about living up to my ideal, but not as much as poor Louis Dubedat and, of course, not for the same reasons. I have in my life to guide me the Declaration of Independence and the Bill of Rights and I believe in them to the letter—to the dismay of some. I, too, can get strength from Michelangelo and Rembrandt and Bach and Mozart and Shaw and Shakespeare, and the teachings of Jesus and Plato and Aristotle. These great makers and shakers have helped me to find reason, majesty, and greatness in the world. They have helped me to drown out the frenetic racket made by the compromisers who try to bend ideals to fit their practical needs and personal appetites and to deprive us of our spiritual salvation. The knowledge that every day there is something more to learn, something higher to reach for, something new to make for others, makes each day infinitely precious. And I am grateful. One thing makes for another. Shaw wouldn't be without Shakespeare, Bach without the words of Christ, Beethoven without Mozart—and we would be barren without all of them. I was proud the day I first learned to make a good loaf of bread, a simple thing which others could enjoy, or to plant a bulb and help it to grow, or to make a character in a play come off the printed page to become a human being with a point of view who can help others to understand a little more; all these things, and the effort to do them well, make it possible for me while "struggling through the unreal part of my life," and being "threatened and blackmailed and insulted and starved," to be true to myself and to fight the good fight.

I survived this time of tapped phones, of the F.B.I. tippy-toeing in one's footsteps, of anxious glances over the shoulder in a café to make sure that no discussion was being overheard. I survived in a healthier state than many others. I had no guilt to deal with since I hadn't betrayed anyone. I didn't bear resentment at having *been* betrayed or "named" to congressional committees, because my accusers remained anonymous. I didn't go to jail, I didn't kill myself, and, as for the blacklists which barred me from TV and films, they simply removed me from any temptations or lures into the commercial world or the temptation to compromise my goals any further than I was already doing on Broadway. But it was the only time in my life when I was made fearful or felt that I had lost control over my own destiny. And for that, I have the right to remain outraged!

The relationship between the vast social upheavals of the sixties and seventies and the theatre is still hard for me to put into perspective objectively (except for my awareness that artists were late in reflecting or illuminating these times). In January 1961 at the inauguration of our new, young president with the poet Robert Frost at his side, we were challenged to acknowledge that our freedoms must be earned by the acceptance of our responsibility for them, that we must again seek to do something for our country rather than just for ourselves. Many accepted this challenge. The Gandhi-like civil rights movement made great inroads on our culture but these promises were dampened by the tragedies of the assassinations of Kennedy and Martin Luther King Jr., and again later by the murder of Robert Kennedy. L.B.J.'s furtherance of civil rights and his ambitious war on poverty were marred by his abetment of our ever-deepening involvement in Vietnam. In the next administration the situation worsened as the war reached into Cambodia and the public learned more and more about corruption in our leadership.

Meanwhile, the silence of the McCarthy generation had been broken by their children in reaction to their parents' lack of social involvement, as well as to their middle-class and often hypocritical values and the importance that had been given to the acquisition of material things. The rebellion of the young, which, of course, involved many moderates, also included two kinds of extremists with distinctly opposite aims. On the one hand were the "flower children" who preached love and peace and looked for the simplest kind of existence, working only to achieve the barest necessities for communal living. Many of them were undone by the failure of their ventures and, particularly, by a further escape from reality into the world of drugs and what they called mind-expanding chemicals. On the other hand, we saw fanatical young political activists who believed they could change the established world by terrorist tactics against villains of their own choosing. They, too, were undone, occasionally by accidentally blowing *themselves* up with their homemade bombs. The events in Asia increased the polarization of our country with ever-growing numbers of conscientious objectors, peace marches, and movements that finally brought the tragic war in Vietnam to an end. Then, after the enforced resignation of the president and, in my lonely opinion, the four-year revival of an *honorable* Democratic presidency, we arrived in the eighties. But what was happening in the arts during the two prior decades?

For many years theatre activity seems to have been only slightly touched by the turbulent times, probably because of the lingering fear of new congressional crackdowns on political beliefs. (If government troops could shoot down students at Kent State, what could Congress do to an artist?) In 1962, Edward Albee's bitter and cynical indictment of middle-class social mores, *Who's Afraid of Virginia Woolf?*, made a big splash and influenced many of his younger colleagues for years to come. But throughout most of the sixties, Broadway flourished with its usual fare and the inclusion of British imports. In one year alone there were sixteen English plays with predominantly English casts creating a shutout of American plays and performers. Off-Broadway had also become recognized as an arena where profits could be turned. Consequently, big business moved in, the unions came with ever-increasing "minimum" demands to make sure labor would not be exploited, box office prices rose, critics attended with regularity, and popular plays were sought out with an eye to moving them "uptown" until, in most cases, there was little difference between being on or off Broadway or, as Herbert used to say, "Now we have small grocery stores downtown trying to compete with the big ones uptown."

An answer to these conditions was temporarily found in a recurrence of the original Off-Broadway movement. In increasing numbers, even smaller stages and workshops in basements and lofts were occupied by young people hoping to escape from the new union demands and the high budgets they entailed, once again reaching out to be heard in experimental works with a minimum of financial risk. These new ventures soon fell under a large umbrella dubbed Off-Off-Broadway. The Café Cino provided a platform for many young performers, directors, and writers like the gifted Lanford Wilson. Ellen Stewart began her Café La Mama, which is still very much alive today with countless experimental productions. But, as a whole, the Off-Off-Broadway movement was quickly infected by marketing practices of one kind or another. The more successful ventures merged with Off-Broadway; many went under or degenerated into being mere showcases. The very term *showcase* speaks for itself, illustrating that members of the profession are putting themselves on display to be bought by the highest bidder, each individual member of the venture serving his own ambitions to attract the agent or talent scout, the producer or author he has usually invited to "case" his worth. The possibility for a fruitful collaboration in the single-minded creative effort necessary to produce a serious work of art is automatically eliminated. Many people consider the Off-Off-Broadway movement a huge success. I consider it a dismal failure. At best it has made way for a few exceptionally gifted individuals who, having begun with youthful idealism, were fed right back into the mainstream of that same commerce from which they were initially escaping and where they usually remain with one foot, teetering, with the pretense that they are serving art. When, on occasion, they *do* achieve something of merit, it is an accident rather than a result of these conditions.*

Joseph Papp began to function on all four burners in the sixties. He is an exceptional producer with an understanding of social theatre plus an incredible ability to arouse the municipality and its philan-

---

* Today actors have the "Showcase Code," and playwrights have new provisions in the Dramatists Guild which specify and spell out the details of how we are allowed to sell our wares.

thropists into a support of his efforts. Free Shakespeare in the Park, street theatre available to all and sundry: What a seemingly impossible achievement. The growth of his people's theatre complex on Lafayette Street is an equally heroic accomplishment. Whether you applaud all the presentations or not is almost beside the point. In 1967, his production of *Hair* was the first to echo and reveal the existing problems of the young. The same can be said for his later success, *A Chorus Line*. I'm convinced that the daily hurdles he faces, the problems that must plague him in bringing about his successive efforts, problems that make artistic growth difficult, are similar to those which plague all projects that begin with honest and idealistic intentions. Among these problems are many for which we actors refuse to take responsibility, the ones with which I'll throw down the gauntlet at the conclusion of this chapter.

In the mid-1960s Neil Simon's comedies, not unlike the truly American plays of George S. Kaufman in earlier decades, began sweeping across Broadway with social insight and compassion, and, so far, they continue to do so. Perhaps in the future, in less farcical productions, they may even be recognized by those who now dismiss them as commercial fare for being plays that have arisen from the tradition of Gogol and Chekhov.

Also in the sixties, new support was coming from philanthropic foundations. Previously, foundations like Ford and Rockefeller had offered help to science and education. Now they extended it to the arts—even to the theatre. Smaller foundations followed suit, and a proliferation of regional theatres ensued. Foundations made it easier for established groups in Washington, D.C., Houston, Boston, and Chicago, to name a few, to expand and continue their work. And they helped new ones get started: in Ann Arbor, the APA; in San Francisco, the ACT; in Minneapolis, The Guthrie, which started off with flying colors; and many others. Foundation support continues, and regional theatre has become a force to be reckoned with, particularly as to the way in which it has moved into the Big Apple. While Nelson Rockefeller was governor of New York, he alone was responsible for persuading the federal government to involve itself in sponsorship of the arts, and the National Endowment for the Arts was the result. Later he created the New York State Council on the Arts. These institutions still extend help to ventures of good will, albeit often meager help buried under bureaucratic restrictions.* They and some of the foundations are sometimes weak in their evaluations of potential talent and skill, so the output of many ventures remains provincial.

In the seventies, often with the help of Joe Papp, new playwrights appeared on the horizon, notably Sam Shepard, David Rabe, and Michael Weller. On the other hand, the Theatre of the Absurd had become increasingly absurd with the arrival of "happenings," plays of audience confrontation, nudity, sexual acts depicted in detail, and actors urinating into the audience—all in the name of "art" or in the name of "liberation" from old-fashioned theatre. In their desperation to perform, actors got so confused that they allowed for unspeakable indignities. Two young men once asked me what they could have done at an audition about being lined up by the stage manager to have their penises measured. Stunned, I answered, "You shouldn't have *let* him!" They were not fully satisfied by my reply.

For most of you, the 1980s will be remembered still unclouded by feelings of past history. Now that we are headed toward the twenty-first century, paying heavily for the extravagant, spendthrift Reagan years, you will understand how the decade's excesses were reflected in the theatrical super-spectaculars of Andrew Lloyd Webber and English imports such as *Nicholas Nickleby*. One theatre was gutted to make room for entire roller-skating ramps and rinks—in the name of "art." On the positive side, we saw the plays of August Wilson and emerging feminist writers Beth Henley and Wendy Wasserstein. Many actors decided that the Method had had its day and reverted to formalism, in imitation of the performers of English importations.

Not only in New York, but all over the country in increasing numbers, "innovative productions" (another phrase I detest) have often been considered to be "modern" theatre. Most of them are based on attention-getting devices and external gimmickry under the

---

* A short lesson in dealing with red tape was given me by that genius, Twyla Tharp. She had applied for a grant and was supposed to fill out a lengthy form including a request for a written proposal for her upcoming project, which the foundation would evaluate to see if she qualified for its support. Diagonally across the first page, in large handwriting, she scrawled, "I don't make proposals. I make dances!" She got the grant.

guise of giving new meaning to the classics. They are perpetrated by directorial "concepts" that place *Troilus and Cressida* in the roaring twenties, *Timon of Athens* in the American Civil War, *As You Like It* in a forest at the edge of a golf course with actors dressed in knickerbockers carrying mashies and putting irons, or *The Cherry Orchard* on a white shag rug, or—more recently—on Persian carpets. Any device is used to disguise the fact that neither the director nor his cast is able to live up to the author's intent. It simply points up the paucity of their vision and weakness of their skills. The "innovations" are still very much with us, encouraged by esoteric critical praise, proving the gullibility of an audience that wants to be "in the know" even while they're yawning out of the other side of their mouths. Perhaps someone will attempt a combination of the fashionable seventies and eighties with a production of an all-nude *Hamlet,* placing Elsinore in a health spa, in order to guarantee the theatre owner months of standing room only.

A healthy, gimmick-free, nonsensational, experimental theatre was curtailed by snowballing inflation, which, incommensurate with wages, put the price even of *Off*-Broadway tickets out of the reach of devoted theatregoers. Production costs spiraled, abetted by growing advertising costs and union demands and the increasing practice of featherbedding—ranging from up-front office expenses to the number of cigarettes allegedly purchased for each performance by the prop department, inflated bids by costumers, designers, carpenters, and electricians to the limo service demanded by stars for transportation to and from work. When challenged, the answers of the featherbedders are based on the philosophy that "everybody does it," always accompanied by the attitude that those who *don't* are "suckers" and fools.

But I firmly believe that the high cost of inflation, as well as the current lack of resources resulting from a recession, are only *excuses* idealistic theatre people make for the plight of the theatre. If your heart pounds, as mine does, at the mere mention of the beginnings of a theatre like the Neighborhood, the Provincetown, the Theatre Guild, the Civic Repertory, the Group Theatre, the Phoenix, or the APA, it must also sink with the awareness of each demise. We may also ask what happened to the promise provided for a time by some of the theatres still in existence. We can place the blame on inflation, recession, depression, problems of profit and loss, the high cost of theatre tickets, lack of audience support—on union restrictions, on exploitation by big business, on real estate monopolies, on egomaniac producers or directors, on weak leadership, on opportunistic visions rather than artistic ones with a clear point of view, even on the critics—and we will be correct. *But* we forget that in our search for the blame, we may well have to place ourselves at the top of the list.

For example: The positive movements in our history, our floating islands of hope, have disappeared because they were deserted by the very artists who had initially sworn loyalty to them. I don't need to name names because they are easily traced, but in case after case, the ones who made the biggest splash in a given production were quickly lured away by the popular, more lucrative offerings of Hollywood and Broadway, having used their colleagues in the collaborative venture merely as stepping stones on which to reenter the world of "show-biz." They always left behind a weakened, demoralized company that grew more and more cynical, rightfully doubting if *anybody* really meant it! That is the *real* reason for our failures in the past and lack of growth in our existing attempts. Nonprofit theatres are often visited by guest players who let the management and other actors feel they are doing them a favor by passing a little time with them between their *really* important work in film or on TV.

Let's face the fact that since the disappearance of the golden age of the actor-manager in the 1800s, the acting profession as a whole has relinquished its responsibility to the theatre. It has willingly accepted the role of subservient child to a kind of parental control exercised by managers, producers, directors, even its own agents. This situation has worsened with the years. It sometimes resembles the relationship of prostitute to pimp, or the migrant fruit picker to the orchard bosses. Taking no position of their own, actors bow and scrape to be hired or merely noticed. Many have befuddled their minds and poisoned their talents with drugs. Many stars have forgotten that, as in sports, they can only win the game together with a strong team, no matter how much they may seem to score personally. We must not fog ourselves with illusions about an ideal theatre but fight for it all the way to the mountaintop. In the examination of our past and present, I've tried to emphasize the swamps, the potholes, and the traps that have strewn all the paths taken before us in the fervent hope that with open eyes we can clear our own path as we climb it.

Perhaps we don't all have the same mountain in mind and must first decide which one we're aiming for.

2

The Actor's Goals

IF we agree that the actor must be aware of the world in which he lives in order to be an artist with a point of view, it must become equally clear that he needs not only to take control of his own destiny, but also to define where his true destination lies.

In their broadest sense, the words of George Bernard Shaw have always been an inspiration to me:

> This is the true joy in life, being used for a purpose recognized by yourself as a mighty one; being a force of nature instead of a feverish, selfish little clod of ailments and grievances, complaining that the world will not devote itself to making you happy. I am of the opinion that my life belongs to the whole community and as long as I live, it is my privilege to do for it what I can. I want to be thoroughly used up when I die, for the harder I work, the more I live. I rejoice in life for its own sake. Life is no brief candle to me. It is a sort of splendid torch which I have got hold of for the moment and I want to make it burn as brightly as possible before handing it on to future generations.*

This is a statement that springs from someone with an overwhelming sense of self-worth and a talent which few can lay claim to. But artists of *any* field can aspire to its aims. They are lofty but not unrealistic.

With the initial guidance of my parents, my personal, more specific

---

* This compilation was given me by a student who found it among the papers of her aunt. Half is from the preface of *Man and Superman;* the rest is probably from another preface which I have been unable to locate.

goals have always seemed clear to me. Rarely have I lost sight of them even while pitting them against the opposing aims of the commercial theatre. I do not forget them because I have not attained them: I am not a member of a fine ensemble or a part of a national theatre, because they do not yet exist. I am still working to improve my craft. I am not steadily occupied in performing challenging roles in worthwhile plays. But I have not given up hope of fulfilling my destiny and will continue the attempt to create opportunities, not *just* wait for them to arise, and to make the most of them when they do. (Perhaps this book will attract more allies to my cause!)

The very clarity of the goals which consume me makes me occasionally forget that they are not necessarily shared by others. For the actor, "the purpose recognized by yourself as a mighty one," as Shaw puts it, can take many forms. I have only to think of some of the performers in the commercial world who have given me pleasure to recognize the many other areas in which one can be of service: Greta Garbo, Spencer Tracy, James Cagney, Marcello Mastroianni, and Anna Magnani in films; Alec Guinness, Anthony Hopkins, Gérard Philipe, and Charles Laughton on stage and screen; Fred Astaire, Mary Martin, Bert Lahr, and Judy Garland in musical theatre and films; Lucille Ball on television; Ruth Draper and Whoopi Goldberg as monologuists, and Emmett Kelly in the circus ring, are only a few of the superb artists who have enriched my life. Masters of their craft, they have served us with tenacious dedication and set examples for everyone in the acting profession. So I happily acknowledge that the goal of a career in film, TV, or commercial theatre can be as admirable as mine and will make equal demands on the skill of talented performers. But I also believe that such a goal is more readily attainable than mine, because it lies within the realm of the status quo. A young performer quickly recognizes that these fields are based on commerce, that each individual venture within them is a product made for sale (including those of many "not-for-profit" theatres that produce tryouts with an eye to moving them into the larger marketplace), and he knows that once he has trained himself in his craft, he must also ready himself with the skills of self-promotion. Of course, the paths that lead to such careers are thorny and fraught with pitfalls and detours, but they don't seem to lead to the degree of confusion confronting the actor who aspires to an art theatre or those who pretend to themselves that they do.

In our society, which seems to equate success with the amount of dollars earned, the performer, abetted by his agent, even his relatives, begins to believe he is failing when he is "not making a living," or earning very little, sometimes even while he is working in the theatre. Rather than gaining confidence through the development of his craft, learning to set his own standards, he leans on the reassurance of good reviews and box office receipts. He looks to the swimming pools, grassy estates, Mercedes, jewels, and limousines which are the symbols of today's success as proof of his worth, giving little attention to the quality or value of the work itself. Judged by such standards, one would have to conclude that artists such as Rembrandt, Van Gogh, Gauguin, composers like Mozart, Bach, or Beethoven were abject failures because they died as paupers. Their gifts to us were the result not only of their talents, but of their obsession to fulfill creative needs. Their rewards lay inevitably in the process of creation regardless of monetary remuneration. The desire to perform in order to attain fame or fortune *or* romantic dreams of starring in the classics are not real goals but notions that rattle in the void. Until you define and *face up to* the challenge of the *specific* field to which you choose to dedicate yourself, you will belong to the large majority who drift into any paying opportunity that presents itself, quickly falling prey to the worst of the turmoil in our profession, becoming a victim of the conditions deplored by all, ultimately being responsible for the continuance of these conditions. You will blame "the business" or "the industry" for your ills and, to quote Shaw, "complain that the world is not devoted to making you happy." Cynicism inevitably follows on the heels of disillusionment, of soured, unrealistic dreams. The ability to better the state of the commercial performer *or* to bring an art theatre into existence is within our power if our goals are clear and *if we join hands to do so!*

Once sure about your personal destination and once you are functioning professionally, there will be many valid reasons for "crossing over" into the other fields: for example, moving from the legitimate theatre to a role in a film, a TV drama, a situation comedy, or perhaps to a TV commercial. One reason may be a simple curiosity to explore the difference in techniques. And it is possible the new techniques will excite you to the extent that you will want to change your priorities. Greta Garbo, James Cagney, Spencer Tracy, among others, found enormous satisfaction in their film careers, and to my knowledge, had no desire to return to the stage. They fulfilled their goals. Monetary reasons are logical ones; to pay the rent or to pay off a debt. (I once accepted three days' work on a film in England because it paid for three weeks of spiritual renewal for me *and* for Herbert.) If working in commercials, which takes a very special skill, is pleasurable and if the financial rewards provide a life-style to your liking, it is perfectly honest to remain in that profession and to be proud of it.

The trouble arises when, for mistaken or self-deceptive reasons, the actor gets sucked into another medium for lengthy periods while deluding himself that it is a temporary stay. He often realizes when it is too late that he has lost his way. Since I entered the profession in 1937, I have heard over and over again, "I'm going to work in films and television only until I make enough money and become well enough known to return to the stage in a position to do what I *really* want!" I have yet to meet the performer who has achieved this goal. Although Henry Fonda is often pointed to as an example of someone who achieved the best of two worlds, he confided to me a few years before he died that he bitterly regretted the eighteen years in the prime of his life during which he made films, many of them "B" westerns, missing out on all the parts he had dreamed of playing on stage. At worst there are the many gifted actors who trap themselves in TV series or sitcoms for years on end with the idea of attaining "high visibility" and large bank accounts in order to be "free" to do theatre. Stuck in the image of the roles they have created, they have not only limited their techniques but their very presence has become synonymous with their roles, making it difficult for the public to accept them as anything else. The young actor who returned East after many years of starring in a sitcom to fulfill his dream of playing Hamlet should not have wondered why he failed so abysmally, but rather should ask himself how those sitcom years could possibly have prepared him for the Prince of Denmark.

Broadway, Off-Broadway, and "not-for-profit" theatres are constant hosts to film, TV, even rock stars, who "cross over" to the stage. Managements' primary reason for the invitation rarely springs from admiration for these performers' abilities. They are relying on the stars' renown to guarantee large advance ticket sales, "to protect their investment," and much of the audience is attracted by the idea of seeing these stars in person with little regard for serious theatre. The familiar remarks of players claiming "I want to return to my first love, the theatre," or, "I need to hone my craft," or, "I have to renew my enthusiasm for acting," or, even better, "I want to prove my loyalty to the theatre" are noble clichés, usually untrue or, at best, self-deceptive. Actors are not serving the theatre when they return with inadequate or rusty theatre skills, when their real motivation is usually to boost their sagging ideals or reputations, thinking that a sense of stature associated with the theatre (which has sadly diminished in any event) will enhance their image. They insist they are making a commitment to a play, at the same time agreeing only to a "limited engagement." "A return to my roots" is not a commitment to the theatre when the limited engagement consists of a few months spent on stage squeezed in between the more lucrative work which they remind us will make for "higher visibility!" Their noble experiments are basically opportunistic ones which only augment the conditions that make our theatre more and more into a hatchet marketplace. These facts are common knowledge. I'm merely trying to put them into a perspective that will help the actor to determine his goals, and to pursue them. Established performers who are content may regard me with suspicion, barely understanding that a problem exists. They are obviously successful in the gambling casino of show business, skillful at throwing the dice that propel their careers. My hat is off to them! But the countless others, with needs like mine, who try to forget or suppress their ideals, thinking they have no choice but to play the game in order to function, are caught in a web of spiritual frustrations from which they often seek escape in liquor, drugs, or trips to the analyst. The pain they experience might be eased by a review of their original values and a consequent change of priorities. Such actors are examples for young performers who must understand their dilemma before they can try to conquer similar problems. They must realize that standing with one foot in each camp helps no one, least of all themselves.

We have arrived at the nitty-gritty of the artist's problem when he insists that he must "make a living!" First, one has to combat the notion that one is only a professional when the profession pays one. On two separate occasions Joseph Papp hugged me and thanked me for a "brilliant" performance while, in the same breath, lamenting how awful it was that I wasn't "working." The first time was after a performance of a play on which I had worked for months at the HB Studio, the other was after an evening of *Charlotte* at his own Public Theatre in a part I had played on Broadway and then toured with over a period of two years. In each instance he meant that, since I had not been paid, it couldn't be called work. I was stunned that not even *he* seemed to see what a ludicrous perception this was. But I remained unshaken in my conviction that one cannot demand of art that it pay you in any other way than in the satisfaction of the work itself. I knew that even those two "not working" performances had reached the hearts and minds of a few hundred people, that I had fed their soul with food more satisfying than the sop of a *Dallas* or *Dynasty* with which I might have reached millions and been paid thousands of dollars.

Those who look for salvation from the endowments and counsel from our national and state foundations for the arts may groan at these organizations' new determination to give help only to those groups who hire actors for pay. They seem to have become an extension of our trade unions.

I believe that when you have achieved great skill, a point of view, and the power to communicate, an audience, no matter how small, will reward you with the respect that makes it all worthwhile. If you are willing to make a true commitment to the making of theatre art, like a dedicated priest or nun you will have to accept the likelihood of poverty in exchange for inner riches. It is the only trade-off you can hope for.

3

The Actor's
Techniques

ARMED with a passion for self-expression, with a point of view about his world and a specific goal to reach for, the actor must acquire a mastery of his craft—or all the talent and good will in the world will count for nothing.

There is a greater lack of understanding and more misinformation about the nature of this craft than in that of any of the other arts, including the notion that acting is merely intuitive, entailing no craft at all. "You're just born to be an actor," "acting can't be learned," "acting can't be taught" are phrases that spring from ignorance and the kind of prejudice that once again relegates the actor to the position of a gifted, rather unintelligent child. They are the opinions of those who believe that the "tricks of the trade" can be picked up while performing in public. These views are even echoed by our trade unions (Actors' Equity, Screen Actors' Guild, and the American Federation of Television and Radio Actors); with no established criteria, they will accept anyone who has been hired or fired, by a fluke or a relative, after just *one* job without any prior training or experience. So we continue to have a theatre of mediocrity, of hacks, of imitation or ready-made acting styles, relieved only by the few exceptional performers who, aside from their gifts, have learned to respect, understand, and perfect their craft.

We have yet to shake the negative aspects of our American theatre heritage* when the only means of learning used to consist of joining a group of strolling players, a stock company, or an established actor-manager's company as an apprentice, playing small parts, occasionally receiving help or advice from the director or leading players, or simply by imitation. Of course the *extraordinarily* gifted survived, developing an intuitive, personal way of work (which they were often unable to articulate) while relying on their experience in front of an audience in order to grow as artists. But they were and remain the exception.

At a ballet, when the audience sees the dancers' pirouettes, elevations, stretches, and lightning-quick entrechats, when they are transported by the content revealed by this artistry, they *know* that what they have experienced would be impossible to achieve without years of training and practice. When they attend a concert and watch the violinist tuck his instrument under his chin, using the fingers of one hand on the strings while stroking the bow across them with the other to make his beautiful phrases, they *know* they could not emulate him. Nor do they pay attention to the technique: They listen to the music, they watch the ballet. When the actors' techniques are visible and audible as in the case of artificial, "effective" theatricality, studied poses, mechanically enunciated words "sung" by richly produced voices, when tears are shed merely for the sake of proving you can cry on cue in public, when histrionics and bombast are reveled in, the audience is often impressed because they *know* that they could not do that either.

I am only impressed when the actor's technique is so perfect that it has become *invisible* and has persuaded the audience that they are in the presence of a living human being who makes it possible for them to empathize with all his foibles and struggles as they unfold in the play. It is my firm belief that when you are aware of *how* a feat has been achieved, the actor has failed. He has *mis*used his techniques. Unfortunately, when he has succeeded, when his work communicates convincingly as a living person, it is just then that much of the audience will be convinced that they can do that, too—the only intangible being, "How do you learn all these lines?" Otherwise they

* See Chapter 1.

consider themselves to be knowledgeable critics, often giving "how-to" advice to the actor. Sometimes the beleaguered, insecure actor even listens, almost always to his disadvantage. The actor must know that since he, himself, is the instrument, he must play on it to serve the character with the same effortless dexterity with which the violinist makes music on his. Just because he doesn't look like a violin is no reason to assume his techniques should be thought of as less difficult. The gossipy curiosity about what makes an actor tick, which is expressed on every second talk show, as well as in endless public seminars, the superficial answers given (often accompanied by "funny" personal examples), only aggravate our problems. The audiences, as well as the talk show hosts, are rarely interested in discussions of a musician's finger exercises, a dancer's pliés, a painter's palette or how he applies a "wash" for a watercolor. Why should they care about *our* techniques? They are *our* business, not theirs. So, for you, the actor, whose entire being is his instrument, let me define what the techniques consist of which make up our fabulous craft!

THE OUTER TECHNIQUES

In Europe, until recently, few actors would have been allowed on a stage before they had received a thorough training of their body, voice, and speech. I, myself, came to the theatre well equipped in all three, and, although I do not teach these skills (nor would I presume to do so), let me explain why I give them such importance and why their neglect, which is so prevalent in our theatre, appalls me. If you are aiming for a television career in roles close to your own persona, parts in which your blue-jeaned slouch and your own regional speech will be acceptable, in which the mike will suffice to pick up your breathy voice, you won't have to worry about these particular basics. But if you are aiming for something more, please trust my advice.

You will begin by recognizing that THE BODY is the outer manifestation of the actor, the most visible of his tools, capable of communicating the slightest nuance of thought and feeling, of regal bearing and Olympian carriage as well as the physical frailties and distortions that may be demanded by a given role, and you will know that years of dogged determination are needed to perfect it. I believe that modern dance is the finest means of attaining correct body alignment, kinetic awareness, and flexibility. Sports such as swimming and gymnastics are extremely useful. Tennis and fencing have the additional advantage of training interaction between you and a partner, alerting you to the give-and-take that is so crucial on the stage. Mime will extend your imagination as well as the use of your body when you learn to produce the absent elements of space and objects through physical movement. "Stage movement," which is so often taught, has the tendency to produce artificial, self-conscious gestures and stances of predetermined shape, whereas dance, sports, and mime make for a body that will respond by reflex to the demands made by a large variety of roles without interfering with the involvement of the actor's human responses.

THE VOICE is in itself an instrument on which you must learn to play. Treat it with the care given a Stradivarius. Use the finest bowing techniques instead of sawing on it. Misuse creates nodes or spread vocal chords which produce the kind of rasping, hoarse croaks so often heard in older players and, on occasion, in younger ones. It brings about the self-induced cases of laryngitis that cause actors to miss performances. Other manifestations of a lack of training are unpleasant nasalities, squeaky or foghorn voices, and poorly modulated ones. Even if God has given you a naturally well-placed voice, you need training to maintain it and to learn how to support it with correct breathing techniques, allowing you to be heard in a large theatre without shouting, pushing, or anxiety about projection. Today most of our Broadway houses have to be miked because so few actors are able to be heard in them.

This mechanical intrusion into the communication of a live performance is sad indeed, and it is only a partial excuse to blame the audiences for not listening properly because they are so accustomed to the blaring television sets in their living rooms. You must be armed with a well-modulated voice, flexible enough to encompass a wide variety of roles and strong enough to be heard in a sizable theatre. To achieve it, I believe that singing lessons will best serve you. "Voice production" for the stage has similar drawbacks to "stage movement" in lieu of dance. Through singing you will learn to understand the vocal instrument and to exercise it without listening to yourself when you speak. You will not be tempted to make beautiful sounds for their own sake but will allow your voice to be at the service of your character without self-conscious contrivance.

SPEECH, that glorious means of communication given to man alone, is given to the actor as the sole tool that sets him apart from all other performing artists. The necessity to master STANDARD AMERICAN SPEECH, which is beautiful, elegant, without artifice or affectation, is acknowledged by our profession as a whole. It is a mark of our laziness, our lack of discipline and commitment, that so few achieve it to the point of its becoming an integral part of their instrument. Even those who for years attend two or three speech classes a week, during which they learn and practice all the correct sounds, fall back into their own distortions the moment they leave the classroom. As a consequence they never arrive at the point of believing it is truly *they* who are speaking well. They only feel like students "putting on" correct sounds. And when they apply their newly learned technique to a role, they feel "unnatural," and the portrayal itself becomes alien to spontaneous human speech. Those who *do* achieve it will be able to put themselves truthfully into any present or historical time or place, into the myriad of characters they will want to become. Hamlet's advice to the players, "Speak the speech, I pray you, as I pronounced it to you, trippingly on the tongue," does not make much sense when delivered with New Yorkese distortions. We have heard the comic overtones, the disservice done to the poetry of Christopher Fry and T. S. Eliot, to the tirades of Shaw by drawls and twangs and slurs. Nor is British speech the answer. It places Chekhov, Ibsen, Strindberg, or Molière in the heart of England. British speech belongs to our colleagues abroad. If it is demanded by a specific character or the milieu of the play, it can be learned with the same relative ease with which other dialects or accents are learned for particular roles. (I say "relative ease," meaning *after* standard speech has become a reflex.) And it is *very* easy to revert to one's original speech if the part requires it.

In order to absorb what the actor has learned in class, he must be willing to take his lessons into the street, to practice his sounds in daily life until they become second nature to him. He will need the courage to combat a society in which it is a sin not to be a "regular fella," a society that considers any word, sound, or movement outside of the familiar to be an affectation or a sign of dishonesty. He must steel himself against the criticism of the friends and relatives who insist he is "putting on airs" or "acting stagey" or "uppity" when he tries to speak well. He must practice his speech until he becomes used to it, until he, himself, becomes accustomed to it and can revel in his newfound verbal freedom, until "Tuh be oar naht tuh be" seems weird and will no longer be necessary for his sense of reality.

The same principle can be applied to body work, when the actor is practicing a perfect body alignment or the fluid movement of a simple walk across the dance floor, but feels compelled, when leaving, to slouch out with his usual round shoulders and protruding stomach to make sure no one will accuse him of seeming "fancy."

There are other ways to exercise your verbal skill outside the classroom. For instance, sight reading can be developed at home, by reading aloud for half an hour every day. Use a friend as a target now and then to see with what dexterity you can communicate the content of the material. See how quickly your capabilities will increase, even after a few months. Choose your material carefully: Use novels that employ fine language or the essays of Emerson and Thoreau. Read poetry, the sonnets of Shakespeare. If you tackle dramatic literature, read aloud only the scenes that do not involve a character you may want to play or work on seriously in the future. Read the prefaces to Shaw's plays. They will familiarize you with the author's ideas and idiom. These useful drills for sight-reading, for voice and speech are *preparations* for the eventual, organic process of making the character's language your own. If you impose self-conscious vocal and verbal effects on a character's language you will damage the deeper work involved when working on the role. In other words, do not confuse such exercising with interpretation.

Such practicing will also increase your appetite for words, for fine language and the ability to make it yours. It will make you reject "all riiiight!" and "coooool!" as the sole means of expressing a response to a profound experience or event. You will reach instead for the endless supply of adjectives, verbs, and nouns available in the dictionary. You will question our society's penchant for the use of "no waaaay!" in place of any courteous expression of disapproval or rejection, or "tsk" and "wow" as responses to a breathtaking sunset or spinning tornado, or the use of four-letter expletives as the sole means of communicating frustration or anger. Read out loud. Learn to relish the explosive ideas and phenomenal imagery contained in a body of contemporary and classic literature. Let language take shape on your tongue until it begins to spring from your soul.

THE HUMAN TECHNIQUES

A belief, still shared by a large part of the international theatre community, is that the actor's training is complete when he has achieved a command of the outer techniques, that he is then ready to acquire what other skills he may need by experience alone, through a kind of sink-or-swim method on stage. Under such circumstances the actor, having been advised to use his "imagination" about his role, learns while rehearsing and performing, by imitation, by borrowing the behavior of his more experienced colleagues, taking their hints about the tricks of timing, illustrated actions and reactions, placing laughs, waiting for laughs, picking up cues, simulating emotions, etc. From the others he borrows suitable behavior for a variety of ready-made "styles"—for drawing room comedy, for slice-of-life plays, for Chekhov, Ibsen, Shaw, Restoration plays, Shakespeare, Molière, and the Greek dramatists. And these conventionally accepted, easily imitated, formalistic approaches are passed on from generation to generation. Eleonora Duse, the great Italian actress, once expressed the fervent wish that all theatres be destroyed so that, after a hiatus of at least fifty years, actors could begin anew, with no stale traditions to copy.

Since the seventeenth century when opinions about actors began to be recorded in letters, diaries, and, later, in critical writings, there have been two schools of thought about what separated great actors from the ordinary. On the one hand, there were traditional performers who were deemed exceptional because of their charisma and panache, their visible and audible skills in effective theatricality, their ringing voices, their chilling screams, their heartrending depictions of grief and terror, the bravado of their startling choices, the grandeur of their gestures, and their ability to *illustrate* many different characters. On the other hand, in almost every generation, we hear about the isolated performers who astonished and captivated their audiences with recognizable human behavior, who seemed to have shaken off all theatrical conventions. Their selected realities, their discoveries of truthful behavior, and ways of communicating it as freshly as though it had just happened seemed mysterious, and other actors found it impossible to imitate.

A preference for one or the other of these two opposing genres continues to make for passionate debates among performers as well as audiences. Theatre historians have given them names that irritate me because they are confusing. I mention them only to satisfy scholarly accuracy. The first is termed representational acting, which I prefer to call FORMALISM, **in which the artist objectively *predetermines* the character's actions, deliberately watching the form as he executes it.** The second is referred to as presentational acting, which I call REALISM, **in which the actor puts his own psyche to use to find identification with the role, allowing the behavior to develop** out of the playwright's given circumstances, trusting that a form will result, **knowing that the executions of his actions will involve a moment-to-moment *subjective* experience.**

The notorious rivalry which raged for more than ten years between Eleonora Duse and the great French actress Sarah Bernhardt at the turn of the century supplies us with a perfect example of the differences between formalism and realism. To help you decide which side to take, read one or more of the countless biographies of Bernhardt with their descriptions of the flamboyance of her performances as well as her personal life, which served to make her an international idol. She played roles as diverse as Camille and Napoleon's son, the Duke of Reichstadt, in Rostand's *L'Aiglon*. She even played the role of Hamlet.

Camille was also one of Duse's famous roles. Later she introduced many of Ibsen's women to Europe and America.* When the two actresses were in London playing the part of Magda in Sudermann's play *Heimat* at two different West End theatres at the same time, George Bernard Shaw wrote a lengthy article in which he compared these two great ladies of the theatre.

---

* William Weaver's fine biography, *Duse* (New York: Harcourt Brace Jovanovich, 1984), is rich with information about her career and impressions of her work by actors, directors, and writers like Chekhov and Shaw. You will discover the realism to which I have referred.

Here are a few excerpts from Shaw's review in *The World,* June 15, 1895: "The contrast between the two Magdas is as extreme as any contrast could possibly be between two artists who have finished their twenty years' apprenticeship to the same profession under closely similar conditions." He describes Bernhardt as "always ready with a sunshine-through-the-clouds smile." He continues with her appearance, complexion, and make-up: "Her lips are like a newly painted pillar box; her cheeks, right up to the languid lashes, have the bloom and surface of a peach, she is beautiful with the beauty of her school, and entirely inhuman and incredible. But the incredulity is pardonable, because though it is all great nonsense, nobody believing in it, the actress herself least of all, it is so artful, so clever, so well recognized a part of the business, and carried off with such a genial air, that it is impossible not to accept it with good humor." He then speaks of Bernhardt's acting as being "childishly egotistical," without deeper feeling, and notes she has "the art of making you admire her, pity her, champion her, weep with her, laugh at her jokes, follow her fortunes breathlessly, and applaud her wildly when the curtain falls."

And then Shaw comes to Duse: "All this is precisely what does not happen in the case of Duse, whose every part is a separate creation. When she comes on stage, you are quite welcome to take your opera glass and count whatever lines time and care have so far traced on her. They are the credentials of her humanity." Later he says, "Duse is not in action five minutes before she is a quarter of a century ahead of the handsomest woman in the world. . . . Madame Bernhardt's stock of attitudes and facial effects could be catalogued as easily as her stock of dramatic ideas: the counting would hardly go beyond the fingers of both hands. Duse produces the illusion of being infinite in a variety of beautiful pose and motion . . . only the multitude of ideas which find expression in her movements are all of that high quality which marks off humanity from the animals." Shaw extols Duse's range "which so immeasurably dwarfs the poor little octave and a half on which Sarah Bernhardt plays such pretty little canzonettes and stirring marches." Later he describes Duse in a scene in which Magda receives a bouquet from a man she admires: "A terrible thing happened to her. She began to blush; and in another moment she was conscious of it, and the blush was slowly spreading and deepening until, after a few vain efforts to avert her face, she gave up and hid the blush in her hands. After that feat of acting I did not need to be told why Duse does not paint an inch thick. I could detect no trick in it: it seemed to me a perfectly genuine effect of the dramatic imagination."

Although not quite as extreme, other historic rivalries existed, for instance that between our great American realist Edwin Booth and his English colleague Sir Henry Irving, whose competing Hamlets became the talk of two continents. Today we have many examples of formalistic and realistic stars whom I choose not to name because of my obvious preference for the realistic ones. I cannot reject *all* formalistic acting because I would have to exclude the many brilliant performers who have impressed me through the years. But I *do* reject formalism as an approach to my own work as an actor and teacher. Eleonora Duse remains my role model: Duse, whose way of communicating was already instilled in me as a child—without my ever having seen her; Duse, about whom it was written—"She has no gift for advertising. . . . She does not gesticulate, does not declaim, does not invent scenic effects, but creates characters, *lives* them with a simplicity never seen before. . . . She has formed herself through the observation and understanding of life. . . . It is simplicity achieved through complexity, through **the penetration of the whole** [emphasis mine]."* And it was Gerhart Hauptmann, the great German dramatist, who called her "the first interpreter of that psychological art that is now making inevitable progress." When Duse was asked about the technique she employed to bring about this "psychological art," she referred to it simply as *la grazia* or "the gift," which is better defined as **the conscious use of subconscious promptings.**†

Duse, although possibly the greatest of them all, was not alone in a realistic approach to her roles. Others, like Tommaso Salvini, the

---

* Alexey Suvorin, a Russian critic, quoted in Weaver's *Duse.*

† On many occasions, alone or in the company of my students, I have gone to New York City's Museum of Modern Art to view the film *Great Actresses*, which shows sections of performances by Réjane, Mrs. Fiske, and Bernhardt among others, as well as Eleonora Duse's short film *Ashes.* Duse's work is an ultimate example of the timelessness of great acting. It is as modern as tomorrow, while the work of most of the others proves that the reflection of prevalent fashion in acting styles quickly becomes passé.

Italian tragedian in whose company she had worked, Joseph Kainz, the Austrian actor, Alexander Moissi, the Italo-Austrian star, and Albert Basserman in Germany, also found their personal way of bringing roles into being, sharing the truthfulness and sense of immediacy in their performances that gave their audiences such a profound experience. It was to actors like these that Constantin Stanislavsky, the Russian actor-director, went in search of the procedures they were using. He wanted to define what they had in common that set them apart from formalistic, traditional actors, to make the seemingly mysterious sources of their work concrete. Where did their *faith* and *belief* come from? Down what paths did their *imagination* take them? What magic did they employ to keep their *concentration* focused on the arena of their life on stage instead of letting it stray into the auditorium? How did they arrive at **a selection of truthful actions**? How did they **maintain such spontaneity** in the continuing repetition of their roles? Stanislavsky tried to articulate and record what he had learned about the creative process used *intuitively* by great actors such as Duse and Salvini. And he made his findings available to the profession as a whole. He longed to raise the level of the actor, not necessarily to that of a genius, but enough to present an audience with an entire cast that could communicate the total intent of the dramatist instead of giving them only the star performances to which they were accustomed, in which the play was used merely as a personal vehicle.

From the great realists, who often had difficulty in verbalizing their techniques or were unwilling to share their secrets, Stanislavsky nevertheless found sufficient material to develop his system or Method. The proof of the pudding was the Moscow Art Theatre, a brilliant ensemble company which, under his tutelage and guidance, reigned for years as a shining example of modern acting. It was rivaled only by the magnificent company of actors that flourished under the direction of the German director Max Reinhardt. Along with the success of his productions, Reinhardt conducted his famous acting seminars in Salzburg and later in California where he was a refugee in the forties, but, *unfortunately*, he did not publish his findings.

As Stanislavsky's *An Actor Prepares* became available, actors all over the world were, for the first time, able to avail themselves of extensive techniques other than the external ones. Today the Method is taught or referred to in professional workshops, as well as in the drama departments of schools and universities throughout the country. It seems to be more open to a variety of interpretations and misinterpretations than the Holy Bible. As we know, Stanislavsky's discoveries were based on *his* understanding of how the great realistic actors applied the psychology of human struggles and drives, their response to emotional, physical, and mental stimuli and to their consequent actions. Sticking slavishly to his doctrines is an injustice to Stanislavsky himself. It is wrong to assume he would have stood still, clinging to the conclusions to which he came at the early part of the twentieth century. We cannot ignore the findings of the many behavioral psychologists that have come to our attention since his death, nor, perhaps even more importantly, the writings of contemporary philosophers and authors who have helped us to understand ourselves in relation to the present, so that we may put *ourselves* to work in the illumination of the human soul. On the heels of Freud, Adler, and Jung came the nonclinical cultural humanists and behaviorists like Erik Erikson, Abraham Maslow, Bruno Bettelheim and his uses of enchantment, Eric Berne, B. F. Skinner's furtherance of Pavlov's theories, Kurt Lewin and his followers, etc. We have the writings of Gide, Camus, Wittgenstein, extraordinarily helpful studies of semantics, even those of body language—all of which can bring about new personal insights and fascinating triggers for the actor's imagination that, I'm convinced, would have fascinated Stanislavsky.

The best-selling work of Allan Bloom, *The Closing of the American Mind,* has been a recent inspiration for my acting and teaching. It has made me re-examine Aristotle, Machiavelli, and Rousseau, each of whom expounded on the human condition in a way that was original in his time, in each case creating a new language for his proposals—as did Stanislavsky for the actor. It must be noted that it is often the *colleague* or *direct disciple* of a new thinker who gets stuck in literal interpretations of the work, tending to freeze the new ideas and language into an inflexible, static condition.

Whatever you learn from the great writers, or even from me, *however* you employ your intellect, *beware* that it does not lead to cold, pedantic answers or inflexible, dogmatic hypotheses. In my own work I always guard against *clinical,* psychiatric analyses. They deaden the creative process. To the psychiatrist, *Oedipus* is a complex, a subject illustrating a particular kind of human deviation or abnormality. To the actor, *Oedipus* (or *Hamlet,* for that matter) deals with the exploration of moral and spiritual anguish. Any psychoanalytical probing of the subconscious that leads to scientific answers and categorization may be of interest to doctors and scholars, but it will annihilate or bypass the emotional and sensory stimuli that the actor needs to catapult him into a creative state.

Modern acting became known on the European continent and quickly spread to America. Passionate debates ensued, which continue into the present, between those actors who espoused the new way of work—from the inside out—and those who defended traditional formalism—from the outside in. Examples can be made of some of the finest actors who firmly believed that a conceptual shape for their performances came first. Laurence Olivier, while acknowledging that he was often attacked for being "too technical," defended this view in a BBC interview, and nobody can deny the brilliance of his career. Once, after playing *The Entertainer* with incredible involvement and spontaneity at a run-through for an invited audience, in answer to the friends who, deeply moved, had rushed backstage to congratulate him, he announced, "I don't like that kind of acting; I didn't know what I was doing." Similarly, the famous nineteenth-century actor Coquelin once apologized to his colleagues in the wings, "Tonight I shed real tears on stage. I promise you it will not occur again." Like Olivier, Coquelin also believed it was inartistic to be transported by a real experience while portraying a character. In my defense of these two artists, with whom I disagree, I am presenting you with a choice. I also wish to point out that if you opt for their direction, the main thrust of this book will be of little value to you.

When I first came on the scene in the 1930s and worked with such giants as the Lunts and Paul Muni, although they didn't want to hear even a *mention* of the Method, I was always surprised to observe that their own work actually went *further* than the recommendations of Stanislavsky in their hunt for reality. In the last act of Chekhov's *Sea Gull,* when the family exits to the dining room to eat while Nina and Konstantin play out their final farewell, Alfred Lunt and Lynn Fontanne took turns complaining at every rehearsal: either that they didn't *believe* they were going off to supper, or that they didn't *believe* they were reentering the drawing room after having eaten. Their solution to this problem was to set up table and chairs, china, glasses, and silverware in the wings and then to improvise an off-stage eating scene every night of the run. A by-product of this work was the brilliant counterpoint provided by the clink of glasses and cutlery and muted dialogue and laughter offstage to the tragedy unfolding on the stage. (The prop list for this improvisation, never seen by the public, was almost as long as that for the rest of the show.)

When I played with Paul Muni in Maxwell Anderson's *Key Largo*, he also rejected Stanislavsky, yet his fanatic search for identification with his character was almost agonizing to watch. His background work occasionally went as far as going to live for weeks with families in the neighborhoods where his character might have lived, in order to absorb, subjectively, the daily habits, the very atmosphere of his character's previous life.

Laurette Taylor was my idol and an inspiration to me.* She believed her work of identification was incomplete until she was "wearing the underpants of the character." Her subjective development of actions and words, which always sprang from her as though for the very first time, her refusal to arrive at quick results, never setting an effect, opening herself to the stimuli imaginatively applied to her on-stage life, were ideal examples of how to work from the inside out—and yet she insisted she had no technique.

These artists' denials of the existence of the specific techniques which came instinctively to them is understandable. They rebelled against the systemization of a process which they considered to be in the personal, subjective realm of their own creations. Their resistance arose from a rejection of the psychoanalytical approach which I have already discussed. And it came from the misuse of these techniques that was so often in evidence. (For instance, when, in the actor's hunt for an emotional experience, he uses the emotion for its own sake, indulging in it, displaying it rather than using it as a springboard to find and feed the selected actions of his character in the given circumstances, he is confusing *feeling* with *doing*.) Above all, what the great actors rejected was the often trivial, *naturalistic* behavior which

---

* Read her biography *Laurette*, by Marguerite Courtney (New York: Atheneum, 1955).

manifested itself in the actors who claimed to be using Stanislavsky's techniques. I have no desire to diminish the importance of Stanislavsky's pioneering efforts: He provided us with a new concept of the approach to our work. He laid the foundation for a common language and gave us the knowledge that tools existed with which to work on our craft. His goals, ideals, and personal integrity, his expression of artistic ethics remains awe-inspiring!

Naturalistic acting is often confused with **realistic acting** but they are worlds apart. The very expression "I want to be a natural" implies a desire to be ordinary and leads to a search for the habitual, for the trivial details of daily life, to an irrelevant imitation of nature. It produces the nose rubbing, the sniffing and throat clearing, the shrugging and scratching, the brushing aside of stray hairs, the casual kicking at something underfoot, the insertion of "uhhh . . ." or "well . . ." as a handle to every mumbled sentence, the fuzzling of words to find a "natural" tone—all the tedious mannerisms, sometimes deliberately acquired, by the actor who wants to feel comfortable and natural on stage. It's small wonder that the audience balks and asks for something more theatrical. But **reality is theatrical,** in the very best sense of the word. When a director (whom I distrusted in any event) once described the behavior he envisioned for a certain play as being "bigger than life," I challenged him with "Do you mean phoney?" I truly believe there is *nothing* larger than life. How often do we greet an extraordinary event with the comment "If we saw that on the stage, we wouldn't believe it"? What a dreadful commentary on the state of our theatre. Is reality too big for it? Must we water down the truth to make it palatable in the mistaken notion that *that* will be an answer to false histrionics?

In the August 1952 issue of *Theatre Arts* magazine there is an article by Christopher Fry entitled "How Lost, How Amazed, How Miraculous We Are" to which I often refer. Although Fry is addressing himself to the dramatist and the poet, every word has pertinence for the actor. He writes, "Reality is incredible, reality is a whirlwind." He pleads with the artists to receive the world with innocence, with awesome wonder, and he attacks "the dull eye of custom" which grinds down our sensibilities to fit ourselves into recognizable molds. He cautions us not to attempt to make sense of reality by tucking away our perceptions into familiar pigeonholes.

Realism entails a search for *selected* behavior pertinent to the character's needs within the prescribed circumstances of the dramatist. We must take *from* life in order to create the reality of our *new* life on stage. What it is that we take is a reflection of our vision, our point of view—and the power of our selection is the measure of our artistry. And, since we have only a few hours of compressed life on stage, our creation has to count! **Naturalism,** which pursues the unselective imitation of life, is the antithesis of art.

The **techniques** (with which I deal in Parts Two and Three) that separate the professional actor from the dilettante and the realist from the formalist concern themselves with an understanding of the self, the development of sensory responses—both physiological and emotional—and their consequent actions. They entail the development of insight into human motivations and **the intersection of psychology and behavior** that will ultimately be applied to the techniques of bringing a character into existence in a play (Part Four).

I will be sharing with you what I, myself, have learned as an actress *and* as a teacher. Unlike some artists who zealously guard the "secrets" that make them function, I love to share the discoveries that have helped my work. (I also enjoy sharing a wonderful recipe and have never understood those cooks who don't want anyone else to know how they make something delicious.) I am enthusiastic by nature and often impatient, even though I won't shy away from a difficult challenge: I learned my best lesson about the patience needed to make something grow organically from gardening. I think this is an analogy for acting: To garden "organically" means to make use of nature's gifts without the addition of synthetic chemicals or anything artificial. First the soil must be tested and properly analyzed, then it must be prepared, fed, dug deeply, raked, and made "friable" (easily crumbled). The choice of seeds must be considered in relation to the light and the environment in which they are to develop. They must be correctly sown, then watered and fertilized. And as the plant sprouts and grows, all the pests and bugs that are its natural enemies must be removed. It must be protected during storms or from other natural disasters. Then it will flourish. And so it is for the actor who wishes to grow, who learns to apply the same procedures patiently, without taking shortcuts, to produce a work of art.

Part Two:
The Human Techniques

4

The Self

As a young performer I read and heard the admonishments of fine performers again and again that "You must *lose yourself* in the parts you play!" It sounded noble—just what a person *should* do who wants to "sacrifice herself for art's sake." But I had no idea how to go about it. I finally understood that it was a warning to the vain and egocentric actors who enjoyed displaying themselves, trading on those characteristics that they believed would appeal to the audience, regardless of the role and the circumstances of the play.

Still I didn't know how to go about losing myself. I wanted to follow in Duse's footsteps. She insisted that the only thing she had to offer the theatre was the "revelation of her soul." I knew that hers must have been a soul of enormous depth and complexity to allow her to shine so far above the others in such a variety of roles. This use of herself was what set her apart from the formalistic actors who chose to illustrate the perceptions they had of the characters they portrayed without any personal, psychological, or emotional involvement. After many years of playing badly, caught between an illustration of the characters with whom I failed to find identification and the attempt to use my own emotions to fill in this illustrative behavior, I finally saw the light: **I must *find* myself in the role!** The light almost went out again when I realized that I wasn't quite sure who I was. What did this soul consist of which I, like Duse, longed to reveal in the service of art?

The soul, the psyche (the Greek word for soul), and the self are one and the same, with different semantic connotations. The soul is often perceived as something infinite, mysterious, not readily definable; the psyche has a more scientific meaning connected with modern psychology. In this age of pragmatism, the self, no matter how complicated, seems a less frightening term than the others, something more accessible to scrutiny for the actor. The self also seems to be less concerned than the soul with things like virtue and evil, making it easier to discover and justify the behavior that results from the pursuit of happiness, of self-gratification—which is at the core of man's existence.

I always believed I had a strong sense of my own identity. Now I tried to define what this identity consisted of: I had an *image* of myself as being outgoing, frank, generous, warmly humorous, gentle yet strong, brilliant yet innocent. This encapsulated, intuitive assessment was accompanied by a *visual* image of myself as a child of nature running through a field of wildflowers, long hair flying in the wind, wide-eyed, eager, with arms outstretched. In point of fact, I have *never* had long hair or particularly wide eyes, and I certainly run through fields only on rare occasions, eagerly or otherwise. As for the admirable qualities that I attributed to myself, I soon learned that these were only a small part of myself and that this total self-image was a cliché. It was perhaps an even bigger cliché than the one I used to arrive at for a role I was to undertake after first contact with it. It became clear that I must learn to enlarge the conception I had of myself, to gain a truer understanding of who I *really* am if my soul is to be of any use, if I wanted to make it available for the many parts I hoped to bring to life.

Since my self-perception was so lopsided with admirable qualities, it became obvious why I was unable to find true identification with the roles I played. I had to be honest with myself in order to recognize the arrogance, ruthlessness, deceit, envy, and selfishness of which I was capable under certain circumstances. I could no longer refuse to examine any stupidities, neurotic impulses, fears, and ambiguities—in other words, the negative as well as the positive qualities that exist in me, as well as in other human beings.

Whenever I criticize students who feel compelled to indicate a character's actions, who comment on the actions rather than really executing them because they've been unable to justify them, I invariably get the same answers I used to make: "But I'm not like that," "But I would never do that," "I'm not shy," "I'm not bossy," "I'm never silly," etc. Then, when I ask them to remember a high school prom at which their slip was showing or when they'd spilled something on their gown or when they had a pimple on their nose, they look down at the floor, sometimes even producing Duse's famous blush, and they are *shy*. I remind them that when they confront a colleague about their right to the rehearsal space they are *bossy,* and that when they make cooing sounds and talk baby talk to their pets they are *silly*. When I am with a scientist, even with an electrician, I am *stupid*, even though my cliché self-image tells me I am brilliant. If a bigoted doorman spouts racist opinions, I pull rank; I behave like *a snob* even though I think of myself as the original liberal and humanist. I believe I'm incapable of cowardice, yet the sight of a mouse sends me into hysterics. It soon becomes clear that **the basic components of the characters we will play are somewhere within ourselves.**

The next thing to learn is that self-discovery never ceases and that it takes a long time to put its results into practice consistently, before the use of oneself becomes a reflex way of working in identifying with the role. I made another big breakthrough when I realized that whenever I behaved *badly,* usually when frustrated in the fulfillment of my wishes, I had given myself—consciously or subconsciously—a *justification* for my actions. I was always in the right. Guilt, or the recognition of cruelty, insensitivity, or manipulation almost always comes after the fact. This learning process doesn't necessarily make you a wiser or better behaved person—just a better actor.

Far easier to recognize and accept than judgmental behavior are the endlessly different aspects of yourself, the variations of your persona that aren't necessarily either admirable or ugly. It is miraculous to discover how your self-perception can change from one moment to the next. There are hundreds of different people within you who surface throughout each day. Imagine that you are on the telephone calling your family and observe how your self-image, even your body and tone of voice, change if it is your mother or father, a sibling, an in-law, an aunt or uncle, a neighbor, or a child at the other end of the line. The next time you call home, see how you change depending on the circumstances when talking to the same people: If you are anxious because one of them is ill, or cross because one of them owes you a letter, or because you need something from them—such as money.

Observe your behavior when you are tidying up your apartment and the doorbell rings: Depending on whom you are expecting, you will present yourself with a marked difference that will already manifest itself in your walk to the door. You will behave one way if it is the janitor or a particular delivery boy, another way if a colleague has come to rehearse, or if someone is making a social call, whether it is a friend from out of town or a neighbor's child who wants to play. You have a different sense of self when you arise in the morning depending on the weather (brisk and sunny or cloudy and bleak), or whether you have a special occasion to look forward to or a dental appointment, whether you had been to a wild bash the night before, or gone to bed early with a good biography, whether your bedroom is tidy or messy.

Another area of discovery that will allow you to mine gold in the expansion of your self-perception concerns the clothes you wear. When I dress for the opera, my self-image begins to change when I put on my sheer hose. It expands further with my slinky gown, velvet shoes, and sparkling earrings, and completes itself as I don my cape and gloves. I feel the essence of elegance, even like royalty, and I already envision myself as a commanding presence seated in a loge or gliding gracefully through the halls of the Met at the intermission. This image might even sustain me until the music starts, but then I sit agog, weeping until my mascara runs, shouting, bravoing, and clapping after an exhilarating aria until I'm hoarse and the palms of my hands are red. My self-image becomes more like the one I had as a teenager sitting in the peanut gallery in hand-me-down finery.

When I dress for work in the garden in sneakers, stained bluejeans, and a man's shirt, I feel and behave like an earth mother. In dressing for a particular occasion, the very act of putting on each article brings about a change of self. Notice how you feel and behave when trying things on in a store, the fantasies that occur when the garment is dowdy and makes you feel older or middle-class, or when it fits a flamboyant image. Note how an outlandish new high-fashion garment can intimidate you and bring about an awkwardness or a remembered sense of teenage gangliness, a feeling of being out of place. Of course, clothing can condition the behavior right up to the point of your removing it to put on something else. When I put on my billowing flannel granny nightgown, I usually have a sense of childlike cozy security. A short boxy nightshirt gives me an image of a cocky, smart kid; a silky nightgown makes me feel like a seductress, etc. In particular, note the difference footwear makes to your carriage, to your entire bearing—for example, slippers, sandals, high heels, sneakers, etc.

You will present yourself in a variety of ways at a fancy party that includes agents, producers, or directors who are in a position to employ you, and quite differently, in another variety of ways, at an informal gathering of friends, with your feet up while guzzling beer. Observe how, by contrast, you will behave at your parents' home when they are entertaining their peers and, once again, how you will transform yourself to suit the occasion of a birthday party for children. In each instance even your verbal idiom changes.

In summation, **you change your sense of self a hundred times a day as you are influenced by circumstances, your relationship to others, the nature of the event, and your clothing.** There is an element of spontaneous role-playing in this procedure that I believe exists in all human beings but to a far greater extent in actors. To all actors—not only those who believe that their own persona is boring, that their character in a play is more interesting than they are, leading them to formalistic character illustration as the only way out—I recommend this **training in self-observation,** in "self-stretching exercises" as I call them. It is the source for a warehouse full of selves that can be called on to fill the complicated characters you will be called on to bring into being.

If you are still in doubt, if a fear lingers that you will be too much the same in every part, it is because you have not tested self-discovery enough or are impatient with it. Or, perhaps, you are confused by the examples of "personality" actors, so many of whom crowd the stage and screen, who use their cliché self-image over and over again, usually because it worked for them the first time with the approval of both audience and critics. In order to ensure their continued success, unwilling or technically unable to move away from their limited self-image, they copy the *manner* of themselves as tediously as formalistic actors copy the manner of their preconceived characters.

To reassure you that you need not fall into this trap, let me offer a personal example. A man who had seen me in a dozen plays—in parts as different as Joan of Arc, Blanche DuBois, Martha in *Who's Afraid of Virginia Woolf?*, and Natalya in *A Month in the Country*— told a friend that he was dying to meet me in person because he couldn't possibly imagine "what *she* is *really* like!" And yet, while performing, I was always living in those particular parts, because I had learned to put myself to proper use.

If you are afraid that the self-observation I propose will stifle spontaneous response and produce calculated behavior, I can simply assure you that, without having a scientific explanation, it does *not*. And you must remember that, in your daily life, **in all forms of spontaneous role-playing, your *own being* is always at the center of it.** You are not copying the behavior of others, but revealing the myriad facets that spring from your own soul and imagination.

Of course there is an enormous difference between the self-awareness that an actor must develop and the kind of self-consciousness that is the mark of an affected human being. Unless we shed the calculating affectations so often acquired during our teens by the time we reach adulthood, we will be bad actors. If someone narcissistically applies the borrowed mannerisms of his daily life, focusing on them rather than on the people with whom he should be interacting, how can he expect to play all the characters who are *un*affected? It is true that most people have a few personal mannerisms. You must pray that your friends and teachers are kind enough to alert you to yours so that you can rid yourself of them one by one or use them only if they are serviceable for a particular character.

I find that the observation of *others*, which is taught and recommended by so many teachers, is useful *only* when that observation enlightens you about yourself, when you *identify* with it. If you watch someone in a fight with the checkout girl at the supermarket and his frustrated, idiotic behavior rings a bell, makes you aware that you have behaved in a similar fashion, it can be useful. If you observe someone tottering down the street with an infirmity, ask yourself what causes it (sore feet, stiff knees, a weak back, or dizziness). If you then examine how *you* walk when you are dizzy or your feet hurt or you have a stiff knee or bunions, it can be useful. *But* the imitation of the outer manifestations of others is as dangerous as the imitation of other actors' styles.

There is a time in the life of every young artist when he falls under the spell of a mature artist whom he idolizes and *will* emulate, consciously or subconsciously, almost by reflex. It is probably the way great art is passed on from one generation to the next. Mozart was influenced by Haydn, but Mozart went on to become Mozart. Beethoven was strongly influenced by Haydn *and* Mozart but developed his own powerful expression. We must hope that we are influenced by the best. We must pray that our taste and judgment will help us to discern between true artists and those who make a temporary commercial splash. Above all, we must try to inherit the *concept* of the work of the great artists rather than the outer shape and form of their expression.

Now, with a continuously expanding understanding of our self, we must learn how to use our discoveries so that we can reveal all the fascinating human beings in dramatic literature within our reach.

5

Transference

Author's Note: Throughout this book, whenever I place "I," "you," and "your" in quotes, I will be denoting the character in the play to differentiate them from you, the actor.

WHEN Laurette Taylor insisted that all that was needed to be a fine actor was *imagination,* I thought: How wonderful, I have a lot of that. The trouble was that I wasn't sure how to put it to use, into what direction to send it. At the first reading of a play, I used to create an image of my new character, or, if it was a familiar classic, I already had one. Then I embellished it. I imagined how *she* looked, walked, talked, suffered, loved, and laughed, where *she* lived, how *she* responded to the conflicts in the play and, in the process, I removed *her* farther and farther away from my*self*. No matter how hard I tried to fill this image with my own psyche, I was trapped into character indication and illustration by the time I got on my feet. At this point in my career, I hadn't yet learned to enlarge the understanding of my own identity, didn't yet know that I was a compound of many human beings, that I had within myself all that I needed to draw on.

Only when I began to use my imagination correctly by starting my work on the role with the magical question—"If *I* were . . . ?"—did I learn to set myself on the path that leads to identification with the character. At every stage of the way I needed to tap my life experience in order to make a selection of relevant *transferences* to those of the character. The difficult journey ended with the creation of a *new* "I." Webster defines the verb *transfer* as: "to convey from one person, place, or situation to another." If, like Laurette Taylor, you want to ensure that you will be wearing the *underpants* of the character, you will have to start at the beginning with transferences from your own life to the very origins of your character, to ensure faith in the reality of your new existence.

Let me take Blanche DuBois as an example since most of you will be familiar with *A Streetcar Named Desire*, the twentieth-century classic by Tennessee Williams. I find that the tendency to shape a general cliché image of a character can take place at the very first reading of a play. You can guard yourself against this by assuming, *while reading*, that *you* are the character you will be working on. The mysteries that unravel during the events of the play, the facts about Blanche's life, which are revealed through the action, will eventually be made personal by transferences from your own life. In the first scene you learn that "you" were raised at Belle Reve, a southern mansion, that it was overly mortgaged and gradually went to seed, that "you" had to become a schoolteacher, using "your" meager salary in an attempt to hang on to "your" home. You learn that "your" mother, father, and other relatives died, some of them in your arms after gruesome illnesses, of rotting cancers, through which "you" nursed them; that there was a long parade to the graveyard, a succession of funerals, for which "you" had to pay until Belle Reve (Beautiful Dream) was lost, "lost, lost!" and that "your" younger sister, Stella, having left home, had not shared in these burdens. Later you will read that "you" had married a beautiful young gentleman, that "you" had idolized him until "you" surprised him in a compromising situation with an older man, after which "your" young, homosexual husband committed suicide.

In an attempt to recapture this lost love, "you" began to seduce young men and to drink more and more. After the loss of Belle Reve, "you" were forced to move into the Flamingo, a questionable hotel, where "your" affairs with men became too much even for the management. The high-school principal became aware of all the gossip and fired "you," and "you" were virtually run out of town. At the play's opening, then, "you" are homeless, penniless, seeking refuge with "your" sister and brother-in-law in their shabby apartment in the Latin Quarter of New Orleans. Unable to face up to the scandal of "your" past, desperately clinging to the illusions of a life of elegant gentility, deluding "yourself" about the existence of any ugly realities, "you" are now confronting "your" last chance of survival in this strange new environment. "You" are convinced that "your" sister and her husband know nothing about "your" scandalous last years, and "you" feel it is crucial to *keep* "your" secrets from them. "You" have arrived via a dirty bus trip, then via a streetcar named Desire, at "your" destination—Elysian Fields, as the streetcar stop is called— and *that* is where "your" life in the play begins! (Of course, you, as the reader and, eventually, the audience will receive all this information only as the action of the play unfolds.)

It is unlikely that your imagination will have been powerful enough to have turned all these overwhelming facts into a sufficient reality for you to have identified with them, but it *will* serve you *now* if you slowly **begin to make transferences from your own experiences to those in the play** *until they become synonymous* **with them.** Start with "your" origin: Ask "Where was 'I' born?" and answer, "In Laurel, Mississippi." This will need immediate clarification since it is highly unlikely that you, yourself, really were. But, you may have traveled through the state, seen the trees laden with hanging moss, passed the antebellum mansions, or even walked through some of them with their musty smells of lost dreams, surrounded by their shaded lawns or lawns gone to weed, spied a bed of your favorite childhood flowers. You may have spoken to a caretaker who shared his nostalgic memories with you. If, on such travels, you were using your actor's imagination to pretend that you had lived there, you now only need to solidify and adorn these events: What games might "you" have played there, indoors and out, and with whom? Which of your actual playmates can you transfer to these surroundings for an imagined game of tag or hide-and-seek? Did you really have a younger sister who could serve as "your" Stella? If not, substitute a cousin or a younger friend whom you enjoyed looking after or bossing around. Did "you" read and study together in one of those imposing bedrooms? Could your personal teddy bear be found on that canopied bed? Might the bed be covered by a favorite quilt? Did "you" and your Stella have dress-up sessions, pretending you were belles of the ball, waltzing around in the arms of handsome officers?

Naturally, any actor born in the South will have many more direct sources to draw on that might seem alien to a Northerner, but even if you have never visited or spent time there, you can avail yourself of countless books and photos of Faulkner country and Southern homes, into which to transfer yourself by using the same imaginative procedure. Or you might use a visit to a Long Island estate or one in an exclusive suburban area of the Middle West, provided it reminds you of a Southern mansion and enhances your faith in realities that surpass a feeling of fiction. In this fashion you will gradually build a solid foundation for your new childhood.

You have learned that Belle Reve went to seed in spite of "your" vain struggles to maintain it before it was taken from "you" by creditors. You must find a substitute for this loss of roots, for the despair that takes hold when your home is lost or threatened. Moving away—even if it is to a better place—can be a frightening experience, creating a sense of insecurity and panic comparable to Blanche's feelings. Taking leave of a summer home, or clearing out a place for renters—any event that made you feel displaced can be useful.

Blanche has coped with the agonizing death of her relatives, nursing them as they clung to her in their pain. Hopefully, you have never experienced anything exactly like it, but you will have sat by the bedside of a loved one while his teeth chattered from chills and fever, or held the hand of a sibling or friend with the flu or bronchitis, or been near a parent who suffered with vomiting or diarrhea due to intestinal flu, etc. Anything similar is sufficient to transfer to the illness of Blanche's cousin Margaret, for example. Attending one dreary funeral is enough to help you imagine all the others; the look of the coffin, the garish floral arrangements, the droning preacher, the stiffness of the other mourners, etc. The greater your own visualizations are for these past events, the more sources you will have when "you" accuse Stella of having abandoned "you" to face these nightmares alone.

Later in the play, when "you" confess "your" deep love for "your" young husband to Mitch, as well as the guilt "you" feel for his suicide, you must first find someone you adored, the perfect symbol of romanticism. If none of your first loves seems appropriate, you could substitute a teenage idol, someone unobtainable about whom you fantasized—just as long as the memory is connected with a strong, sensory image of a suitable man. If the horrifying moment of discovering "your" young husband in the arms of his lover seems impossible to identify with, then think what this moment represented to Blanche: To her it was an aberration, something repulsive, comparable to coming across a slithering snake, a giant spider, or a snarling, scruffy rat. You can transfer whatever spells out revulsion to you. In other words, you will want a psychological trigger for that moment of recall. It will be necessary to link the suicide of "your" husband to a disaster for which you feel responsible, for which you carry the blame because he shot himself after "you" had accused him of disgusting "you." Try to recall if someone was fired because of something you said or did, or if someone was robbed because you left the door unlocked, or if someone was hurt while driving after drinking and you hadn't stopped him. Actually *anything* horrible you feel you could have prevented can now be transferred to the sense of guilt "you" have for Allan Grey's death.

By now, you should have an idea of how to pursue this task of taking personal realities to put in the place of fictional concepts, how to weave them imaginatively into the circumstances of the character's past life. You will continue in the same way to find substitutions for Blanche's sexual exploits (one actual affair or one affair you *almost* had is enough to suppose there were more), for the escape into alcohol (not too unlike an obsession for sweets or for pizza orgies), for an identification with having been gossiped about, for being exposed for scandalous behavior (it has happened to all of us), for being penniless, stranded, and in need of refuge (something familiar to most actors), or anything else you may need to solidify your identification with Blanche's life prior to the beginning of the play.

The next step, which you will already have begun intuitively, is to find identification with Blanche's basic character traits, with her *main* needs, the driving forces that propel her into action throughout the play. You will have discerned a need for beauty, elegance, and gentility, for delicacy, a need to be loved and protected, and the seemingly dichotomous desire for sensuality, the necessity for self-delusion and self-deception in the face of harsh realities, the need to escape into fantasies in order to avoid anything ugly, etc. If the sum total of these human traits seems alien to you, if it again conjures up an image of a Blanche removed from yourself, deal with each need individually in the hunt for *your* reality. Remember the times when you indulged in poetry orgies, when you sighed or wept with Browning, Keats, or Rilke. If you have ever attended a tea or cocktail hour at a hotel or a resort where dainty tea cakes or hors d'oeuvres were served on fragile china while a string ensemble played in the background, pretend now that this was a daily routine. If you think you are basically a careless dresser, try putting on a pair of snow-white cotton gloves fastened by tiny buttons and make it important to yourself to keep them spanking clean while you proceed on an errand. See how these dainty gloves influence your sense of self, what frustration occurs when they get smudged. Take a leisure hour to bathe in bubbles, smooth your skin with baby oil until it feels satiny, douse yourself with a floral scent after you've toweled off, put on your best lingerie while imagining that this is habitual behavior to maintain confidence in your femininity. Brush your hair until it shimmers. If, like me, you feel most at home in sandals, sneakers, or bare feet, put on sheer hose, high heels, and a frilly dress in place of your usual shirt and slacks. Set the table with your loveliest linen and dinnerware for an imaginary supper with a new beau. Light a candle. Hold it up to a mirror to see how its glow flatters your face and seems to erase the little lines around your eyes. Try to recall a time when you lied about your age because you believed you were too old to be cast in a wonderful role. Try to recapture the feeling of danger at being caught out to transfer to Blanche's hypersensitivity about her age. Remember that the exposure of a single line or even a tiny wrinkle might give you away or put you in jeopardy of missing out on a great opportunity.

The need to be loved and protected is at a peak when we feel abandoned and are particularly vulnerable to difficult circumstances. Most people will have experienced something comparable more than once before they have finished their teens, so it should be relatively simple to find a transference for this reality. The same might be said for a sexual desire or lust for a primitive, macho person with rippling torso gleaming with sweat who evokes wildly sensuous fantasies. And it is not a contradiction to have a powerful need for a sensitive, intelligent, romantic, and gentle partner side by side with such erotic yearnings.

As for self-deception, we have many examples in small daily occurrences. We check ourselves in the mirror and see what we *want* to see rather than what is actually reflected. We hear only positive things at a job interview, ignoring negatives in order to keep up our courage; or we block out unpleasant incidents during which we behaved badly that, when brought to our attention, may cause us to invent new facts to convince ourselves that we were blameless, and so on. It is not unusual to find escape or diversion in other "more important" activities when we want to avoid finishing a distasteful task, or when we have a dentist's or doctor's appointment at which we expect to be hurt, etc.

Transferences for Blanche's need for gentility, propriety, and decorum can be fortified by identifying with her abhorrence of crudeness, vulgarity, brutality, and violence—easy enough to find for anyone who has spent time in a large metropolis. It is necessary to apply a revulsion for such ugly manifestations to the creation of "your" relationship to Kowalski, to the couple living upstairs, and to the poker players, as well as to the neighbors, passersby, even to the street noises. It applies to the very milieu of the Latin Quarter and the Kowalski apartment in which "your" life will be revealed.

Until now I have dealt mostly with the homework of imaginative transferences, which should help to substantiate an identification with the character's *past*. From the time that work begins on the *present*, from the moment the character appears on the set, so to speak, a new element arises, one that is essential to combine or alternate with forthcoming transferences. This is *not* homework but a part of the actual rehearsal procedure. I call it **particularization:** the making of each event, each person, and each place down to the smallest physical object as particular as possible, exploring these things in detail to discover in which way they are relevant to the character, in which way they are perceived, in which way they further or hinder the character's needs, and, consequently, how they will condition "your" behavior. Nothing should be left general or taken for granted. Everything must be made specific. First examine what is *there* by defining it in detail.

Let me give examples for a few seemingly unimportant objects used by Blanche when she is left alone in the apartment at the beginning of the play: After taking in the shabbiness of the room, having seen that there is only one narrow unmade bed with no place for her, she spies some liquor in a cabinet with its door ajar and helps herself to a stiff shot. At your rehearsal, examine this bottle. Is it a cheap blend or a good whiskey? Is it full? Will the amount "you" pour be missed? Does it have a screw top or a cork? Is the glass you handle from the dime store? Is it thick and heavy or thin and easily cracked? Or is it a beautiful glass that Stella had brought from Belle Reve, out of place in these seedy surroundings? Is it clean or murky? There will be either tea or water in the bottle, which must be endowed with the taste of real whiskey when "you" gulp it down. When "you" wipe the glass with your hanky before replacing it in order to hide the fact that "you've" used it, will the hanky be damp and smell of liquor? Can it be hidden in your purse? For the hanky itself you might make a transference from a dainty one given you by a special beau or, perhaps, your mother. If you have given sufficient consideration to these objects, you will quickly grasp that *how* you will consequently *handle* the bottle, glass, and hanky will have been determined by the properties with which you have endowed them.

Everything in the place must be made particular. Although the set is dictated by the writer, designer, and director, you alone can make it real to yourself. Blanche asks Stella what she's doing in this "horrible" place. What is horrible about it? The poverty of the furnishings, the mess? The empty beer cans, the stale cigarette butts? What does it remind you of? A debasing tryst with someone in similar surroundings? What does the broom lying on the floor mean to you? Are the windows curtainless? Do you feel exposed? What can you see through them? The railroad tracks, the passersby? Which chair has a rough or splintered leg that might snag "your" hose? Is there one which allows you a sense of propriety when "you" sit in it? Is the table covered with crumbs, the refrigerator dirty? Do the bedsprings creak? If these suggestions open the doors to your own imagination you will see that transferences and particularizations are continuously intermingled in this process of creating your faith in the place.

I have already dealt with examples of transference for aspects of "your" relationship to some of the characters who don't actually appear (relatives, playmates, the young husband, other beaus and lovers). I have touched on the relationships to "your" sister, Stella, and brother-in-law, Stanley. All the other characters with whom you will be interacting, with the exception of Stella, are new to "you" when "you" meet up with them during the course of the play: the neighbors, Stanley, Mitch, the young collector, the poker players, the doctor, and the nurse. Study the play from Blanche's point of view to examine "your" basic relationship to the others, first defining them in broad terms: affinities and aversions, advantages and disadvantages. For each one, try to determine who leads and who follows and under what circumstances the leading and following occur. Does competitiveness enter into it? Is it reciprocal? (Who takes, who gives?) Next, consider "your" assumptions, right or wrong, about each of them, as well as those "you" believe they have about "you." Explore how "your" assumptions change during the unfolding action as the relationships come into conflict within the context of the play. Consider what "you" like and dislike about each one and what "you" think they like and dislike about "you."

The homework you bring to rehearsals is based on possibilities, on *considerations* about these relationships and for transferences which should eventually make them real to you. Beware of opinionated, inflexible *decisions* that could put you out of commission when they differ from those of the director or those of the other actors or when they don't fit in with your live partners. Most of the specific work on "your" relationship to the others, how they develop and are in flux as "you" come into a variation of conflicts with them, will occur during the actual rehearsals with your colleagues.

The complexity of most human relationships, and the actor's problem of coming to grips with them in a given play, deserves an entire section of its own.* But, for the purpose of this chapter, which is based on the use of transferences, I will deal with the process at a simplified level.

In your homework, construct elements of "your" past life with Stella by using a substitution of an actual younger sister, cousin, or friend whom you enjoyed caring for and, at times, lorded it over. Imagine how Stella left Belle Reve. Consider the parting: Was it friendly? Was she going to New Orleans to look for a job? etc. Now apply these imaginings to your actual partner when you meet up with her in rehearsal. The actress may be your own age. Then use your substitution in order to treat her as though she were "your" junior. Otherwise, particularize her physical presence, tone of voice, per-

---

* See Chapter 24, pages 262–277.

sonality. Evaluate in which way her being enhances your faith in the relationship. If she is willing, let her show you a photo taken several years earlier to help your awareness of the changes in her. If she agrees, improvise scenes from your past: dressing and making up together for a double date, for example. Explore how you might have pulled rank, competed, or simply shared in an enjoyable experience. Improvise her leave-taking. Help her pack, etc. These adventures will powerfully influence how you first greet each other in the play. Now *"you"* need *her* protection, are vulnerable to her appraisal of *"you."* "You" have much to hide from her and much to justify in "your" desperate hunt for shelter; consequently, the relationship has shifted, and there are times (when "you" ask where she will find room to put "you" up, or when "you" confess that "you" are "not very well") when she will become almost a parental figure for which you may need a different transference.

Until the actor playing Stanley has developed his character, he may at first strike you simply as the personable, sensitive, educated man he really is, but if you endow him with the qualities of the brawny, dirty, bigoted mechanic at the corner filling station, imagining this man to be married to "your" gentle little sister, you will be on the way to making an initial transference to "your" Stanley.

At the end of the first scene of the second act there is a crucial scene between Blanche and the young collector. The collector must symbolize romantic dreams and evoke in Blanche all the nostalgia for her lost youth, her yearnings for gentility. He is probably working his way through college by means of his newspaper route, and his gentle good manners seem quite out of place in this section of the Latin Quarter. It is unlikely that the actor playing this role will supply all the needed elements to provide your Blanche with a sufficient stimulus to induce the correct actions. You will want to transfer to him a person from your own past. (I, myself, imagined him to be the French actor Gérard Philipe, who was to me the epitome of a gentle prince.)

On occasion, a particular partner may seem to have most of the requirements you intuitively sensed as being necessary for your character's relationship to him. Then conscious substitutions from your own life become unnecessary. One of the four Mitches with whom I played during my two years as Blanche DuBois was a friend who looked up to me, felt inferior to me socially, was awkward yet gentle, treated me with kid gloves in our social contact, and was, consequently, ideally suited for many aspects of "my" relationship to Mitch. I had little to do to endow this actor with the character traits needed in establishing my basic relationship to him.

At the age of eighteen, I played Nina in *The Sea Gull* with the Lunts. Nina is a naive middle-class girl from the country who is drawn into the life of her neighbor, a famous actress of whom she is in awe, and the actress's lover, a noted writer whom Nina hero-worships. I was in awe of Miss Fontanne and hero-worshiped Mr. Lunt. These particular character relationships were mirrored by my own, and I used their reality directly for my role. When I played in *Who's Afraid of Virginia Woolf?* my character, Martha, was the daughter of a college president whom she adored. My own father was a professor and chairman of his department, and I adored him. She was raised in a college town; so was I. At the opening of the play, she is just returning from a faculty party. Making these things particular was easy in the initial stages of my work on the play. In other words, in any area where the playwright's creation meshes with your own life, your transferences are ready-made and can be easily adjusted to the details of the variations in the play.

Classical roles pose the added problem of *historical* distance, in which time, place, fashion, and social conditions must first be researched before being adapted to the existence of your character. Periods of history can be made real by transferences from your own life experience when *combined* with the sources you find in traveling, in appropriate historical novels and biographies, in trips to museums, and in films about the period.*

The examples I have given in this chapter for a number of characters, in particular for Blanche DuBois, do not pretend to be based on any kind of definitive interpretation and should not be taken as such if you were ever to work on these roles. *No one* can supply you with personal substitutions. If they are to be truly useful, you must find your own. If any of my suggestions have stirred you, it was by accident. **Start to build your own storehouse of transferences and**

---

* The historical exercise (Chapter 20) concerns itself in detail with this fascinating aspect of transporting yourself into a distant time and place.

learn to make them an integral part of your homework and rehearsal procedures.

Beware of the trap of wanting to confide your sources for the transferences you make to the director or your colleagues. Such things as "Guess what I'm using here," or "Do you know what I'm using for my relationship to you?" are only helpful when they remain private. If you satisfy the natural curiosity of your partners, they will immediately become *observers,* testing how your substitution manifests itself, instead of finding their own relation to your action for their interaction. Sharing these secret aspects of the work will make you self-conscious about their application until finally they will become useless.

Let me stress, because it is so often misunderstood, that **finding the source for a transference is not an end in itself.** It should not lead you into private feelings and reveries when you are on stage. **A transference is incomplete until the original source has become synonymous with the material in the play.** To give you a simple example, let me describe something I demonstrate in class to make this point. I select a student as a partner and place him at the opposite side of the stage. I ask him to come toward me as if we were meeting accidentally on the street. Just before we shake hands, as I become aware of his presence, I assume that he is Alfred Lunt. Invariably, my face reddens, I become shy and instinctively **bob my knee in a semi-curtsy as I deferentially shake his hand.** I repeat the demonstration, this time imagining that the same student is a rather crude and impertinent pal of my daughter. As we approach, my body stiffens, **my head pulls back** and **I give his extended hand a perfunctory shake.** A third time, I make believe that my student is a peer, a close friend from abroad whom I haven't seen for years. **My step quickens, I take his hand in both of mine** and finish the greeting with **a bear hug.** In each instance, I have substituted Mr. Lunt, my daughter's acquaintance, or my old friend as **an initial stimulus which resulted in specific behavior applied directly** to the student. I have not hung on to an image of Mr. Lunt or the others or dangled their images before my eyes. That would cloud my awareness of the partner and my influence on him. Each time, something brand-new in my relationship to the student is established for which I would no longer need my original source. **I have completed the transference by finding**

the behavior. I have used the past to make the present real. On stage I will be living in the present, not in the past.

I would like to emphasize that whenever an actor's imagination flags in his hunt for appropriate transferences to the material in a play, when he is stopped by the notion that "*I* never did . . ." or "*I* never would . . .", it is because he is being literal-minded about the *events* of the play, about the given circumstances, looking in vain into his own life for a parallel to the events in which the character is involved. You may have noticed that my examples of transferences do not mirror the exact events in the play. Instead, they are connected with the *essence* of the character's experience made real by the transference of comparable, personal, sensory, emotional, and psychological experiences. If I hunted for the remembrance of a lover who, like Allan Grey, was found lying in a pool of blood after having shot himself in the head, I would be at a dead end. But recalling the agonizing death of my beloved little poodle, abetted by the guilt I felt for not being able to prevent it, is enough to transfer to the essence of Blanche's experience. Illogical as it may seem externally, internally it is comparable.

If, on occasion, an actor has a strong, natural affinity for a particular role or for certain aspects of it, and a vivid imagination, it is possible that he will find identification without having to make meticulous, conscious substitutions in the way I have described. I, myself, have sometimes made a few initial transferences which have catapulted me into areas of the play and sustained my sense of reality for long stretches. These times, when the magic "If I were . . ." carried me along without a violation of the truth of "my" existence, are the exception. And the *instant* I catch myself thinking in terms of "her" instead of "I," when I begin to illustrate how *she* ought to feel, what *she* would want and do, and when I realize I am laughing *about her*, weeping *about her* plight, actually relating to her as an audience rather than participating in and grappling personally with the character's problems, I stop short and return to the examination of specific transferences from my life to hers. Never confuse the enormous difference between the kind of involvement we have when we are *participating* in the character's actions and that of the involvement entailed in the kind of muscular, emotional acting springing from an observer's *sympathy* for the character. And remember that although the director will always be your guide, he will be unfamiliar with your personal life experience. Making everything true to yourself remains the actor's job.

In summation: Transferences are a part of your homework and during the rehearsal period they are in flux until the performance is complete. The purpose of making them is twofold. First, *to find identification* with all aspects of the character's past and present, *to substantiate your faith* in the time, place, detailed surroundings, and circumstances in which your character will be living, and to endow the relationships to the other characters with appropriate realities. The second purpose deals with the discovery of the character's behavior, justifying it while alerting you to every circumstance, to every animate and inanimate object that stimulates you to act, to do something consequential about what you feel and want. Thoughts and feelings are suspended in a vacuum unless they instigate and feed the selected actions, and it is THE CHARACTER'S ACTIONS which will REVEAL the new "you." Each stage of this work should ultimately bring about personal, relevant, justified, revealing actions. It is, in a literal sense, a process of "make believe," to make you believe in "your" existence. Then the audience will have been made to believe in it, too.

6

The Physical
Senses

Before we learn how to transfer our senses to the role, we must first understand how they function. We know that a part of being alive entails the full employment of all of our senses. Yet, in this age of social alienation, we are deadening them. We stare straight ahead or look to the ground to shield our sight from the homeless sleeping in doorways. We turn from the brutalized children and stray animals that roam our parks and streets, from our graffiti-smeared walls and vandalized buildings. We wear dark glasses, often indoors. Our perception of others is frequently distorted by vanity. We evaluate *our* effect on them rather than *their* effect on us. An interchange of ideas becomes almost impossible when so much of the conversation must be shouted above the racket of the radio or TV that seems to be turned on at all times, or above the din of most restaurants. When we are alone, we cover our ears with Walkman headphones to drown out "noise pollution" when actually we are blocking out thoughts and suspending all imagination. Rock and roll has become today's opiate of the masses. Acid rock has deafened the young, and in the discos they dance alone, never touching, only peripherally aware that others are also writhing around by themselves. Therapy groups attempt to teach people how, simply physically, to touch one another again. Cigarettes and overly spiced foods have dulled the taste buds while cheaply scented room deodorizers mask the smell of flowers, not just the cooking odors. Drugs have wrecked lives and careers, and even the moderate user has desensitized himself and befuddled his brain. All in the name of "coping" with the world. "Cease and desist" from these deadening habits. Open your senses, no matter how painful it may be. Doing so will heighten your sensitivities, which are an integral part of the actor's talent. It will also increase your understanding of the world in which you live and may even induce compassionate actions in your daily life.

While walking through a little park in Greenwich Village in the spring, you may come across a discarded crack vial—if you look *down*. If you look *up,* right next to it you may SEE a flowering fruit tree with endless variations of white, cream, and rose-colored blossoms. Perhaps you will TOUCH its smooth bark and chiffonlike petals, pick a bloom to TASTE the sweetness of its nectar, SMELL its heady fragrance, and HEAR the gentle rustling of the leaves in a breeze. Your very soul will be moved by such a miracle and you might wonder whether the crack user would have taken the drug at all if he had been able to perceive the tree in all its glory. Human beings can affect you even more powerfully than the tree. If you open all your senses, contact with them might bring about "But soft! what light through yonder window breaks? It is the east, and Juliet is the sun!" or Richard's outburst in *The Lady's Not for Burning:* "Oh, God, God, God! I can see such trouble!" when Alison first walks into the room, or Blanche's cry of "Stella, oh, Stella, Stella! Stella for Star!" at the moment of reunion with her sister.

The five sensory organs (eyes, ears, nose, tongue, and skin) *are our receptors of external stimuli.* The more "sensitive" we are, the more intensely we respond to the stimuli that induce in us everything from spiritual ecstasy to excruciating pain—because the *physical* responses evoked by these stimuli are, of course, accompanied by *psychological* ones.

Too often our sensations are taken for granted and remain unexplored. They are easy to recall when they are extreme: when we touch a hot stove, when we cut ourselves on a razor or a piece of broken glass, when we bite into a lemon or a piece of creamy fudge, when we smell perfume or raw sewage, when we see a flaming sun rise or a wounded animal, hear a trilling bird or the screech of a siren. But something as seemingly ordinary as a handshake can only take on meaning when the actor sensitizes himself to the very texture of the skin he contacts: Is it warm or cool, damp or dry, rough or smooth? Is the proffered handshake firm, friendly, limp, aloof, pumping with anxiety, or gently sensuous? Alert yourself to the objects with which you deal in daily routines: the textures and smells of soap, cleaning equipment, cologne, leather, wood; the smells and taste of food, both raw and cooked, of liquor, sodas, juices, etc. The sound of your phone, doorbell, buzzer, street noises, pigeons cooing on the windowsill. Observe how you respond to these stimuli. Observe your physical and psychological responses to the weather, the light, the humidity when you open or shut the window at night or in the morning. Note how strongly they can influence your ensuing behavior. *Anything* dormant that can be awakened by attention to the sensory process will help give meaning to what you are capable of receiving. How you deal with the reception of sensory stimuli can be stored in a treasure chest to be recalled and transferred selectively to a particular character's stage life.

In learning how to bring our physical senses into play, to have them at our beck and call so that a real involvement with them will manifest itself in motivated character behavior, we must understand the difference between TRUTH IN ART as opposed to TRUTH IN LIFE. The *formalistic* actor tends to illustrate his character's headaches, fatigue, chills, and sweats, to devise pieces of business for cramps after taking poison, or cliché staggers and slurred speech to indicate drunkenness. He artificially recoils when attacked, without *any* employment of his own senses. To avoid this, the *naturalistic* actor often falls into the trap of demanding the wrong kind of truth. In a fight scene, for example, he may ask that his partner actually assault him and he may actually hit him back, thereby risking sending his colleague into the orchestra pit or to the hospital, or being sent there himself. He may think it truthful to drink real liquor on stage, but the liquor will prevent him from fulfilling the truth of his character's actions. Even the character's words will soon elude him. The actor who ran up and down the backstage stairs, so that he would actually be out of breath for his entrance, succeeded so well that he fainted and the curtain had to be rung down before he had a chance to utter his first line. If Othello actually strangled Desdemona and then stabbed himself to death, we would need a new cast of characters at every performance.

This is no more ridiculous than the use of *any* external reality that can take control of the actor during the course of his stage life. If we bring real snow into the theatre to provide "truthful" behavior during a blizzard, we will see it melt before the curtain goes up. Directors are often as guilty as actors in introducing naturalistic effects into a play. I have watched scenes on Broadway in which milk on the stove boiled over on cue, and in which actual steam came out of an iron. Each time, buzzing voices were heard in the auditorium: "That stove really works," "How did they *do* that?" "Gee, that iron is really plugged in," etc. In place of a distilled artistic truth that might have furthered the reality of the play, these devices *dis*illusioned the audience, interrupted their involvement in the play, and made them speculate about the achievement of the effect. Unless it is presented in a burlesque house, nudity on stage affects me in the same way. I always get clinically analytical about the sag or lift of the breasts, the size and tint of the nipples or the male genitalia, and I become acutely aware of the actors' self-protection from possible embarrassment. The *characters'* validity flies out the window when the continuity of artistic illusion is broken. The audience stops believing. Similarly, when actors actually slug it out in a fight, they will become anxious and worry about the *actors'* bruises rather than those of the characters they are portraying. A believable fight must be as carefully defined as a pas de deux if the performers want to execute it with *spontaneity* night after night. **The *realistic* actor learns that, at will, he can induce specific, imagined stimuli to produce an organically correct behavioral response in order to arrive at the essence of the experience.** That means being true to art instead of naturalistically true to life.

Let me begin with the simple physiological process (organic process, if you prefer) of **waking up** from a deep sleep, which is so often called for in dramatic literature. When the actor has a long time to prepare before being discovered on stage in bed at the opening of an act, he may intuitively bring about a correct physiological process. But he can "put himself to sleep" and seem to awake in a matter of seconds, if necessary, when he has just finished one scene, changed into pajamas, and run from his dressing room to leap into bed as the lights come up on the next, although his heart is pounding and his whole being is alert. First, rather than assuming *general* snuggling or relaxation, use a particular part of your body to settle down—your back *or* behind into the mattress, *or* your shoulders into the lower half of the pillow, *or* plop a knee across the extra pillow under the covers. While doing this, close your eyes, rolling them upward into sleep position as though you would be looking straight ahead under the lid, not downward. Next, direct your inner attention to an isolated image such as a tuft of grass *or* a fleecy cloud *or* a wave crashing on sand. From this object, direct your inner attention to something relevant to the given circumstances such as: What time do you think it is? Have you overslept? *or* What day is it? What must you do today? *or* Did you hear the phone or doorbell ring? Who might it be? *Now* open your eyes and sit up to verify the speculation. Consider your first destination, for instance, the robe or slippers near your bed. As you begin to move, your eyes and limbs will feel heavy, your whole body will respond by reflex to serve the ensuing physical actions, and you will *believe* that you have just wakened from sleep.

Fatigue, which is another sensory condition commonly called for, has endless variations depending on what *caused* it. General fatigue, trying to feel tired all over, makes for general actions and unfocused behavior. Your selection will, of course, depend on the given circumstances. If you have just awakened, are you still tired because you had too little sleep? Do your eyes burn? Recall that sensation before blinking and rubbing them gently to make the burning stop. Or has your leg cramped up in bed? Localize the muscle in your calf. Rub it to get the circulation going, stretch it out before putting on your slipper. Or did you have too much sleep? Does your head feel logy and hollow? Recall the feeling before shaking it slowly to clear it. Or, under different circumstances, are you coming home from a hard day's work? What kind of work? Have you been sitting for hours at a typewriter until your shoulders and the back of your neck are tied in knots? Hunch your shoulders, roll them back, stretch your arms to alleviate the condition. Or have you been doing hard labor that has made you stiff and sore in the lower back? Locate the sorest spot, press your hand against it as you lean back to ease the ache. Or have you walked for hours on hot cement streets in thin-soled shoes until the balls of your feet feel tender? Try to take the pressure off them with each step as you go about your task. In *each* of the above instances, the *rest* of your body will follow suit to respond by reflex without your having to give it further attention, and you *will* feel fatigued as you pursue your actions.

Even the manifestation of a **simple yawn,** which is so often badly illustrated by the actors who open their mouths wide while *ex*haling, can be correctly produced after realizing the physiological *cause:* We need oxygen in the brain. Consequently, we must *in*hale deeply as our mouth opens and our jaw drops down and back for a maximum intake of air before it can be pushed, with an exhale, high up into our head. This organic procedure may even make your eyes water when the critics are in the auditorium.

Many actors have a tendency to hypochondria. It is almost an occupational hazard because, understandably, we are interested in our sensations. Some actors are so suggestible that at the very mention of a particular illness, pain, cough, itch, chill, or toothache, they are momentarily convinced that they are afflicted with the same condition. This can be an advantage, provided that they are *aware* of the way in which they can make use of this hypersensitivity in their profession and as long as it doesn't send them to bed or to the doctor. With or without this tendency, the actor can master the technique of imaginatively producing physical sensations at will.

No matter what sensations we wish to induce to put to use in our characters' lives, the principle remains the same: From the play's given circumstances **determine the precise cause of the condition and its effect on the particular, most suggestible part of the body. Then find the physical adjustment needed to alleviate it or overcome it.** Here are a few examples.

The play dictates that it is **hot.** Where do you feel it most strongly? Perhaps under the arms. Imagine that the perspiration is oozing from the pores and starting to trickle down one side, that your shirt is sticking to your skin. Raise your arm a little while pulling the sleeve away. Try to let in some air. At the moment of executing this action, at the moment of trying to *ease* the condition, you will feel hot. For the sake of emphasis, let me repeat: First give your attention to the imagined stimulus, then move quickly to the physical adjustment to it. Do *not* wait to feel hot. You might sit there forever. If you are very sensitive, you *might* have the correct sensation, finding an adjustment intuitively, but, as a rule, it is not until you have selected a consequential adjustment to the condition that you will be able to repeat it at every performance with full faith in its existence. On the other hand, do *not* skip the initial attention given to the imagined stimulus, jumping mechanically to the outer adjustment, or you will end up illustrating the sensation. Even the old cliché of indicating heat by wiping sweat from the brow can take on reality if you first simulate the recall of prickling moisture at the hairline, the feeling of sweat running down toward your eyes so that you *need* to wipe it off with the back of your hand. Or, for the same reason, you might assume that your breath is cooler than the air and, with protruding jaw and raised lower lip, blow it upward to cool off your face. **The sensation will occur most fully when we are occupied in overcoming it.**

The apartment is **cold.** Where do you feel it most? Perhaps a draft from the cracked window hits the back of your neck. Your shoulders hitch up, you clasp or rub your hands. Sometimes you even *make* yourself shiver to get the circulation going. Or you might feel the cold floor through your slippers. You step gingerly on the way to your cup of coffee, or stop to hop lightly from one foot to the other to warm up a little. Or you are out of doors and the wind is biting. You avert your face from it. You try to snuggle your mouth into the collar of your coat. You will believe you are cold all over.

You have a **cough.** Recall and localize an exact spot in your throat where you imagine it tickles or scratches and you will *have* to cough to relieve it. You have a head cold. Your nose is stopped up. Contract the uvula, the little lobe at the back of your soft palate, and try to swallow. Your nose will feel stuffy and you will want to blow it.

You **burned your hand** on a hot iron or pot on the stove. Recall how the skin tightens before it blisters, how it stings. Blow on it, flip your hand back and forth to ease the pain, and you'll believe you just burned it.

For **dizziness,** recall the sensation of a spinning in the head and the loss of control of the neck muscles that hold your head steady. Give in to this feeling for a split second, then try to steady it. Sit or lie down to gain control over the feeling. You are supposed **to be nauseous.** Pinpoint the quivering queasiness in your stomach, slightly inflate your cheeks, imagine how the saliva gathers in your mouth. Try to breathe deeply. It will be real to you.

You have **a headache.** Where? Is it throbbing at the temples or is there a dull pain at the back of the eyes, or a stabbing at the lower back of the head? How can you ease it? Do you raise your head slightly to get above the feeling or push into it or pull away from it? Do you close or expand your eyes? Do you gently rub the pain? Experiment to see which is your tendency, and you will soon find the adjustment that makes you believe in its existence.

On occasion, actors complain that they have been so successful in recalling a sensation such as that of a headache that they actually get one. Then I always suggest that, since they have dictated the pain, they might just as readily suggest to themselves that an aspirin had just taken effect. Then they can experience the pleasure and relaxation that sets in when they realize the pain is gone.

I must warn you that in the rare case during a performance when you are actually experiencing the same condition with which your character is supposed to be afflicted, avoid it by shifting your attention to another part of your anatomy or the condition will control you instead of the other way around. If an actual headache is pounding in your sinus area, imagine that your character's headache is at the back of the head. If you are nauseous, give your character stomach cramps instead because if you give in to the actual nausea the curtain may have to be rung down.

As with transferences, remember that sensory recall is not an end in itself. Heat, cold, weather, illness, drunkenness, etc. are the *conditions* under which the actions of the play unfold. Rarely is a scene *about* a cold, a headache, or fatigue.

Sensory recall must be used with faith and accuracy **to condition the character's actions.** Some of the exercises in Part Three are devised solely for training in this technique: the re-creation of sensory responses to imagined stimuli. In part of Chapter 15, you will learn how to cook on a cold stove, how to deal with putting imaginary polish on your fingernails, how to burn yourself on an unplugged iron, to cut yourself on a rubber knife, to drink water as if it were steaming coffee, brandy, or bitter medicine (even poison, if need be), to give a few examples.

In Part II of the same exercise, you will discover that you can believe in the necessity of groping around in a dark room although the stage is sufficiently lit for you to be visible from the balcony. You will put to the test what you have learned here—that you can be aching with fatigue or illness although you are in peak condition, that you can respond to stifling heat in an air-conditioned theatre or shiver in an igloo on the stage of a hot, stuffy Off-Broadway house, etc., etc. In the first section of the outdoor exercise, Chapter 16, you will learn how to bring about sensory realities and adjustments to rain, sleet, snow, to glaring sun on the seashore or up in the dizzying heights of mountains, to rocks, mud, or sand underfoot, to splashing waves, etc. Eventually, you will be able to emulate the great actor Albert Basserman, who, during an argument between the director and designer about producing an actual downpour on stage, interrupted with "Pardon me, but when I enter, it will rain!" And, without "special effects," it did!

For the purpose of this chapter, I hope I have provided sufficient examples to help you find your own way for most of the sensory problems that may arise. Of course, there is always the magic "if" when, with the help of some physiological research, you can find the faith to answer even such questions as "If I were in labor . . ." or "If I were dying . . ."

7

The Psychological Senses

Is it not monstrous that this player here,
But in a fiction, in a dream of passion,
Could force his soul so to his own conceit
That from her working all his visage wann'd,
Tears in his eyes, distraction in 's aspect,
A broken voice, and his whole function suiting
With forms to his conceit?

(Hamlet II.2.)

Hamlet's amazement at the Player King's ability to produce the passions that suit the action of his own conceit (or concept, as is meant here) is still echoed by contemporary audiences as well as by many of today's actors. Even scientists are mystified by many aspects of human emotions. They can trace the sources of mental and physical functioning to various sections of the brain but find it difficult to understand all the causes and effects of feelings and the complex way in which they are connected to thought and behavior. So, not unlike the artist, the psychologist continues to explore the intangible psyche, the soul. However, even when scholars and psychologists *succeed* in defining aspects of our passions and their causes, they remain observers. They remain in the audience. They are not able to produce their sensations at will in the service of a character on stage. *Actors* can. This creative process remains in the artist's domain.

The individual's character is shaped by specific, inherited genetic traits, and their interaction with the environs determines specific concepts about such things as good and evil, justice and injustice, honor and shame, truth and falsehood, success and failure, beauty and ugliness, pride and guilt, power and weakness, kindness and cruelty, morality and immorality, and so on. And **the perception of these concepts** during the individual's life experience is the determining factor of his values. Therefore **the five senses are the avenues of our psychological as well as of our physical perceptions.** They are the avenues to our body, and to our mind and soul.

I want to repeat my warning about the deliberate deadening of the senses that takes place in the name of "coping" with the world. It should be clear that this tendency erodes the very core of our talent, which has roots in vulnerability and high sensitivity. We should also guard against the aspects of an American upbringing that deem it socially unacceptable to shed tears, laugh too loud or in other ways reveal spontaneous feelings. We must strip the cover, the hard-boiled mask, the thick skin used as a protective covering around the soul if we want to regain an artist's innocence and the intuitive responsiveness necessary for a limber, truthful, emotional instrument.

My old friend the dictionary, which often provides such clear answers to acting problems, defines the noun *feeling* as **a psychic and physical reaction, subjectively experienced, which involves physiological changes that prepare the body for vigorous action.** This also answers those who conceive of physical and psychological feelings as being two separate entities. They occur in conjunction with one another. Physical sensations such as heat, cold, pain, or fatigue are *accompanied* by psychological feelings. For example: A muggy night can make for feelings of depression, irritation, annoyance, along with the perspiration. The simple smell of leather or soap might make you feel invigorated, romantic, even sad—depending on your past association with the smell. The taste of a cloying cough syrup might make for self-pity or resentment, while that of a gentle pasta can create a sense of being comforted or, if you are overweight, a sense of guilt. The sound of a church bell can make you feel serene, wistful, or perhaps frightened, while the howling of a distant dog might make you feel abandoned—again depending on past associations. The vision of a starry night can create feelings of awe or tingling excitement.

The sight of a car accident can bring about horror, panic, or sick fascination. *Conversely,* a psychological response is accompanied by a physical one: The car crash can make for quaking knees, the starry night can create goose pimples, the cough medicine can make you nauseated, and the howling dog can give you a chill. An argument can bring on a headache, and a lover's rejection can produce a sweat. In order to describe our emotions, we often use physical terms such as "It hit me like a ton of bricks," "I felt as if I'd been slapped," "as if the rug had been pulled out from under me," "as though I'd been kicked," "as if a bucket of cold water had been dumped on me," "as though I was floating on air," and so forth.

Our feelings and emotions, our physical and psychological responses to external stimuli, are the result of an *accumulation* of life experiences. In infancy, within our first few *months* of life, we have already experienced feelings of anxiety, impatience, resentment, even rage, while waiting for our hunger pangs to be assuaged. We will have been hurt, if only by the prick of a safety pin, and so develop a fear of danger, of possible pain. We will have felt love, comfort, tenderness, sensuality while being nursed, clothed, and tended to. We will have discovered feelings of accomplishment and failure, even during the simple action of sucking a thumb. We will have had moments of being ignored or felt a sense of abandonment when no one answered our crying, of joy and laughter when being dangled, tickled, or otherwise pleasingly communicated with. We will already have asserted our will and tested our strength in demands for attention and will consequently have felt exultation in winning, disappointment in losing, even the galling acceptance of submission. We will start to become aware of the approval of parents, as well as the tension, annoyance, and anger we sometimes evoke in them and the ensuing feeling of satisfaction or guilt.

We soon begin to **make associations that link our feelings in the present to similar ones in our past.** This process of linkage, of associating one experience with another, continues throughout our lives. When the time arrives that we seriously decide to be actors, usually after adolescence, we believe our souls to be a hotbed of feelings, of emotions crying out to be expressed. And we are right. We have accumulated all the emotions we will ever need. **We will find *no new emotions*** although **we will continue to encounter *new*** *events* under *new circumstances* and will cope with them in the main by trying to *understand* our emotional responses to them. Even though we may have become conscious of the connections of sensory associations in our daily lives, we may not have realized how crucial this actor's tool is for evoking an emotional recall *at will.*

Let me cite a few personal examples that can evoke strong feelings in me during the course of seemingly unrelated events. The lingering scent of a particular perfume left behind by someone in an elevator or taxicab can transport me in a flash into the middle of a ballet performance that thrilled me many years ago. Evidently, someone sitting near me in the theatre at the time was wearing the same scent. I remember riding through the countryside in Italy, taking in deep breaths of a marvelous smell that was coming through the open window, wondering why it proved to me that I was really back in Europe. I laughed aloud when I realized it was the smell of sewage running in the open ditch at the roadside. I had associated the stench with a similar one that existed at a farm in the Tyrol where I had spent a happy week of my childhood. The sight of a yellowing gardenia always transports me into the moment of a tender farewell from a beau on a sultry summer night. The smell of old sneakers brings back the gym at a high school prom where the aroma left behind by sweating athletes must have been more pervasive than that of the floral arrangements.

Everyone has a popular tune which he associates with a romantic moment. He has others that represent a particular happy hour, a few bars of classical music that bring back a beautiful, shared experience, and others that recall hours of enforced practicing or of a foot that fell asleep during a concert. We all have our favorite flowers, as well as those we detest because of previous associations with them. For me, petunias, particularly purple ones in straight rows, are linked with sensations of being trapped in a rigid, puritanical suburb. The sight of sunflowers or hollyhocks instantly fills me with a sense of desolation because I first became aware of them on a journey through Madison's shantytown, where they grew straight and tall in the sand, between tin hovels and ash cans, as symbols of hopeless poverty.

In each instance, the stimulus, the *thing that triggered anew* my feelings of exuberance, exhilaration, romance, tedium, oppression, or desolation, was supported by an *inner* logic rather than by any *ex-*

ternal aspects of the total experience. It was always a particular smell, sound, or sight that had been perceived subliminally at the time of an event, something only peripherally connected with it. As a young actor, I occasionally stumbled on this strange kind of trigger for a correct psychological transference to my role, but I didn't understand why it seemed to function so well in an emotional scene. Most of the time I would try to think general sad thoughts, or try to recall an entire sad story. For example, in trying to recall teenage misery, I would go through the entire events of my first prom: how I had coaxed my brother into escorting me because I didn't have a proper date; how unpopular I felt; how enviously I watched the lovely girls dancing, fantasizing that it was I who was whirling around in the arms of the school heroes, the football captain, the head of the debating team; then my awkward acceptance of a dance with the chunky, pimply C student; and my final bitterness about what the evening might have been. It all overwhelmed me with misery, and I rushed to lock myself into a cubicle in the gym's shower room. Whenever I tried to stimulate an emotion by reminding myself in this way of the sequence of events, I ended up either with a blur of general emotions, or else I became objective about them while trying to pump up some feelings. I didn't understand why the stale smell of sweaty sneakers could bring back a rush of feeling, an immediate sensation of miserable teenage awkwardness. Nor did I understand why the sight of a hollyhock or sunflower should make for desolation rather than the remembrance of the poverty-stricken people themselves and their children with whom I'd identified as they huddled against the corrugated tin walls of their shanties. Why would a purple petunia oppress me, or the smell of raw sewage be exhilarating? I couldn't figure it out, but since it was operative for me, I learned to trust this particular way of rekindling sensations that gave cause to my character's actions. I trusted it sufficiently to teach its use. I also discovered how many gifted actors used the same procedure as intuitively as I had, even when they hadn't consciously verbalized it. Not until I had to put it down on paper in my first book did I feel compelled to look for a scientific answer. I went for clarification, which was immediately supplied by my good friend Dr. Jacques Palaci, a psychiatrist, humanist, and someone with a profound understanding of the artist.

When something happens to us in life that momentarily suspends our reasoning and prevents us from coping logically, we have been **taken by an emotion.** (Actors, please note: THE EMOTION TAKES US, **we do not take it!**) At the instant of the suspension of control over our reason, **in our struggle to control it,** we are *overcome* by tears or laughter, rage or joy, etc. Since the human being does not want this loss of control, his reason provides him with a censor that blocks him, telling him not to give in. Once I had understood that even in the course of my daily life this little censor was at work fighting any loss of control, fighting my being overcome by an emotion at the actual moment when something was happening to provoke it, I realized why it was difficult to *recall* an emotion, to experience it anew in the service of the character's action. Dr. Palaci explained that the recall of something seemingly unrelated to the event, **something only peripherally perceived at the actual time, was the *very* thing that had escaped my reasoning censor, thereby allowing the recall through the *association*. It brought back the emotion as a summation of the memory.**

As actors we can make use of this knowledge by consciously using such triggers, by finding personal release objects drawn from our life experience. If you haven't already found them, if you aren't already aware of how many you have at your fingertips, or if you want to augment your treasure chest for future use, if you aren't sure how to go about it, you will need friends (preferably nonactors) to help you with the experiment. Let them in on what you're doing, tell them what you're up to. Think about an unhappy event in your life. Make sure it is an occasion about which you've talked before, about which you have some perspective. Tell them only the *roughest outline* of the story, not its details, something as simple as the external facts about the time when someone you loved tried to walk out on you—or you tried to walk out on him. Then describe *everything* you can remember about the **surrounding circumstances;** the time of day, the weather, the light, the pattern on the wallpaper, a grease spot on the carpet, reflections in a mirror or on the windowpane, street sounds or the music on the radio playing in the background, the details of your lover's clothing, what after-shave he was wearing, what you'd been eating or drinking, and so on. Inadvertently along the way you will probably touch on *the* object, something as unimportant as the recall of an ink spot on your index finger, which will release the censor. The emotion will take you and you will weep or rage again. You will have discovered a new inner object, a new trigger to store away for future use. In the event that you don't succeed with this first experiment, "try and try again!"

Here I would like to warn you about probing into any past experience that may have traumatized you to the point of your still being unable to deal with it. I am referring to an event about which you have never spoken or *wanted* to speak, from which you have no objective distance. If you do probe this, you will be on dangerous ground. You will risk becoming hysterical. And hysteria is a state to be avoided by the actor at all costs. It is a state in which one is flooded with truly uncontrollable emotions, in which one becomes illogical to the point of losing awareness of any contact with surrounding realities. It is of no artistic use. It is anti-art! My criterion for deciding which of my past experiences can serve me is that they must be experiences about which I have achieved a degree of objective distance by talking about them, airing them until I have understood how they affected me. I do not tamper with those that want to stay hidden. Palaci assured me that this rule of thumb was correct. By objective distance, I don't mean to imply a distance measured by the passage of time. I might have a terrific row with my husband in the morning about which I have talked to someone during the day until I understood it. I might already have isolated a trigger object which I can use in a rehearsal or performance the very same evening. And I can have had an experience twenty years before which is still shrouded in unexplained fears and pain. That one I will leave alone.

Many experienced actors, as well as students of acting, once they have learned to identify with their roles, are emotionally free and limber, finding support for their actions in the play as long as the psychological circumstances are familiar to them. The irritations and annoyances they truthfully experience while performing a scene in which they are getting themselves ready for a job interview, for instance, the kind of love and tenderness they manage to feel during an intimate dinner scene with a lover, the outbursts of anger they can release in a scene about a confrontation with a rude employer or bus driver, the tears they let flow when the soup is supposed to have boiled over—all these feelings seem to be at their beck and call and they employ them without tension or anxiety. But the moment they arrive at a point when they think a "big" emotion is demanded, like an outburst of grief, or tears, or a shriek of terror, or a fit of laughter, etc., they are derailed. They are frightened by it. When such manifestations are asked for by the playwright, the director, or the actor himself as interpreter, the actor has a tendency to wave a red flag by qualifying the emotion, by visualizing a *result* and then weighing this result against whatever response he tries to stimulate within himself. Thus he creates feelings of inadequacy which can block him as strongly as his mental censor. (As a matter of fact, any self-examination of the *degree* of emotional intensity while it is in progress will be a guarantee of bad acting.)

A similar trap presents itself when an actor confronts classical themes in "big" plays, believing that nothing in his own experience can match the enormity of the events that befall the characters in the play. Just as many directors do, he refers to these plays as being "bigger than life." He is convinced that his emotions and actions should therefore be "bigger than life." He may have forgotten that anything bigger than life is *dead*. He hasn't yet learned that **the making of art consists of the selection of appropriate life realities** to create a new canvas, to make a new living, breathing statement. Unless we resist preconceiving the emotional results and actions which are always born out of editorial, fictional, audience responses to the material, we will be lured into conventional pushing and illustrating, in other words, false theatrics. (At best there are the extremely gifted actors with a bent for externalizing who belong to the camp of formalism, who pride themselves on their ability to execute preconceived actions, to illustrate how tearful, terrified, agonized, how wounded, angry, ecstatic, or terrified their character is without any psychological involvement of their own.) I myself have learned to trust the bottomless well of sensations and emotions from which I can draw, the seeds of which were planted in my soul in infancy. I trust the process that allows me to drink from this well, to find the appropriate psychological associations whose essence I can transfer to any "big" moment, thus providing more than enough sources for a "big" play. I now know that, by my late teens, all the emotions I would ever need were already somewhere available to me. At that time, I was simply lacking the human understanding that would later help me to find the corresponding passions that would "force my soul to my own conceit."

It is not only that we have been insufficiently trained in our understanding of the human condition to evaluate the psychological similarities between a past event in our own lives and that of the character in a play, but the fault often lies in our American literal-mindedness, which bogs us down in a hopeless search for similar *events,* similar story lines. Now, having understood that emotional recall is supported by the inner logic of association rather than by the outer event, we should be liberated from such trappings to find instead the psychological essences that feed the imagined circumstances of any scene no matter how "big," without fear of our own lack of experience or fear that our choices will be illogical.

To give you an example: When I was eight years old, I had an experience which has served me again and again in a variety of roles. On my way home from school one dark, bitter winter afternoon, I found myself suddenly pursued by a group of neighborhood children who, using me for vicious sport, pelted me with snowballs frozen hard as rock. As I tried to flee from them, the snowballs' impact on my back and shoulders almost knocked the breath out of me. One that hit the side of my face drew blood. But even more terrifying was the epithet the children yowled at me like snarling wolves—"Atheist! Atheist! Atheist!"—because they knew we didn't go to church. As they caught up with me, among the leering faces in the dim light I noticed one with frost-spotted spectacles that made him appear blind. The recall of those spectacles brings back a flood of terror, of senseless shame, of being hounded, of never reaching safety. And yet this is only a story about children who bullied a patsy one winter afternoon. Those frosty eyeglasses have served me for Blanche at the end of the ninth scene of *A Streetcar Named Desire,* when Mitch's accusations and attempted assault catapult her into the screams of "Fire! Fire! Fire!" They were equally useful for the role of Io in *Prometheus Bound,* in which she is eternally pursued by the stinging flies that Zeus has set on her. Io has a desperate need to run from them and wildly attempts to ward them off. (To prove what a generous teacher I am, I can now tell you that in sharing this example with you, in *reasonably* explaining the way the eyeglasses have served me, I have relinquished their usefulness to me for the future. I now understand them too well, objectively speaking. Thank God I have a thousand inner objects just as serviceable. But be sure to keep your sources to yourself, once you have found them.)

In giving you other examples for application to the dramatic events in plays, events so overwhelming that we often fail to understand that we have psychological parallels in our own lives, let me stress that the *first time* we are caught in a particular, brand-new crisis in our lives— such as a brush with death or the loss of a loved one, a natural disaster such as fire, flood, or hurricane, a man-made disaster such as assault or robbery, a serious illness or accident, or the first powerful attraction to another human being—our responses all have something in common. They involve a struggle *to cope with the event, to understand it,* to fight for normalcy, to regain control over the seemingly illogical emotions we are having because we do not yet understand the *consequence* of such events on our lives and souls. It is these responses of amazement, this fearful incongruity, and the actions of fighting for *normalcy* which we must unearth and bring to the character's life in a similar dramatic crisis—*not* the response of the onlookers who are able to evaluate the human consequences of the disaster. Let me explain: Years ago, I was in a car that went through a yellow traffic light and was hit broadside. It overturned and then landed upright again. For months I tried to come to grips with this event, not only with "Why me?" which is such a common reaction, but more importantly with the seeming illogic of my feelings, or lack of them, at the time, as well as my unexplainable behavior. On impact I must have shut my eyes because I can remember seeing nothing, only hearing the deafening sounds of splintering metal and shattering glass. The first thing I became aware of was the driver, who had been thrown into my lap in the backseat of the car. She was transparently gray, and I thought she must be dead (she wasn't) but that it was not my concern, that I must try to push her off so I could find my puppy who had been thrown out through the broken window. I couldn't understand why the crazy people outside kept shouting at me not to move her. After being pulled from the wreckage, after retrieving my pup from a bystander, I became aware that something hot and sticky was running down my face. After one particular gush, I was sure that it was something from my eye, that I must have lost it. But after a mere twinge of anxiety, I quickly told myself it didn't matter because it didn't hurt. I was curious about the onlookers who had gathered around the wreck. It was *they* who were moaning and screaming "Oh my God!" until I felt compelled *to reassure them* that I was all right. I made jokes with the police even as they insisted I must be rushed to the hospital. I told myself that they were interfering with a nice, ordinary weekend in the country. Later, I realized I must have been in shock, that blessed protective covering provided by nature, because I felt no physical pain for twenty-four hours and was blocked from any understanding of the effects of all this on my life and career. As an actress I discovered once again that how I behaved and what I felt in crisis was totally different from the feelings and behavior of the nonparticipating observer, the audience of the event. For many months after the accident I felt compelled to share this experience with friends, talking about it endlessly, questioning my responses and my behavior over and over again, until I finally arrived at the objective distance which made me understand it. *Only* after working through this was I able to isolate the yellow traffic light as the release object for the trauma into which the assault on body and soul had thrown me, so that I dared to use that trigger to recall the eeriness, the suppressed panic, and the desperate need to behave "normally" all over again.

If we are lucky, the loss of someone dear to us, a first realization of death, does not occur until we are at least on the way to adulthood. I myself was nineteen. My most vivid recollection is that of a *lack* of feeling, of once again trying to cope earnestly with routine tasks, of being grateful for anything that seemed familiar and ordinary. There was a kind of numbness from the time of the death until the funeral was over. I was consciously curious about my absence of grief, which, according to everything I had read and heard, was supposed to accompany such a devastating occurrence. I pumped deep for the expected feelings, feeling guilty when I couldn't produce them. I even *pretended* to cry. I envied those whose faces I studied intently when they were pinched with suppressed sorrow or flowing with tears. I stood obediently ready, allowing others to hug me compassionately. I marveled at the speaker at the funeral who turned ashen, standing next to a tall vase of stiff, ugly bronze chrysanthemums, trying to support himself on the shiny coffin, unable to begin the eulogy. About six months later, my loss started to become concrete with daily reminders of the physical and spiritual absence of my beloved. I went through periods of seemingly senseless weeping, self-pity, feelings of futility, and of tremendous guilt, and a belief that the only person to whom I was accountable was gone—in other words, deep depression. As the years went by and others close to me passed away, a comprehension of the finality of death, of the irrevocable loss and the implications of the effect on my future solidified until I, too, would turn ashen, my knees would buckle and, at best, the tears would flow, sometimes even upon receiving *news* of a death. Today, the visualization of a spiky bronze chrysanthemum can trigger the same feelings of unreality, of suspension, of deadly numbness. In the case of the young actor who has not yet had such an experience, I would like to assure him that the death of a pet or the abrupt, permanent departure of a loved one can be perceived in a similar way.

When powerful desires are frustrated or become impossible to fulfill during a love affair, or when there are conflicts with parents, or even in one's career, some people become so emotionally boxed in that they no longer cope rationally. The future looks so bleak that they can no longer envision it. Then they may be led to acts of violence either against the party they believe to be responsible, who has created the devastating sense of frustration, or against themselves through suicide. I have yet to meet the teenager who has not *contemplated* such acts. And, since the contemplation or speculation about them may seem not far removed from the reality, they can easily be transferred as a psychological essence to the many imagined events in dramatic literature that reflect such events.

I remember telling a friend that in the course of my life I had faced everything from giving birth to being married and divorced, from hurricanes, deaths of relatives, near-fatal illness to accidents but, thank God, I'd never been in a fire. One week later I was in one. My first response was of disbelief. My first ludicrous action, after grabbing the dogs and running barefoot into the hall to escape the roaring flames, was to rouse my neighbor with a quiet but urgent request that she "call the police! I'm having a *fantastic* fire!" A little later I remember sitting disconsolately on the floor of the downstairs hallway clutching my animals, staring at the deflated hose while one of the firemen stood casually by as his colleagues attempted to get the water flowing. (He insisted that I ought to remember him because we'd worked together for a whole season in *The Country Girl* at the Lyceum. When I politely asked what part he had played, he replied impatiently, "I was the fireman backstage, don't you *remember?*") Since then, the vision of the deflated hose arouses immediate feelings of stunned hopelessness in me. During the next few weeks, I relied on the assurances of sympathetic friends to make me grasp that our home was really gutted, that we were lucky to be alive, that it was truly appalling and a miracle that we could function at all, with no stove or fridge, huddling together in the least damaged small bedroom with our three dogs. I understood many things. First, I found I could now identify with the problems of poor families who have to live with too many in too little space. My husband and I never argued as much. In the attempts to grapple with our disrupted lives, looking for normalcy in the midst of chaos, we behaved as idiotically as the couple does in Neil Simon's *The Prisoner of Second Avenue* after they've been robbed. Like them, we tried to grasp what had happened, experiencing similar irrational upsets, the same insistence on answers from each other about irrelevant matters to which there *were* no answers. In the fire we lost many prized possessions, heirlooms and paintings; but it was the loss of old, raggedy souvenir programs and travel folders that finally undid me and brought about uncontrollable tears. If you study the behavior of the characters during and after the fire in Chekhov's *The Three Sisters*, you will find a perfect example of truthful behavior of people caught in a crisis and how they struggle to cope without yet being aware of the consequences.

Any event over which you have had little or no control, which has temporarily or permanently altered the direction of your life, can have relevance for transference to a variety of plays in dramatic literature. For the enormity of something like the trial of Saint Joan, I personally was able to make direct use of the time when I was hounded by the congressional investigating committees during the McCarthy period. But any occasion during which you were unjustly set upon, during which you were compelled to defend your beliefs, can supply you with recognizable psychological truths, serving you far better than the emotions you might pump up through empathy with Joan arising from the knowledge that, after all, the poor girl was burned at the stake. Joan did *not* know this until she was in the flames. During the trial she is struggling with each inquisitor in defense of her position. The understanding of the consequence belongs to the onlooker. Forgive my repetition of this crucial point. I will make it *again*. There *are*, of course, times when your character in the play *is* the onlooker of a dramatic event. Then such compassionate feelings are appropriate and usually easy to come by. They also lie in the realm of the members of the Greek chorus that moans and weeps while observing and explaining the consequences of the tragedies as they unfold. *Self*-pity is a perfectly common and acceptable human emotion, but pity for the character we are playing usually evokes criticism such as "That actor feels so sorry for himself."

Dr. Palaci provided me with another interesting answer when I asked him why I only had to *think* of a mouse or a rat to feel ice-cold shivers, shudders of revulsion, and a compulsion to scream, leap in the air, or run away when I wanted to induce a sense of terror on stage. He explained that human beings often have one object that acts as a collective symbol for the many fears we encounter in our daily lives, fears we repress or don't fully understand. When I told him how useful the rodent was to my acting and asked what I could use instead, if, through analysis, I were to rid myself of this fear by discovering its initial source, Dr. Palaci patiently assured me that, first, there was no need to rid myself of it unless I had to *live* with rodents and, more importantly, within a week I would probably develop another kind of fear because human beings tend to use such a catchall symbol as an escape hatch for other fears. I was delighted. Since then I have enjoyed playing games with those who claim that *nothing* unreasonable frightens them by listing snakes, spiders, roaches, maggots, worms, until something—perhaps something as idiotic as a moth—will make even a great, swaggering macho man shiver and turn pale.

I have left the turbulent experience of love for the last of my examples because it seems to entail emotions that are most readily available for the actor. From the first turmoil we are thrown into as teenagers, from the first crisis brought about by "falling in love," we will recognize that our passions recur again and again with few variations, that we associate present feelings with those in the past, that we weigh our present obsessions against those of the past, valiantly trying to correct past mistakes. We attempt to control unreasonable impulses of possessiveness, the twinges of jealousy and fears of being deserted, all of which embroil us until we arrive at the faith in the continuance of the relationship, the security in believing that we are loved in return. The recall of trigger objects for such transferences is seldom elusive. The problem of falling in love instantaneously that occurs in a body of dramatic literature, whether it be in *Romeo and Juliet, The Lady's Not for Burning,* or a domestic comedy, can be difficult. To create an exceptional transference to the partner for such an event, I myself have been successful with such psychologically similar sources as my response to an unexpected, phenomenal sunset or sunrise, the sudden appearance of a rainbow, or a shower of shooting stars.

I would like to make a final observation about my *personal* selection of release objects. The most serviceable triggers that I transfer to my stage life are always *visual* (the yellow traffic light, the frosted spectacles, the bronze chrysanthemum, the deflated fire hose, etc.). Even though I have confidence that my other four senses are highly developed, I find that smells, sounds, touches, and tastes are difficult to recall on command when I need a particular emotional release. (This does not hold true when, as in the previous chapter, I bring them into play in connection with my *physical* behavior.) Perhaps, if I *first* tried to visualize bacon sizzling and curling up in a frying pan, I might be able to recall the smell. Or, if, in my mind's eye, I *first* imagined the sight of the church spire in the Alps from which the ringing bells had resounded, I might be overcome with the same feeling of mysterious awe that enveloped me at the time when I actually heard them. But I have found this method too circuitous. However, if *you* are able to bring the recall of any of the other four senses into spontaneous existence to trigger an emotional moment, don't let me discourage you.

At this point, if you have freely availed yourself of the many examples taken from my personal life, hopefully, they will have suggested endless parallels in your own. If you are still doubtful about the relevance of their application to your roles, I suggest you reread Chapter 5 on the use of transference. **The psychological essences you will want to substitute are manifold as they relate to your character's background, the surrounding circumstances, and the given events of the play, as springboards to the various relationships with the other characters, and as motivations for your character's**

main needs and pursuits, as well as for the individual moments of crisis. You will need to supply personal psychological realities *only* when direct contact with the events, the objects, and your partners fails to stimulate you, when the imagination alone fails to support your specific actions during the moment-to-moment give and take which will prove that you are alive on stage.

The *mis*use of the emotional instrument is flagrant on today's stage, in films, and on television. Many of our contemporary stars make it a primary goal to prove to themselves and to the audience that they have feelings, that they can produce tears. They induce general emotions, think sad thoughts, leave the stage, so to speak, while doing their incorrect homework in public, as they push for sources that, usually without relevance to the action, make the water flow. They hang on to a mood, mistaking attitudes for actions. They pump themselves up into neurotic states in which they ride unintelligibly through a scene with muddy actions or none at all. Someone wisely observed that if crying were acting his aunt would be Duse! And the audience, which usually remains unmoved in the presence of such displays, will at best stop to whisper, "Look! That actor is crying real tears." Another error, which used to be popular but is now, thank God, going out of fashion, occurs when the naturalistic actor, who is supposed to be angry with another character in a scene, decides just before his entrance to pick a personal fight with his colleague in the wings; or when, in order to bring about sufficient passion in a love scene, he deems it necessary to make love to his partner in private. Let me repeat my earlier statement that this is just as idiotic as finding the reality for murder on stage by first trying it out in life. The sole purpose of developing a limber psychological instrument, and the correct technique of spontaneous emotional recall, is to discover and execute the consequent *actions* (what we *do* about what we feel) and to give substance to the *actions* which are the true communicators of our character.

The technique of psychological sensory recall is identical to that used for physical sensory recall. You might now want to review the previous chapter with this in mind. Remember how you use imagined stimuli at will to move you into the discovery of correct *behavioral responses*. Remember that the play's circumstances determine the cause of your psychological as well as physical condition, that your identification with the cause must be motivated, and, above all, that the sensation must produce an action. Do not *wait* to feel and do not *skip* the initial attention given to the stimulus if you want to avoid mechanical or illustrative actions. The sensation will occur most fully while you are struggling to control or overcome it. At times an action, whether it be verbal or physical, can generate an emotion in itself. The simple act of banging a fist on the table can produce a sense of rage, provided it is logically motivated. Pleading with someone for forgiveness, begging verbally, or stroking physically might even produce tears. If you tickle someone, you might find yourself joining in with a fit of giggling. I don't recommend this predetermination of an action to supply an emotion, but I would like to add that, just as the emotions feed the actions, so the **emotions are furthered by the action.**

On the many occasions when actors come to me for advice about dealing with the recurring problem that their imagined stimulus, a particular inner object, now fails to trigger the required emotion because it has "worn out" or become stale through repetition, I give them a list of reasons, any of which may be the cause. They may have failed to connect their inner object with the actual stimulus provided in the play. They may be anticipating how or at what second the emotion should manifest itself, consequently forgetting the cause. Most often, they are dwelling on the emotion rather than using it as a springboard for the consequent action. Or they are weighing the degree of intensity they are experiencing against the previous one. Simple anxiety and fearfulness that the emotion will elude them is another guarantee that it will not occur. To correct these errors is easier said than done, and any or all of them may recur even for the experienced artist. But the longer we work, the more we understand these pitfalls, the more we aim for a perfect technique in applying emotional recall, the sooner we will learn to hurdle them.

In conclusion: We must continue to gain perspective about our psychological senses and clear the way for truthful responses to them in order to avoid generalities, false theatrics, and irrelevancies. We will then be able to open ourselves only to what we need in the play, to that which will animate body and soul in the pursuit of our character's life on stage.

8

Animation

THE BODY

IN my introduction and particularly in Chapter 3 where it has to do with the *outer* techniques, I stressed the importance of training the body to be ready for many roles, whether they be Apollo, Richard III, or Biff Loman, Saint Joan, Rosalind, or Laura in *The Glass Menagerie*. Every actor should strive for the agility that allows him to leap into the air for joy or across table and chairs to accost an enemy, to race up a flight of stairs, or to collapse in a heap. He will want the grace to dance a minuet or a tango, as well as to rock and roll, the skill to duel and fence, even to mount a horse and gallop off into the sunset in a western—if he so chooses. But, more importantly, if he wants this limber instrument to be at his beck and call, to be **animated** during his character's struggle to achieve his objectives, responding freely and intuitively to the imagined circumstances and surroundings and to the characters with whom he is interacting in the play, he must understand *all* the things that bring his body to life. In the earlier chapters I have already given many examples of ways in which the body is influenced by such things as changes in self-image, by clothing, by one's relationship to others, by weather and time of day, by physical conditions such as fatigue and pain, and by the psychological causes that "prepare the body for vigorous action" as my dictionary so aptly puts it. I have not yet dealt with the crucial issue of the body in motion.

We have all experienced those miserable moments of awkwardness and self-consciousness on stage when our hands hang stiffly at our sides feeling like appendages that belong to someone else, when our legs are leaden and our feet seem to be in the way, when our concentration becomes solely centered on an attempt to protect ourselves from a sense of naked exposure by assuming theatrical positions or naturalistic, "comfortable" bodily arrangements. (Such states usually harken back to the same ones we had wrongly acquired as amateurs or in a college drama department.) This kind of disoriented panic can take hold at the very moment of an entrance because we don't know where we have come from (except the wings), because we don't know where we are (except on a stage), or when our first move to the couch has no other motive than that it was a given piece of blocking. Once seated, the actor may momentarily regain a faith in a reality by instinctively settling back in the cushions and finding a connection with his partner that enables him to involve himself with the content of the interchange. But if he rises again without motivation or destination for no other reason than that it was a stage direction, the same self-consciousness will flood over him.

I learned the hard way that all my diligent work on identification with the character's life went for naught if I was unsure of truthful, motivated PHYSICAL DESTINATIONS. And when I remembered that the body is the visible tool with which I communicate a living character, and since it is my goal to avoid illustration, I must remind myself that **voice and speech, the soul and the mind, are not separate from the body but originate from it,** emanate through it. Therefore, if the body is inert, unmotivated, and artificially positioned, the soul will also be deadened, the mind will freeze up, thoughts will become occupied with external irrelevancies, the throat will tighten, and we will produce mechanical or unintelligible words. We will be exposed actors on a stage, not human beings in a room, a palace, or a garden.

The famous director Arthur Hopkins said something long ago that some contemporary directors might well take to heart, and that every actor ought to pin up on his wall: "The reason for walking is destination!" I have learned that unless dead or dead asleep, the human being is *always* in motion. During fleeting moments when he seems to be temporarily arrested, he is atingle, trying to determine his next destination. **Many physical destinations are *consciously* motivated**

by events, by basic wishes, by what is done to us and by demands of others. These are relatively simple to define. But **countless others, ordinary ones of which we are only** *subliminally aware while psychologically occupied,* **are determined by habit,** such as heading for the stove or refrigerator for food, to a table to eat, the desk to write or phone, the bathroom to wash, a chair or couch to relax in, to read or socialize. We rarely think them out, but follow habitual and instinctive needs. (Of course, we also have many complicated subconscious psychological motivations, which I will discuss in Part Four: The Role.) In life **we know where we have just been, where we are at the moment, and where we plan to go next,** unless we are insane, drugged, or in a coma. Destinations based on reflex, habit, and personal eccentricities, of which we are usually only subliminally aware, must be *unearthed* if we want to be truthfully animated on stage, to eliminate those arid stretches when the body ceases to serve us. If we learn to understand and to **define the causes of our destinations and the consequent behavior** under ordinary circumstances in our daily lives, we can apply this procedure to the *extra*ordinary, the dramatic circumstances given us by the playwright. For example: At this moment, **I am seated** at the typewriter with my legs crossed in my nightie and slippers. **I have just come from** the kitchen where I prepared a cup of coffee to bring to my desk. Intuitively, I know that after trying to solve a few problems of this difficult chapter, **I will head for** the bathroom to wash and get dressed for an appointment. While working, my body is occupied with the task of typing, with adjustments to the slight chill in the room, with smoking my hateful cigarettes, and with sipping coffee. I also follow through on many smaller destinations of which I would be unaware if I were not trying to unearth them for you, because my mind would be *primarily occupied* with the task of clarifying my ideas: I get up to empty the ashtray, to get a fresh cup of coffee or pack of cigarettes. I half rise for a box of tissues that is just out of reach or for the typing correction fluid. These things are arrived at by reflex. They are *secondary* to the struggle with my primary, psychological objective, which is to make this chapter helpful to you. Here is another example: If **I have come from** the store, while **I am unlocking** the front door, I know that **I will head for** the kitchen with my groceries—unless a dire need to go to the toilet makes me dump the groceries on the floor en route.

While doing these things, I am *primarily, actively considering* how to resolve a recent argument with a friend, instinctively knowing that my next physical destination will be the refrigerator to store the perishables before I start cooking dinner, and so on and so on. If the logic of these examples seems childishly self-evident, ask yourself how often you have ignored such basic principles of human behavior when you are trying to put your character into action. How often have you made an entrance with no knowledge of where you were coming from, or when you have answered this question only with a little intellectual lip service? How often have you lost animation because you had no immediate destination and no inner plan for the next?

The influence of the surroundings on your physical life may also seem obvious, but they are manifold and often profound even in their subtleties. Let me share a few observations about myself which may ring a bell in you. When you live with someone else you establish your own territory right down to which side of the bed and which side of the shelves in the bathroom cabinet are yours. Without discussion, you will have determined your favorite chair—in every room. In the living room, the right end of the sofa is *mine* with *my* pad and pencil at my elbow and *my* ashtray ready at my side. When a close friend is visiting, he knows that this place is reserved for me so he sits down in *his* chair, the same one in which he always sits, the same one in which I had probably invited him to sit the very first time he came to call. If a new guest comes to see me, I always steer her away from *my* place and if, before I have a chance to prevent it, she inadvertently sits there anyway and I must sit elsewhere, I feel momentarily as discombobulated as I do in a strange place. The next time you visit someone for the first time, observe something you are ordinarily unaware of, how much reflex attention you give to the newness of the place—not just the decor, the paintings, or the books, but in orientating your body to the comfort or discomfort of your chair, to a place for your purse or other belongings, to the distance between yourself and the coffee or end table that dictates tiny destinations toward a drink or nosh or an ashtray—before you attain a sense of physical equilibrium. Then notice how, on your next visit, you will head for the exact spot in which you had finally felt secure the last time.

This takes me to that actor's nemesis when he follows the ghastly stage direction "He wanders about aimlessly," which is often given when a character is restless, in despair, or doesn't know how to solve a dilemma. If the director or playwright would at least say, "he walks to and fro," the actor might be smart enough to ask himself, "to what" and "fro(m) what" is he moving? The psychological state of restlessness, boredom, indecision, or despair which on occasion gets us on our feet, unable to settle for long in any one spot, is accompanied by voluntary and involuntary destinations which hinge on our familiarity with the place.

Let's say that you are at home, routinely seated at your desk to pay some bills, but more importantly involved with the psychological struggle you are having with your job. *You may hardly be aware* that you rise from your desk to head for the window, that you move the curtain aside to check the weather or the cop on the corner, that you go to the liquor cabinet but reject the reflex to pour a drink. You change direction and walk to the phone and adjust the receiver before heading back to your desk but decide instead to go to the kitchen for a glass of water. All the while you have been grappling with your problem at work. Even if you should catch yourself following the same path several times, from your desk to the window and back again, you are never moving "spacelessly," as so many unskilled actors do. Since our physical life on stage should evolve out of findings for selective actions pertinent to the character's problems and his circumstances, any mere naturalistic imitation of a restless state must be avoided. Even the act of truthful "wandering" must be substantiated by *meaningful destinations*, focused on relevant objects. Let me use the previous example to suppose that the event occurs during a few moments in a play. Everything is the same except that you are now waiting for a phone call, possibly a visit, from an agent bringing news about an important job. The room is in readiness in case the agent comes in person. Again you are at your desk trying to pay bills with the need to keep yourself occupied. This fails, so you walk to the window to see if the agent is in sight. You go to the phone, pick up the receiver to call him, but reject the notion because you remember he wouldn't be in his office now. You take out your impatience on the receiver when replacing it in its cradle. You go to the liquor cabinet, pick up a glass but put it back with second thoughts, knowing you must be on your toes for the interview. You cross to a mirror and check your appearance before sitting by the phone, praying that it will ring, etc. Meanwhile, your mind is racing with the possibilities of the job, the things that might go wrong, the reasons for the agent's tardiness, etc. The *seeming* illogic of the wanderings and the strangeness of the sequence must be substantiated by the logic of the play.

If you are now convinced by Arthur Hopkins's dictum that the reason for walking is destination, I pray that you will be equally persuaded by my addition: **So is standing!** I have seen this fact ignored again and again, even by experienced players from one end of the globe to the other. Unfortunately, the performances in which actors stand artificially posed with glass or teacup in hand, or in which they are draped across the backs and arms of empty sofas and chairs, have still not gone totally out of fashion. Then there are the endless problems that arise when the actor must stand in *empty* space and has found no relationship to the *imagined* landscape or bare room, hallway, or palace, leaving him defenseless, reliant on arbitrary positioning to save himself from exposure.* In life, we always try to fulfill a basic human need, that of finding a place to alight, even in a crisis. Once seated, if we rise to our feet, it is in order to reach our next destination. Rising to *stand* is only connected to a few possibilities: to stretch our limbs before sitting again, for instance. Or at home I sometimes stand as a signal to a guest that I have many things to do so I wish he would leave. In someone else's home I sometimes stand to signify that I must go, a stalling tactic as a preparation for proper leave-taking. I may stand for a moment when I've forgotten where I was going next. I stand when there's no place to sit—at a crowded party, for instance. Or when I'm not sure where I'm supposed to sit. I often stand when en route to a particular place and something momentarily arrests me, as when, on my way to the kitchen to get something for a guest, he stops me with a piece of news. But even while I'm held in place to listen, my body intuitively knows that when he has finished talking, I will continue to the kitchen. It is also possible that the news is so startling that I will forget my original errand and return to my seat. Outdoors, I may stand while waiting for a vehicle or a meeting with a friend. While waiting, I am not

* I will present this problem in Chapter 17 of the exercises.

standing in a rigid position but am pursuing small destinations: to the curb to see if the vehicle is in sight, to a store window to check out the merchandise, and so on. Therefore, let me repeat that the body is always in action or poised in the direction of the next physical destination.

Of course the *total* animation of the body hinges on a correct incorporation of the circumstances, the weather, the time, character needs, relationship to people and objects, on the very clothes we wear, on our immediate needs, and on an active mind.

THE MIND

An alert mind is an actor's prerequisite. It must be exercised as continuously and with the same discipline as the body. Slothful habits, drugs, or other personal excesses are destructive to mind and talent. According to the dictionary, to be *intelligent* means "to reveal good judgment and sound thought, to be alert, to be quick-witted." It also means to comprehend information, to be successful in dealing with new situations, and to apply knowledge so as to cope with one's surroundings. On the other hand, to be *intellectual* is to be "chiefly guided by the intellect rather than by emotion or experience." Therefore, it is important that the artist leave intellectual concepts, theories, and conclusions to scholars, scientists, critics, or to discussions about other matters than the work on his roles. Treatises should be confined to libraries, lecture halls, and parlors, not brought to the theatre. Creativity depends on maintaining innocence and a never-ending curiosity about the human condition. We must use our total *intelligence* rather than our intellectuality to come to an understanding of the play and its conflicts, making sure that all our discoveries lead to identification with the character and the circumstances in which he lives to animate our thoughts and senses in order to *act,* to *do.* If anything in this book leads you to an intellectual approach to the work, you are misreading me—or I have failed.

Let me add that, if you want to fulfill an artist's obligation to be mentally alert at every rehearsal and performance, make your personal life subservient to your work. Leave your lovers' spats, problems with the landlord, and interesting lunches with agents behind you when you enter the theatre or rehearsal hall. Otherwise you will be doing your colleagues and yourself a great disservice. You will also find it difficult to **concentrate** and **focus** on the creative process. Save your energies, clear the deck, and ready your mind for the job at hand.

Obviously nothing in the last four chapters has excluded the thinking process in acting. Everything we perceive and experience psychologically and physically is accompanied by a battery of *thoughts* as well as actions. The necessity for giving special attention to **thinking** arises from the misconceptions so many actors have about the functioning of the mind on stage. For those who don't already know it, **thought moves with the speed of lightning.** Also, it cannot be deliberately slowed down. An example: You are at a party given for a producer. It is finally your turn to be introduced to the great man. In your wild desire to make an impression, you reach out impulsively to shake his hand, knocking the drink out of his hand instead. A little later, off in a corner with a friend, you confide all the things that went through your mind at that horrible moment. It may take ten minutes to put all the things you were thinking in that split second into words.

Thought is not based on verbally organized ideas. I have known actors who, with mistaken diligence, actually wrote out their character's thoughts as though they were dialogue or stage directions. This can only result in illustrated actions and facial grimaces made to fit the surprise, puzzlement, pleasure, or disgust inherent in the words that have been jotted down.

Another major flaw of the untrained actor **is to attempt to separate thoughts from actions,** from basic behavior. He will stand seemingly in limbo or sit in a state of suspension and, when asked what he was *doing* during these moments, he invariably answers, "I was thinking." He must learn that if he stands, his reason is to head for a logical destination, that if he sits, it is probably to get a load off his feet, and that when he rises again, it will be to go to his desk, or the phone, or to the kitchen for a glass of water. In accompaniment with this behavior, he is thinking. When awake, we are *always* thinking. Our thoughts travel even during certain hours of sleep.

Once we have learned that intellectualized thinking belongs to scholars and philosophers, as actors we must also avoid the kind of *passive*, "natural" thinking that occurs in life while routinely occupied with the dishes, answering the mail, or even while reading uninteresting sections of books or newspapers—when the mind may be occupied with irrelevant or straying thoughts. Instead, we must find the "real" thinking that should take place on stage. **Real thinking is preceded by, accompanied by, and followed by action.** Let me stick to those definitions and synonyms for *thinking* in the dictionary that are *active* and that will *animate* us, such as "to form an intention, to hunt for a solution, to form an expectation, to attempt to comprehend, to speculate, to make a mental plan, to call to mind, to imagine, **to envisage,** and **to form a mental picture.**" It is not as difficult as it may sound **to animate our thoughts,** to muster them, **to keep them traveling toward our targets as they interact with our physical, psychological, and verbal actions** to the exclusion of those which are irrelevant and disruptive.

Let's assume that you have rehearsed correctly, are in tune with the character's needs, have particularized the circumstances and surroundings, defined your relationship to the others, and that all your senses are selectively alert to what moves in on you so that you are involved in the specific conflicts of the scene. You will be in action; you will *not* have to concern yourself with what you are thinking. It will have been taken care of. **Your thoughts will be alive, relevantly interacting with what you are giving and taking.** However, it is often during moments when our objectives and behavior seem routine, when the conflict is not self-evident, that our concentration can flag and the attention will stray—into the audience or to irrelevant areas of our personal lives.

As a young actor, I used to kick myself, blaming such moments on poor concentration. It was simply that I hadn't learned *what to concentrate on.* I didn't know how to instigate real thinking, how to trigger pertinent thoughts, those that were drawn from the given circumstances, how to exclude those that scattered all over the place. Once I had figured out for myself how this process occurs under ordinary circumstances (something I certainly don't recommend borrowing as a mere naturalistic device), I learned how to apply it to the extraordinary circumstances given me by the playwright.

Let us suppose that you are at home getting ready to go out to market. You are having company for dinner and have already planned your menu and written out the grocery list. You will hardly be aware that you have buttoned up your coat (unless there was a problem with a loose button or a sore finger). You may consciously check your wallet to make sure you have enough money, and you may be only subliminally aware that you are taking up your purse and putting on your gloves (unless they were mislaid). You may not know how you get out the door and into the elevator.

Now, if you are hardly aware of such reflex behavior, what *are* you aware of? Perhaps of the unmade bed, which ought to be straightened up before you start cooking, of the time when you should start the roast, considering that one of your guests is usually unpunctual, of the brand of toweling you might have to settle for in case your favorite is not on the shelf. You may weigh whether to pick up flowers for the centerpiece or to count on one of the guests bringing you a bouquet. You may wrangle with a decision about which tablecloth needs the least ironing so as to shorten the job of setting the table. You may speculate about the availability of your favorite butcher and whether you will have the patience to wait until he's free, and about the PBS *Masterpiece Theatre* which you hope to con the guests into watching with you. Without your knowledge, such mental activities may manifest themselves in your physical behavior. (You might have yanked at a button while worrying about a tardy guest.) This mental planning, speculating, and problem solving, including the likelihood of much more (which might take another page to describe), can take place in less than the minute it takes to button a coat, put on gloves, gather your belongings, and leave the house.

All of this *thinking* has been arrived at by alertness to the realities of the upcoming dinner party. It moves like greased lightning and is *never* verbally organized. It is at the heart of total involvement in the moment. When I had to execute a similar task on stage, before I had learned how to stimulate active thoughts, I would fight desperately for concentration while giving my total attention solely to the *physical* activities. With intense exaggeration, I would examine and struggle with each button, the clasp on the wallet, and each separate finger as it was pushed into the glove—all the while thinking miserably that everything was taking so *long*.

In order to set you on the path of animated thinking on stage, let me sum up what you can take as examples from this hypothetical preparation for the trip to the grocery store. In a similar situation in a play, it is unlikely that the dinner being planned would be an ordinary one. It would have heightened importance, making it easier to give attention to the selected mental activities connected with it. **When I say "selected" I do not mean regimenting, blueprinting, or scripting the order in which the thoughts are arrived at.** The examples of mental actions were given in random order with no concern for organized logic, but they *were* connected with the surrounding circumstances of the upcoming party, which substantiates their inner logic. At each performance you should arrive at them anew, freely allowing them to change, letting them stimulate others that are related to the event. Each problem and speculation will further the next. Under similar circumstances in a play, you must create a new and particularized familiarity with such things as the unmade bed, the off-stage room and kitchen, the oven timer, the grocery store, the meat department, the face of the butcher, the corner florist, and, obviously, every guest, so that your visualizations will continue to activate your thoughts—your attempts to make plans and solve problems.

Inner Objects

In giving the definitions for *thinking,* I stressed "to envisage" and "to form a mental picture" for a specific purpose. Much of my personal nonintellectual thinking is visual, and long ago I discovered that by **bringing to mind pertinent, specific images, I contacted the sources that triggered actively traveling thoughts** which kept my attention on the events of the play. When these mental images had reality for me, they stimulated my inner actions in all the areas where actual contact with my partners and the place were insufficient to keep my concentration in focus. I began to refer to these images as INNER OBJECTS to differentiate them from those that are actually present, those that I am tangibly, visually, and verbally connected with while playing. I have already referred to inner objects in conjunction with the psychological senses as triggers for emotional recall and, hopefully, you will now understand how essential they are in the use of transferences. I make use of them while listening and also when giving a story about the past substantive reality, a problem that occurs in almost every play. I sometimes use them to instigate a state of being, evoking terror, for example, by visualizing a snarling rat.

I would like to describe and specify here the *inner objects* that can trigger the various mental activities connected with the preparation for the dinner party while buttoning up to go out. (They will be **bold.**) I picture the **unmade bed** in the **bedroom,** which makes me consider when I will be able to **straighten it up.** I make visual contact with the **raw roast** in the **refrigerator** in my **kitchen,** which can trigger speculations about the weight of the meat and the two hours it will most likely take to cook through and the hour at which I must put it in, remembering to set the **timer** if I plan to have it ready for dinner at eight. I picture the small amount of **toweling** left in the **rack** above the **sink** before considering the particular **shelf** at the **A&P** which is usually short of the large rolls of **Bounty** I prefer. Then I see the **Viva** stacked next to it and decide to settle for just one roll of that. I envision the little bunch of **white sweetheart roses** standing in the **containers** under the **awning** at the florist's at the **corner of 8th Street and 6th Avenue.** I argue with myself about spending money on the **blooms that will droop,** probably by the next day. I picture my little friend **Sally** standing at the **front door** offering me **six anemones** as she has done on several other such occasions, and decide to count on them, even though the **colors** won't go as well with my **tablecloth,** and so on and so on. The only reason I have stuck to this order for arriving at the inner objects is to help you draw a parallel with the first description. But no exact order must *ever* be demanded. In the process of re-creating them on stage, they must remain fluid and be given free rein while staying connected to the event. Within each plan, I have provided several inner objects, any of which can precede the other and can suggest even more thoughts, can *trigger more active thinking.*

In summation: **The actor's thinking depends on the subjective process of weighing his course of action by contact with inner and outer objects.** Both of these must be connected with everything that has happened, is happening, and that you *expect* to happen within the events of the play. They must be clothed in substantive *realities* or they will have no consequence. The larger your selection of plausible inner objects, the more food you will have for involving, *active* thoughts. The visualized objects will help you to channel your attention into your character's life and give meaning to your actions—because we must continue to remind ourselves that **to act is to do!**

LISTENING

In Chapters 6 and 7, I talked extensively about hearing, one of the five senses, as an avenue to our perceptions. It should no longer be a mystery that the buzz of a particular doorbell, the tolling of bells, the lowing of cattle, the sound of nails scratching on a blackboard, the din of acid rock, or the strains of a Bach cantata can have a shattering effect on us. So can a child's soprano or a silky baritone, even a nasal twang, when our ears are open to the tonality and melody of the human voice. But, for the purpose of this section, I would like to give special attention to the process of **animated listening** which is essential for total participation in any dialogue. When you consider that in a scene between yourself and only one other character *half* of your life will depend on listening, you will realize how crucial it becomes to be in action while you hear. In preparing for a role, ask yourself how often you have worked only on the things *you* have to say, mistakenly believing that when other characters speak, it is "their turn," thinking it is your obligation as a good colleague to remove yourself from the action by assuming a courteous *attitude* of listening.

When I was a young actress (in the olden days, as my daughter used to refer to this time), when you were hired for a role, usually you received the "sides" of your part instead of the complete script of the play. They contained only the lines of your character and the cues that preceded them, usually the last three words of the other characters' speeches. You were expected to come to the first rehearsal having worked on your part, particularly in summer stock. If it was a new play or one that was not in print, you were left guessing about its content, even in the dark about *who* was delivering the cues. Your sides read like this, the cue indicated by the three dots in front of it:

> . . . spice of life.
> What?
> . . . out of life!
> You talk like a courtesan, Frank.

. . . nuts anymore.
Let's see, where would I be if I were a pair of glasses?
. . . without me, Georgiana!
Someone's feeling mighty good today.
. . . good night's sleep.
When did you get them?
(from Clifford Odets' *The Country Girl* I.4.)

To prove we were pros, we memorized our lines, practicing them out loud with interesting variations of emphasis. We put "feeling" into them. We also memorized our cues. The first rehearsal usually exposed the insanity of our approach, as we discovered in what context we were speaking and what we were answering to. Most of the time permanent damage had been done to the acting by the mechanization of the words and meaningless cues. Sometimes the felony was compounded by an old-fashioned star who insisted, *"No one moves on my lines,"* so that you sat or stood stiffly by with an illustrated manner of listening, waiting anxiously to pick up your cue, the signal to start acting again. In today's theatre, you will still see the residue of such outdated ways of working, sometimes, because even with the best intentions, the actors haven't learned *how to listen*.

Among my other problems of concentration when I was still inexperienced, I had trouble staying connected to my partner when anything he said to me was longer than a few sentences, even when I listened to every single word. I didn't understand that the "single word" was at the heart of my problem. **We do not hear the outer word or words, but rather what is inherent in them.** When my students remain in doubt about this, I tell them to listen to *each* word as I relate an anecdote so carefully that they will be able to repeat it in the exact order in which it was delivered: I say, "Yesterday I went to see Mastroianni in a film on Eighth Street, and his performance was extraordinary, really an exemplary one. I decided again that, more than any other movie actor, he is perhaps the finest. . . ."

When I ask them to tell me what I was talking *about*, they have no idea, with the possible exception that it had something to do with Mastroianni. But they actually heard a mere jumble of disconnected words, rather than the content.

Unless we are philosophizing without dealing in concrete examples, much of what we hear is visual. We form mental pictures (as our thinking travels). In my anecdote, if you had really heard what it was about, you would have had your own inner objects of the street, the movie house, and of Mastroianni in a particular film. To further this point: Recently a young actor came to me in despair about an audition at which he felt he'd made a fool of himself; he feared such an important director would never call him back. Reminded of my own foolishness at such an occasion, to cheer him up I told him about my first audition for Alfred Lunt and how happily it had ended. As I was trudging hopefully through the streets on my way to the Shubert Theatre, it had begun to drizzle. I was dressed to the nines, with an added touch of theatrical glamour, a veil pinned to my hair in place of a hat. The stiff tulle turned limp and damp in the rain and stuck to my face. When I entered the backstage hallway, the doorman looked at me askance, obviously convinced I'd strayed into the wrong place. I yanked off the offending veil and it ripped, catching on the stem of my watch. On the verge of tears, I blurted out defensively that I was a legitimate *actress,* that I was extremely *talented,* that I had a verifiable *appointment* with the famous Mr. Lunt, that I'd walked in the rain only to save the *bus* fare, etc., etc., until he finally calmed me down with a pat on the shoulder and a reassuring "I'll tell Mr. Lunt you're here." The occasion continued to evoke even more outlandish behavior on my part, but I won the part. After I finished this tale, I asked the student how much of it he had personally visually imagined: the veil, Forty-fourth Street in the rain, Shubert Alley, the backstage area, an old doorman? "All of it," he answered, "and much more." While listening, he had loaded the story with his own "inner objects."

Animated listening entails the interpretation of what is being said to us as it interacts with our own battery of psychological and mental actions such as the ones I described in a previous section, The Mind. We weigh the content, approve or disapprove, empathize with it or reject it, speculate on how it furthers or interferes with our own wishes, hunt for solutions to problems being posed. We make discoveries, try to cope with the unexpected, and confirm or reevaluate what we have heard. Often our assumptions change, so that we must consider things within the altered frame of reference until we are compelled to answer audibly. When participating in a dialogue **on**

stage, we listen, from our character's point of view and expectations, to the meaning and intent of the verbal actions of the other. If we remind ourselves that our mental activities, our thoughts, move with the speed of light, that they must remain focused without regimentation or blueprinting, they will manifest themselves only in our concentrated involvement in the events on stage. Although the face and body may spontaneously respond to what we are hearing, **any tendency to mark, indicate, show, illustrate, or externally react to what we are hearing is the mark of someone not really listening.** We must never try to illustrate the ways we are surprised, puzzled, challenged, delighted, depressed, saddened, etc. It is as flawed as the other passé manner of mechanically clicking off the facts with our auditory sense while waiting for the cue to speak.

The exploration of the meaning and intent of everything said to us should begin at the first rehearsal. The validity of our own character's verbal action is dependent on it. We also **listen with our eyes** to interpret the expressions that spontaneously accompany active words. "You're a big ham!" might annihilate me when sent with an arrogant sneer and produce the need for retaliation. But the same words, accompanied by a mischievous grin and a tickle under the chin, could very well bring about gales of laughter and the wish to counter in kind. In point of fact, we listen with our entire being when we are engaged in a truthful dialogue. Once we understand how to listen, the need to answer will become inevitable.

If you want to test the ultimate challenge of animated listening (if you are a woman), you might consider the part of the mistress in Strindberg's one-act play, *The Stronger.* On Christmas Eve, in a tearoom, she is confronted by the wife of a prominent man with whom she is having an affair. The wife challenges her, provokes her, inadvertently gives herself away, pleads with her, threatens her, and lords it over her with every tool at her command. The mistress answers with compassion, with regret, with envy, with doubt, with contempt, with surprise, with vengeance, with pity—and with total silence. She does not utter a word. She is listening, alive in body, soul, and mind. It is a magnificent role.

The need for **spontaneous verbal actions,** for the compulsive *talking* of the wife, can only be sustained by her dependence on and alertness to the behavior of the mistress, what she reads in her eyes, how she interprets every move, and, of course, her silences. This dialogue, this human interaction of the two women, leads the audience to speculate which of them is, indeed, the stronger. (Please note, it is *a dialogue,* or duologue if you want to be pedantic. It is *not* the wife's *monologue,* as so many actors mistakenly dub any long speech that is uninterrupted by the actual words of another.)

TALKING

Now that you have understood that truthful listening hinges on our character's interpretation of the content and intent supporting the words being sent to us, it will be self-evident that when *we* are the senders, *our* words must be supported by meaning and sent with an intention. **The need to talk is instigated by our wishes and substantiated by the experience we are having in the present or by a reminder** (in the present) **of a past experience, or by what is being done to us at the moment, verbally or otherwise.** As actors, if we want our words to spring from us, from our body, mind, and soul, with spontaneity, urgency, and inevitability, we will automatically reject the tedious, old-fashioned manner of working from our "sides" to deliver "line readings" of words that have been mechanically memorized with predetermined, formalized intonations sonorously projected into the audience. We ought to be equally appalled by the so-called modern method of mumbling the words, of riding through them on a general emotion, or of gliding into naturalistic verbal attitudes. We need to come to grips with truthful verbal communication with the other characters in the magic circle of reality on stage, with the mastery of the technique of **animated talking.**

Herbert Berghof said that "words are the messengers of our wishes." This is wonderfully true (even when it conjures up in me the fanciful image of Mercury, almost as though I could see words leaving my mouth with tiny wings attached to them, flying across the room to land on my partner). In order to travel, to further one's wishes, the words must be active. In fact, the dictionary defines *verbalize* as "to convert into a verb." And a verb is *active.* You can make someone laugh by tickling him—physically or verbally. You can soothe someone by stroking him physically or verbally—or both. You can bully verbally or with a fist or with both, etc. And, since I'm on the subject of the actor's grammar, beware of *all adjectives and descriptive adverbs!* Strike them from your vocabulary as well as from all printed stage directions so that they can in no way influence you. *Angrily, sadly, happily, sullenly, like a moth* all belong to the descriptive novelist and his readers and to the *readers* of plays, not to the actors. Our greatest playwright, Shakespeare, simply says *he enters* or *he exits,* without any need for embellishments such as *anxiously* or *thunderously.* Such qualifying words are at the core of the problem of those who mistakenly believe that words are solely the expression of thoughts and feelings, which result in muddied, self-indulgent, inactive words that travel nowhere. Consider *what* you do, *never how* you do it. If something is done to you that makes you mad, you may verbally want to strike back, to defend yourself or to prove the other person wrong, but if you predetermine or *qualify* such actions, you will miss your target. (Apply the philosophy *I am therefore I do,* which applies to any psychological action, whether it be physical, verbal, or a combination of both.) **What is done to you by someone or something will evoke thoughts and feelings and what you do about them is the "acting." And the actions must be instigated by your wishes, needs, and objectives, with the hope and expectation that your wishes will be fulfilled.** Look and listen for your partner's responses, make your words dependent on them, otherwise you will be listening to yourself and the words will, inevitably, become mechanized.

In order to substantiate what we say, every person, thing, event, and landscape, even the weather about which we talk in a play, must be particularized, must be made real to us before we can bring the words to life truthfully.* As you make your particularizations, much of what you have to say will become inevitable, and, when followed up in rehearsals by the discovery of your verbal intents and expectations, the words will be further validated until "learning the lines" has become a byproduct of the work, replacing the outmoded method of mechanical memorization.

Observe that in life, during any dialogue, your words are never

---

* You might now want to reread Chapter 5, Transference, with this in mind.

organized before speaking, but develop and take shape as you are sending them, induced by the lightning-like thoughts and inner objects that feed what it is you want from your partner. Even on the rare occasions when we prepare a speech beforehand (when, for instance, we plan how we will impress an agent, director, or lover), when the time is at hand, during the actual confrontation, the speech never comes out as planned, but is spontaneously evoked by the specific realities of the occurrence.

Words are preceded by an immediate source and sent with an immediate need. In many plays, the actor faces the fascinating problem of animating a long "speech" or "tirade," often the revelation of a traumatic experience from the character's past. Even in this day and age, I hear actors (and some directors) refer to such a speech as one in which the character is *reliving the past*. This notion is an old-fashioned cliché based on theatrical claptrap. Unless a person is insane, he does not lose awareness of his immediate surroundings, or of the person who is the target of his revelations. **He is dealing with the past—in the present.** After having made the past experience real by particularizing every detail of it at home and in rehearsals, the actor must unearth the causes that make him need to examine and share the past experience under the present circumstances. When a particular *memory* moves him, it moves him now, not then, and differently from the way the event did at the time. And his verbal actions are intended for the character from whom he now wants answers, understanding, approval, comfort, etc. Even when the other character is a sounding board rather than the direct object of his wishes, the actions remain dependent on the listener.

During any dialogue, contact can be made through the use of all five senses. Even when someone is behind us seemingly silent, we may feel his presence. Many eager actors believe that when they are talking, they make a truthful connection with their partners only by making **direct eye contact** with them. They keep their eyes glued to them, not realizing that this is why they are having difficulty with the words. To prove this point, I will ask a student to tell me something as simple as what he did just before coming to class without taking his eyes from mine. Unless he has just told the same story several times, he cannot do what I ask. Before beginning the first sentence, he will already look away, or rather into **his *mind's* eye** in order to visualize the inner objects he needs to reconstruct the event and bring it to his words. While communicating any past experience, we look *intermittently* at our partner when we hope or expect to confirm that the listener understands, approves, or disapproves of something we are saying, is entertained by us, or has answers for us. **Eye contact is intense and active in itself.** What we read in the listener's eyes as well as in his behavior conditions the continuance of our verbal actions.

I am assuming that everyone who wants to earn the right to call himself an actor is working continuously to achieve fine standard speech so that he will be able to talk spontaneously, "trippingly on the tongue," and not "mouth it as many of our players do." It should be at his beck and call for a wide range of parts. Nevertheless, he may face certain problems in finding his own reality when the character's idiom is not his own, or in the language of the noncontemporary playwright. This sometimes applies to the American actor, to the very one who has an innate sense of truth. His imagination fails him in finding the faith, the belief that he can speak as his character does. Some of our finest star players have this problem when tackling Shaw, Shakespeare, or Restoration comedy, for instance. Sometimes it is because they don't perform plays of extraordinary language often enough, but more often, and more importantly, they are unsure of making the language their own.

They fall into one of two traps. Either they ignore the specifics of the extraordinary words as though they had no particular import and glide into naturalistic tonalities, or they shape the words externally, formalistically, without the truthful, psychological reality that brings about verbal action. Let me make a primitive example of the differences between the *ordinary* use of an idiom today and long ago. When we first hear something like "That's cool!" we may be puzzled or amused by it until we become accustomed to it. Eventually, we may test it on our own tongue, at first awkwardly, a little embarrassed by it. Within a few days we will use it with such frequency that we get annoyed at ourselves, but eventually it becomes a part of our vocabulary. We are no longer self-conscious about it. The same principle can be applied when instead of asking someone "Where are you going?" we must ask, "Whither art going?" Or if we challenge someone with "Don't deny it!" we might just as well do it with "Thou canst not gainsay it!" Such differences are readily bridged by the mere *habit* of usage.

When we approach the verbal action demanded by poets, it may seem more difficult. Here is a sample from Christopher Fry's *The Lady's Not for Burning*. Jennet is pleading for understanding from Thomas while, at dusk, she tries to cope with her dilemma:

> If I try to find my way I bark my brain
> On shadows sharp as rocks where half a day
> Ago was a wild soft world, a world of warm
> Straw whispering every now and then
> With rats, but possible, possible, not this,
> This where I am lost. The morning came and left
> The sunlight on my doorstep like any normal
> Tradesman. But now every spark
> Of likelihood has gone. The light draws off
> As easily as though no one could die
> Tomorrow.
>
> (II)

When the fabulous images of this cry for answers, for the need to make order out of chaos, is made real by the actor, when she draws them from her own inner vision and from the gloomy shadows of the evening that engulf the room, from the memory of the morning light at the start of the day backed up by forebodings about the given circumstances, she will be able to evoke this verbal plea for solace from Thomas, inevitably, from her own soul. There will be nothing normal or "natural" about it, but it will have *reality* when it travels. I have also heard the speech delivered by a famous player with magnificent cadence and resonance at the expense of the content and was unable to understand a single word of what the hell the beautiful tones were all about.

As for the free verse in this play, or the rhythm, meter, and rhymed couplets of others, I have always believed that when you have found the specifics of the *content* and the actions that communicate it, any external form takes care of itself—when the poet himself has merit. You do him a disservice by stressing such externals. Leave all profound theories about them to scholars and critics. I used to get reviews about my perfect iambic pentameter when playing Shakespeare and can truthfully say that I *never* took it into consideration, nor did

I ever deliberately, naturalistically, try to break up rhyme or meter as some modern actors do, or land on it in the old-fashioned manner. I stuck to the meaning and the need to communicate *what* I was saying—not *how* I was saying it. When working on the plays of great language, I apply another rule of thumb that may be helpful to you. I know that the playwrights are not presenting me with ordinary circumstances; therefore, I cannot assume that what I have to say is ordinary. I don't want to find the natural way in which I *usually* talk, but rather **a reality for the need to talk *now*, as I have never talked until this moment.**

In tackling the problem of language in the social satires of Molière, Oscar Wilde, Restoration comedy, certain plays of Shaw, even some of Noel Coward, which may seem alien, stilted, or artificially mannered to our ears, it is important to remember that the characters' behavior and their very choice of words often springs from a need to prove that they are socially masters of their etiquette, in tune with the fashion of the times. Our first task is to make the social mores of the given society—whether it be lower, middle, or upper class—real to ourselves. We must find identification with what is expected by the society, what will make us shine in it, and where the pitfalls lie. It also helps to remember that, nowadays, we are as guilty of wanting to be "in the swing of it," just as influenced by peer pressure as human beings have been by their peers since time immemorial. Only the externals of what is fashionable at a given historical time and place change. Today, even when we resist the excesses of the current fashion, when we rebel against them or think of ourselves as children of nature, we are not totally immune to them, unconsciously adopting some of the clothing, behavior, and idioms of "popular" language. Our own psychological need to be a part of "the scene" can be transferred to the character's needs, justifying and motivating the specifics of even the most outlandish words and deeds that belong to the fashion of another time.

Most actors enjoy playing parts that require a regional dialect or foreign accent. A few of our most prominent actors even consider them to be the ultimate proof of fine acting, using them as the mainspring of their character. However, some of the actors I have most admired—Alfred Lunt, Laurette Taylor, and Albert Basserman, for instance—have given them little or no attention. Nevertheless, I have my own convictions about dealing with them. I believe that an accent or a dialect must be made a part of me before I have voiced a single word that the character utters in the play, whether I am working on the part at home or in rehearsals. If the required accent or dialect is brand-new to me, one that I have never tried before even by "kidding around with it" (as so many actors do when they are role-playing by themselves or with their colleagues), I consult a specialist about the particular speech pattern of my character. Those actors who are not blessed with a fabulously good ear can learn the phonetic sounds as well as the rhythm and melody inherent in any dialect or accent. I also listen to recordings that may contain the same speech pattern on which I'm working. I go to movies in which they speak the way I want to. And I am audacious enough to practice it around the clock on everyone in earshot. I risk annoying my friends and relatives, even the tradesmen in my neighborhood, until I become used to my new way of talking, until I no longer check myself for accuracy or hear myself speak. Then I am ready to work on the character's lines, to test them for *meaning,* not for sound. I often tell a story about myself which took place at the first rehearsal of an English play with an all-British cast. I was the only American. When I started to speak to them with an English accent immediately upon being introduced I was greeted with amusement and a little disdain. However, they got used to it and when the rehearsal began, when I spoke as the character, they did not laugh but accepted me as one of them. We must authenticate our new speech in the same way that we put on the clothing belonging to the character rather than his costume.

Let me urge you once more to develop the appetite for verbal communication and for extraordinary language. Let it take shape on your tongue as it springs from your soul.

9

Expectation

WHAT was it about the acting of Laurette Taylor and Albert Basserman that electrified me (and everyone else in the audience), that mesmerized me, making me hang on to their every word and deed, that astonished me and helped me to understand something new about human beings every time I saw them, no matter how often, even in the same play? It was something that surpassed star radiance or charisma. It went beyond the ability of other artists I admired who were also able to portray a human being on stage without artificial theatrics. It even went beyond the uniqueness of their interpretations in various roles. Their genius manifested itself in the utter spontaneity and unpredictability of their actions. You believed their existence in the present, that everything was happening to them **from moment to moment,** as if for the first time. They seemed as surprised by the events that stormed in on them during the course of the play as the audience. *This* was what I wanted to find in my own work, and I went to see them again and again to learn how they did it. And each time, I left the theatre in despair, having learned nothing because they had again succeeded in involving me subjectively in their "new" life experience. I did understand why they, like Duse, could not be imitated.

Years later, I realized what courage it takes not to hang on to the shape of an action, even when it means relinquishing a very special big moment. I remembered that every time I took another friend to see *The Glass Menagerie,* just as Laurette Taylor was about to execute one of those extraordinary actions, one that had etched itself on my mind, I would poke my companion and whisper, "Wait till you see what she does now!" It was no longer there. However, that same evening, there were ten *new* unforgettable moments in other places. Let me add, for anyone who might misunderstand, that there was nothing chaotic, loosely improvisational, or willfully different to be different in the work of Taylor or Basserman. They were not so much different from performance to performance as newly alive. They *never,* as many pseudo-Method actors do, violated the logic of their character's behavior or their relationship to the others, and they did not alter or ignore the given circumstances. They were alive in the present—in the play!

The technique of playing in the moment, which these geniuses understood intuitively, a technique which disallows the anticipation of what is to come (any thinking ahead to the next line, action or cue), is one I have striven consciously to perfect for most of my career. Theoretically, I always understood what I must do: use my imagination to achieve what is possibly the actor's greatest gift, the childlike innocence and faith that "I," the character, am living now, suspending all knowledge of what is to come, to leave myself open to surprises, vulnerable to everything done to me, so that my actions will become necessary. Once in a while, during a performance, these essential precepts sufficed to send me flying to the end of my journey in the role. More often they failed to sustain me. I felt there was something missing from my score, possibly something I was leaving to intuition at the very beginning of my work on the role. I was right. Eventually I learned to incorporate the essential ingredient that I had discovered in my personal life, my *expectations.* I had learned that although I never *knew* what would happen next, I always had expectations about it. Just as importantly, I learned that *everything* **I do is conditioned by my expectations, and that what actually happens is never totally in tune with them.**

Let me remind you of a few of the examples I have made in previous chapters to demonstrate this point (aside from those I have already given for thinking and listening): how our self-perception changes depending on whom we expect when answering the phone or doorbell, and the adjustments we make when it turns out to be someone else; in which way a new room surprises us because it differs from our expectations; how we change destination when unexpected things move in; how our plans change during a routine homecoming because something else takes precedence; in which way a new relationship develops because of our continuously changing assumptions and expectations about the other person; how even something as simple as burning ourselves on a hot iron or pot occurs because we *expected* it to be cool.

Let me repeat: **We never *know* what the next moment will be, but we *always* have expectations about it.** Even when what actually happens is close to our expectations, nothing is ever a carbon copy of them. Alert yourself to what happens when you ask or are being asked a simple question. When you think you have not heard or understood something said to you, if you ask "What?" or "Where?" or "When?" while you await clarification, your mind is not blank but racing with possibilities about what was meant. When someone asks, "Guess what I did?" and your answer is "I don't know" it is not that you know nothing, but that you are speculating on what it could be, and if the answer surprises you, it is because you had expected something *else*—not nothing.

Performers are often most fearful about anticipating when the script dictates that the upcoming event *must* surprise them. For instance, when they have to discover a telegram that has been slipped under the door. In order to avoid anticipating the sight of it, they often look the other way or at the ceiling. They must then struggle with the ultimate problem of anticipation, how to get their attention to the floor at all. Their visual attention must be there *first*, for a logical reason *other* than discovering the telegram; *then* it can surprise them. At the beginning of *The Cherry Orchard*, Varya interrupts herself while talking to Anya by noticing, "Oh, you have a new brooch, shaped like a bee!" If she is not looking at Anya with the brooch in her line of vision, she will be forced to anticipate and illustrate surprise by externally directing her attention to it. In a play, **whenever the actor anticipates what he will see, hear, and feel and what the others will be doing** (because he has seen, heard, and felt them doing the same thing since the early days of rehearsal), **it is because he has failed to include the logical expectations that condition his actions, or merely paid them lip service.**

In a broad sense, the problem of anticipation arises the very first time we have finished reading the play we are about to work on. We now know how it ends! Too often, we allow this awareness to influence every step of our character's development during the course of his or her life. Most productions of Chekhov, for instance, are doomed from their inception because the characters are played (usually as directed) from the perspective of the final event. Throughout *The Three Sisters*, Olga, Masha, and Irina should be struggling to escape from their stifling lives in the provinces. They desperately want to go to Moscow. Never, at any time during the play, should they already know what only the author knew when he wrote it, what they and the audience should only know at the end: that they will never attain their dream. In other words, if they are *commenting* on the author's intent, they usually have nothing left to do except to whine about their disappointment. And then who cares? I have often seen *The Cherry Orchard* fail because the characters knew at the outset that their beloved home and orchard would be sold at the end of the play, so that when Lyubov and her daughter return from Paris in the first scene, rather than playing the actions that further the excitement of the homecoming, they drench themselves in wistful nostalgia, treating everything as though it were already lost. Then the play becomes a rather tedious, undramatic mood piece, dusty with age and irrelevant to our lives. When, on the other hand, the characters really act in the present with human hopes and expectations about the future, we in the audience will find all the extraordinary parallels to our present day, enlightened by a recognition of ourselves.

To answer the criticism that nothing happens in Chekhov's plays, a wise person once said, "Nothing—except that one world is coming to an end as another begins." That was certainly true at the turn of the last century, and Chekhov's genius in presenting us with the frailties and foibles of human beings who blindly pursue their own wishes in the midst of crushing changes is painfully echoed in our lives at the turn of this present century. Today most people are aware of social upheavals; of threats to the environment, to the air we breathe and the water we drink; even of the possibility of the destruction of our planet. Just as Chekhov's people did a hundred years ago, some are actively trying to stem the oncoming disasters, but few make it the sole purpose of their lives. Many who are mired in poverty must simply struggle to survive from day to day. Most are ignorant of what lies ahead. Others who are better off play ostrich, not wanting to know. Some lull themselves with intellectual theorizing, while the jet set, the royalty of our day, as well as those who aspire to be a part of it, fight for the status quo and make it a point of honor to maintain and further enrich their materialistic life-styles. Obviously, all of our lives are strongly influenced by our changing times, and we struggle with them just as Chekhov's characters do, each in our own way—and our behavior manifests itself in similar ways. It can also be likened to our behavior when any crisis becomes personal, such as fire, the death of a loved one, or a serious accident; we attempt to cope with each moment, unable to comprehend the final consequence of the disaster. Our actions are the result of immediate needs and expectations. We cannot know or foretell the next *moment* with certainty, let alone the future.

If it is clear that the anticipation of the outcome of the play brings about attitudinal commenting rather than truthful human action, it becomes evident that the same principle holds true for each act, each scene, and each moment of the life on stage. In rehearsals **we must discover and test the actions that are needed from moment to moment in conjunction with what we expect from them.** In performance the validity of our selected realities, whether they sustain us from moment to moment, will be put to the ultimate test.

Many talented actors manage to find the right things in their rehearsals because they *intuitively* incorporate their character's assumptions, speculations, and expectations of what is to come in their actions. Their intuition often sustains them, as it did me in the early stages of my career, through previews and a short span of the run of the play. But with repetition, sometimes in the actors' own words, they become "stale," "tired," and "mechanical." They often complain, God help us, that they are "bored" with the job or "exhausted" by the role. Long ago, when such things happened to me, the only enjoyment in repeated playing rested on watching myself as I made the actions "effective," or in proving to the audience that I could do such things as produce tears on cue or predictably "time my laughs." (I have seen an actor calculate how long he could stretch a pause every night before the audience got restless. As proof, the stage manager was asked to clock it in the wings. Even sadder, the pause had *once* had organic cause.) No matter how pleasurable such expressions of vanity may be to some, they are certainly unrelated to my reasons for wanting to act; they have nothing to do with a desire to reveal a living soul.

My passion for acting returned, never to desert me again, once I had understood how to **suspend knowledge of what was to come by unearthing the character's expectations.** I was *finally* able to use my imagination to achieve the innocence and faith needed to find a new life in rehearsals and to be spontaneously alive on stage when executing the actions from one moment to the next, caught up by the surprises that move in on me. Then every performance becomes a challenge, a new adventure of playing as if for the first time instead of a repetition of the night before. I can honestly claim that I will be more alive on stage at the end of a year's run than I was at the beginning. The effort does not exhaust me—it exhilarates me! If you want to soar, try it: Surprise yourself.

Part Three:
The Exercises

10

The Exercises

GENERAL PURPOSE

I remember thinking as a young performer that, if according to the metaphor the actor himself was the instrument, if indeed I was like the musician's piano, it was clear that I must put myself into top form—until I became as good as a Steinway or a Bechstein. I knew that I could do so by tirelessly exercising my body, voice, and speech. So I worked like a dog in my singing, dancing, and speech classes. Even better, I could set my own pace by practicing all the exercises my teachers prescribed by myself at home. I could sharpen my skills and strengthen habits of self-discipline without having to rely on anyone else. But something gnawed at me about accepting the fashion of the time that, once the piano was in tune, one needed only talent to play on it in public, that *how to play on it* could best be learned through performing. I wanted to know which notes to strike and how to finger them, how to make the music sound in and through me. Although I played many parts to critical success, I was left frustrated and dissatisfied by the problems that arose over and over again that related to the human techniques, regardless of the role I was playing: a sudden loss of privacy or concentration, momentary physical self-consciousness, getting trapped in externals and mechanical actions, the anticipation of a particular response or action, an inability to tap the correct stimulus, pushing for the emotion—to mention a few. When I was not playing, in between parts, I was even more frustrated, believing there was no way for me to function as an artist in the absence of rehearsals, performances, and my fellow actors. In those days, a place to work with teachers and one's colleagues was a rarity. I had learned that I couldn't blame my technical difficulties on the role, the director, or the other actors. In the acting texts I consulted, I found too many theoretical answers (many of which I used to underline, adding "so true" in the margin when so moved) and too few answers that I knew how to put into practice.

In desperation, I came on the idea of working by myself at home to devise corrective exercises for all of the problems I was having by **exploring personal behavior under a variety of circumstances.** I soon discovered that each of my problems was based on a misunderstanding or an omission of something fundamental to human behavior and response. Later, after I began teaching, I shared the things I was practicing with my students. These exercises have developed and undergone constant change over the past forty years. I offer them in their present state with the hope that they will also be helpful to you. They may make the impatient actor uncomfortable and will probably be dismissed by those who think of the theatre as show business, but for the rest of us I believe they have value. They incorporate much of what I have covered in Part Two on the human techniques, allowing you to test and practice what may have seemed only theoretical until now. The application of the techniques must become second nature and an inherent part of your work. The order of the exercises is given deliberately. Don't jump around in them. Above all, don't skim through them, but work on each one until the problem it tackles has been solved, until your ability to apply these techniques to *all* of your work becomes a reflex. Only the last exercise deals directly with a character in a play. When all of them have been completed, they can be combined in many ways as you reach for higher goals in learning to play on your "instrument." Always remember that the answer to "How do you get to Carnegie Hall?" is "Practice! Practice! Practice!"

Self-observation was the first step in unearthing my intuitive behavioral reflexes as well as conscious actions. I needed to find all the things that influenced them. In order to lay down guidelines and give a form to the exercises, I decided first to define and then **to re-create two seemingly routine minutes of life when alone at home,** two minutes spent in **the execution of a simple task in pursuit of a normal objective** such as getting up in the morning or getting ready for bed at night, tidying up a room for company, fixing lunch, or preparing myself for work. I learned almost at once that there was no such thing as doing something "the way I *always* do it." If I tried, I could only illustrate it in generalities. No matter how similar a task seemed to be from one day to the next, no matter what comfort I took in the very familiarity of my habits, my behavior varied enormously because of **the particulars of the past, present, and upcoming circumstances of the specific day.** The more exact I was in determining these circumstances, the easier it was to define what I was really doing and, consequently, to do it again as if for the first time. Gradually, I learned what the essential components of two such minutes consist of, all the things I have to pin down in order to function correctly, whether it is in a role or in the re-creation of my personal life.

If I am working on a *play,* the first of six essential questions, "Who Am I?" entails a search for the understanding of my character and my identification with it. This aspect of the work is an ongoing process, starting with the homework and ending only in final rehearsals. The ensuing questions must all be answered from the character's point of view. For the purpose of the exercises, I will be asking and answering them based on an expanding understanding of myself and my personal point of view. Questions and answers will continuously overlap. They are dependent on one another. You cannot finish the work on one before the next is introduced. On the following page you will find the six steps we have to explore.

Here is an example in which you will see how my exploration of these six essential steps has helped me to define a few minutes of my life. (I will not be pedantic in pointing out exactly where or in which order the various steps fall as they influence my behavior.)

On the days when I teach for six hours, it is my habit to relax for a while after I get home, to get a second wind before proceeding with the chores that usually fill the hours of the late afternoon and evening. My routine is to collect my mail and, after entering the apartment, to dump it, along with my coat and purse, on the bed before heading for the kitchen to fix a drink or

THE SIX STEPS

1. WHO AM I?
   What is my present state of being?
   How do I perceive myself?
   What am I wearing?*

2. WHAT ARE THE CIRCUMSTANCES?
   What time is it? (The year, the season, the day? At what time does my selected life begin?)
   Where am I? (In what city, neighborhood, building, and room do I find myself? Or in what landscape?)
   What surrounds me? (The immediate landscape? The weather? The condition of the place and the nature of the objects in it?)
   What are the immediate circumstances? (What has just happened, is happening? What do I expect or plan to happen next and later on?)

3. WHAT ARE MY RELATIONSHIPS?
   How do I stand in relationship to the circumstances, the place, the objects, and the *other people* related to my circumstances?†

4. WHAT DO I WANT?
   What is my main objective? My immediate need or objective?

5. WHAT IS MY OBSTACLE?
   What is in the way of what I want? How do I overcome it?

6. WHAT DO I DO TO GET WHAT I WANT?
   How can I achieve my objective? What's my behavior?
   What are my actions?

---

* If this puzzles you, reread Chapter 4, The Self.
† Not only the relationships, but all six steps are given separate sections in Chapter 24 as they pertain to the role.

a cup of tea. Then I take the drink to the bedroom and flop down to watch TV, usually a game show, while sorting my mail during the commercials. That's what I think I "always" do.

But what do I *really* do if I pin down the circumstances of a *particular* day? It is a bleak, sleety Tuesday in mid-January. I arrive at a little after 4 P.M. instead of the usual 3:30 because a pesky student delayed me at the Studio. Because of the weather, I couldn't find a cab and had to walk home. My spectacles are fogged up. My hands are numb with cold and I keep dropping the mail as I try to get it out of the box. In the elevator, I spot an envelope from NBC and, hoping that it will contain a residual check, I stop outside my front door to open it. Again the rest of the mail drops to the floor. I set down my purse and impatiently yank off my cold, damp mittens with my teeth. I slit a finger on the edge of the envelope and when I discover a W-2 tax form instead of money, I begin to curse. I am shivering as I fumble with the door key. Finally, the door is open and, quite disgruntled, feeling sorry for myself, I scoop up my purse and scattered mail and bang the door shut behind me. *I stop to consider going out again to rehearse what I just did in those two minutes in the hall because it would be a good exercise.* I decide otherwise. I dump the mail and my purse on the floor next to the bedroom and head for the bathroom. There I remove my sodden coat and hat and hang them over the tub. I sit on the closed lid of the john eyeing my good boots which are covered with slush and grains of rock salt. I start dreaming about the Caribbean. I wrestle to get off the boots, then wipe them with the rag under the sink, delaying a proper cleaning for another time. I run my hands under lukewarm water because hot water makes them sting. *While doing this, I once more contemplate rehearsing these two minutes in the bathroom as a plausible exercise,* but a hot cup of tea has become a dire necessity. As I enter the kitchen, on my way to the stove, I become aware that the sink is filled with dirty breakfast dishes, that the table is covered with rumpled sections of the *New York Times,* scattered breadcrumbs, and two cups containing coffee dregs. The refrigerator is humming, the windowpane rattles slightly from the gusting winds. The kettle still has water in it. Before heating it, I warm my hands for a second above the flame. While waiting for the water to boil, I get my fuzzy slippers and a warm robe. Back in the kitchen, I massage my feet before slipping them into the cozy slippers. I put on my robe, cross my arms and rub the upper part vigorously to get the circulation going. I feel like a drab grandma—older than old. I look around at the mess, brooding how much I'll have to clean up before I can even start to fix dinner. I brush off a few breadcrumbs into my hand. The kettle whistles. I rinse out the old coffee cup and grumble when I notice that my husband has left the canister of tea bags open. While the tea is steeping, I cheer myself up by getting a bottle of rum from the bar. As I add a stiff shot to the tea, the aroma fills the air, and I sigh with contentment. I trot off with my cup to savor it after I have tuned in my game show and snuggled up in bed.

Now let me take the particulars of another day during which I also come home from the Studio with the need to make myself a drink before watching TV.

Once more it is a Tuesday, but this time during the third week of May. The skies are cloudless; the temperature is almost seventy degrees. The sidewalks are scattered with pods and the dropped blossoms of fruit and magnolia trees. Cooing pigeons scuttle for crumbs in the street and in Washington Square Park. New York is nice! With a pang of guilt, I have stopped teaching five minutes before three and finagled a student with a car into bringing me home so I could still catch some of the televised tennis matches of the Italian Open. With the mailbox key poised in my hand, I leap out of the car, my open jacket flapping in the breeze. I check my watch. It is five after three. I grab my letters and, rather than wait for the elevator, bound up the two flights of stairs in my springy sneakers like a thirty-year-old. I take note of a particular envelope with European stamps which must be a letter from my best friend, and I plan to read it immediately after satiating my lust for tennis. In my haste at the mailbox, I have misplaced my key—I know not where. Panting from the climb, in a frenzy of frustration, I put down my purse to check the pockets of my open jacket without success. I empty the entire contents of my purse on the welcome mat and squat down, scrounging around in my belongings, mumbling, "I don't *believe* this!" No luck. I rise to check my pockets again. This time I discover the keys in the patch pocket of my shirt. *While emitting a victory yell, I think what an excellent lost object exercise this would make.* Now, soaked with perspiration, I shove my stuff back into the purse, scoop up the mail, and get myself inside. I throw my things on the bed, turn on the TV and stand mesmerized, waiting to see if the match is still on. It is. Noah is playing Agassi. Within a minute, I discover that they are in the second game of the fourth set. Noah is ahead, thank God. The score is at 6-4, 3-6, 7-5. Noah is serving after having broken Andre in the first game of the fourth set. I have an urgent need to go to the john and rush to the bathroom to relieve myself. Then I run to the fridge to empty an ice tray. The freezer is crusty, in need of defrosting, and it is hard to get out the top tray. It sticks to my fingers as I dump the cubes into the clean sink. I note with pleasure that the maid came today and the kitchen is spotless. The fresh spring air is wafting through the half open window next to me. Lovely! I grab a piece of toweling to mop my brow, reach for a glass. It is chipped, and I toss it, ruefully, into the garbage can. I get another one and fill it with ice, putting the remaining cubes into the ice bucket. I pour a shot of vodka over the ice and fill the glass with bubbly tonic water. I think I deserve a slice of lime but find only a dried out, brownish piece. Oh, well. I remember dinner and quickly take out two small steaks from the fridge, leaving them on the counter to come to room temperature. I take my drink, holding it gingerly so it won't spill as I rush off to the bedroom. I pause to affirm that Noah is on a roll. He's now at four games to love. I kick off my sneakers and prop myself up on the bedspread to watch with baited breath as he serves two aces in a row, his dreadlocks flying, his beautiful face set in deep concentration. I'm hardly aware that I am gulping down the refreshing vodka and tonic.

From these detailed examples of behavior and actions while in the pursuit of an objective, as well as the many others I have given throughout Part Two, you should now have a million ideas of your own for things you are itching to explore and re-create. You may have observed that I have selected "normal" tasks that become "unusual" by dint of self-exploration when all six steps have been taken into consideration.

In turning an examination of a few minutes of life into a practical exercise, remember to define the physical and psychological sensations inherent in the circumstances. Devising an exercise for a task that occurs when you are alone at home depends on your surroundings remaining more or less constant so that you can pin down their specific influences on your action. In the later exercises you will learn how to apply the same principles to someone else's home, an office, a restaurant, or a railway station, for example, as well as to the outdoors, to streets and parks, to hill and dale, and sea and sand.

FOR THE PRESENTATION

When I started working on the exercises, I made amazing discoveries in many technical areas that had always been problematical. The work itself also gave me an outlet for my thirst for self-discipline. Soon I wanted to test my discoveries on my peers. After all, the proof of the pudding is in the eating. I wanted to know if what I cooked would taste good to others. At first, I presented my re-creations to a peer right in my home. I asked for criticism: Did he believe what I had executed? If not, what did he disbelieve and why? Later, studio space became available because I started teaching. I could garner an audience of a few peers for the same purpose. To show them my work, I transferred as many aspects of my own home to the new space as I possibly could. As I increasingly appreciated the value of the exercises, I included them in my teaching regimen in conjunction with the study of scenes from plays. They have become popular and are now practiced and taught in many places throughout the country. They have often been misunderstood and misapplied, perhaps because, in *Respect for Acting*, they were explained inadequately.

The new space in which I first taught was provided by my husband who had been acting and teaching much longer than I had. He had seen to it that it was equipped with the *essentials*, no matter how primitive, that made it possible to re-create the living conditions needed for a wide range of plays (which also served my purpose in the exercises to a tee). Once we understand that human beings don't exist in limbo, that everything on and around us predicates our behavior and actions, it becomes obvious that no one can "act" or learn the principles of acting in empty space.

When rehearsing in the privacy of your own home, you should already be making considerations for your selected actions, avoiding those that can*not* be transferred to your studio or workshop, such as opening or closing doors or windows that don't exist there. In fact, avoid anything that would force you into pantomimed actions. Use real objects, endowing them with the physical and psychological properties that will make them your own until you believe that the place you have re-created in the studio is *where you live now.* Let me warn you not to use the wonders of the furnishings merely to decorate or "dress a set." And be sure to use the objects as tools to further your actions, not as "props," a word I dislike because it suggests the crutches used by the disabled to "prop" themselves up. Conceiving of your *objects* as props leads to an illustration of boring, naturalistic pieces of business rather than to the discovery of the truthful behavior that results when we *need* the objects to further our life.

Eventually, with time and practice, you will develop a heightened sense of artistic selection, choosing *only* what you need to communicate your intention. In his distilled impression of *The Green Apples,* Cézanne is able to awaken all the mysteries of adolescence, of a promise of things to come, and Picasso's abstraction of *A Boy* epitomizes a child's innocence and wonder at the world with only a few brushstrokes. Such works of genius can serve as examples (not recipes) of selectivity as long as we don't forget that the perfection of the "impression" was possible only *after* Cézanne had understood and mastered the anatomical composition of apples, had tasted, eaten, and digested them. Picasso had achieved the skill to see and paint a child in detail, had identified with its soul, had held and hugged it before he could give us its essence in an "abstraction."

Let me add a few warnings about the errors and misunderstandings that most frequently occur when the exercises are presented. A minor misconception is to think they are intended to be mute. If in action you discover that you sigh, grunt, or groan, use expletives or otherwise verbalize your wishes, don't hesitate to include such responses in your score. A major error is to concern yourself with the *effect* your presentation will have on your teacher and fellow students. It will defeat the purpose of the work. Unless you keep the *event* of your chosen task simple, you will become a bad playwright, devising soap operas or melodramas. I have seen actors writhe on the floor from gunshot wounds or poison, in the wild desire to perform, writing suicide notes after a phone call from a lover, wracked with sobs because they must face an abortion, or raging and stomping about like a provincial Lear because they had been unjustly excommunicated. If you discover that you burst into tears because you spilled coffee on your new blouse, emit a shriek because you spotted a roach in the sink, tear up and trample on your photos and bio because an agent was rude to you, you will be on the track of unearthing truthful behavior. Some actors balk at the idea of using themselves for the reasons I brought up in Chapter 4, The Self, because they think they are boring, far less interesting than a character in a play. They will learn that when they are really involved in a simple task, that **when they are *interested*, they will be *interesting*.**

Remember that you are learning a craft, that you are presenting work for constructive criticism, not looking for approval or disapproval. Therefore, I ask you not to sit in judgment of your fellow actors. In order to benefit from their work, identify with their problems. When they make technical errors, ask yourself how often you make the same ones, and, when you hear the teacher's corrective answers, apply them to yourself. When something is convincing and involves you as a spectator, ask yourself how it was achieved and how you could accomplish the same reality. Then you will be learning during the entire session rather than just waiting for your turn to perform.

Before presenting an exercise in the re-creation of two or three specific minutes of your life, you should have rehearsed it at home for at least one hour. By rehearsing, I mean *doing* it, not just thinking about it. A quick improvisation will be of little value in establishing the correct behavioral reflexes we are all hoping for, those that will be so useful to transfer to our roles. I have continually stressed that an exercise must be no more than two or three minutes long. This is not an arbitrary choice. It has *not* been made for the sake of expedience, as some actors believe, so that more work can be crowded into each class. I have arrived at this time limit for a number of reasons, the main one being that **learning how to select pertinent behavior,** finding meaningful actions, is an essential part of our technique. When we first set out on the paths of self-discovery through self-observation, it is easy to fall into the trap of warming up with irrelevant, naturalistic activities or stringing them out self-indulgently. This tendency can become an ingrained bad habit. The last few times you work through each exercise at home, before bringing it in to class, **time it!** (Actors are notoriously bad judges of how long something takes—on stage and off.) If it is too long, reevaluate the need for the actions, sharpen the selections, pare down everything you don't need to fulfill your objectives. Avoid unnecessary preambles.

Let me digress to explain my position on IMPROVISATIONS. You may have wondered why I did not include them in the basic techniques of Part Two. If we agree that acting is based on our response to imaginary assumptions about the character and his or her relationship to others, about time, place, and surrounding circumstances, we will realize that improvisations of a kind are taking place at every stage of the work, even as we test the words of the text when reading aloud at the first rehearsal and as we open up an imaginative playground when we get on our feet. A degree of improvisation is involved in defining each moment of our life, whether it be in a scene or an exercise. We should always be guided by the same game of make-believe that we played so well as children, using the magic "If" in endless variations. Of course, improvising can be an art form in itself, but for those techniques that are useful to actors in a written play, we must see that our improvisations serve us for a better understanding of the play's realities and above all to arrive at the *definitive* actions of our life on stage.

The principles of spontaneous give-and-take, of being surprised by what we receive and propelled into action with our partner, are taught in improvisation classes and then often **ignored by both teacher and student instead of being applied to the work on a play.** They are frequently dealt with as separate rather than interrelated techniques. For use in a play, I personally find extensive **improvisations most helpful in establishing my reality for the previous circumstances** and those that exist in the time lapses between scenes and acts. They also help me to find my relationship to those characters with whom I have had a *life* before the play begins. I *never* improvise aspects of the scene itself that would lead to paraphrasing of the author's words. It is a dangerous detour that delays or prevents one from making those words inevitably one's own.

With all this advice and a few admonishments, you should now be ready to rehearse and to put your discoveries of life under a microscope to be presented for self-evaluation and evaluation by a teacher and your colleagues, to bear fruit in the perfecting of a fine technique.

11

The First Exercise: Physical Destination

PHYSICAL and psychological tension, self-consciousness, awkwardness, loss of concentration, privacy, and faith—any or all of these can set in when the actor lacks humanly motivated physical destination. The purpose of this exercise is to test those things that send us from one place to another, that determine the logic of our physical life. It should rid us once and for all of any notion of stage "blocking," of arbitrary, external positioning. Instead, we must get it into our very bones that every move we make, and every place at which we choose to settle before rising to head for the next, evolves from specific needs under very particular circumstances.* I am also asking you to tackle the enormous problem of making AN ENTRANCE and the lesser one of making an EXIT.

When the PREPARATION FOR THE ENTRANCE is *in*correct, waiting in the wings to take the first step into a life on stage can create anxiety, panic, sheer terror. The natural desire of every actor to give his best can make for knocking knees when he faces his "moment of truth" in making a first contact with the audience. Intensive, creative homework and rehearsals ought to bear fruit in one's moment-to-moment

---

* On pages 101–106 of Chapter 8 this problem is addressed in detail. Review it carefully before working on this exercise. It should answer most of your questions about setting yourself in motion.

existence on stage, and, theoretically, once this work has been done, one should be ready to take flight in performance. But the takeoff for the journey can be bumpy, even abortive, when we depart before making sure the runway is clear, or when we fail to notice that it is still muddy or pitted with holes. Even in a workshop atmosphere where no one is paying to watch and no media critic is present to make a judgment, an incomplete preparation and a need to impress the teacher and one's colleagues will destroy the validity of an entrance.

Until we learn how to cope with them, the conditions backstage may seem like a deliberate conspiracy to make concentration impossible and to destroy our faith. They are totally unrelated to those on the stage or the set we are about to enter, every inch of which we have endowed with realities that will sustain our character's actions. While waiting in the wings, we need to *believe* that we have just climbed the flight of marble steps that leads to the portals of the stately chamber we are about to enter, or that we have just plowed through the snowdrifts outside the farmhouse door, or that we are toweling off from a luxurious bath before running into the bedroom to answer the phone. It is difficult to maintain belief in these kinds of preceding circumstances while stagehands are scurrying about and the stage manager is throwing light cues to the electrician, while other performers are whispering and kidding around at one's elbow. Even in the backstage area of a studio, when no such visual and audible distractions exist, while waiting alone or with a partner who is willing to participate in correct preparation, an actor may have to adjust to being squeezed against a brick wall so the door will open, or to the radiator hissing at his side, while trying to convince himself that he is about to enter the summerhouse from a stroll on the beach. Before dealing with the solution to such problems by examining the essential steps of preparation for an entrance, let me review the correct *preparation for the performance as a whole*, which begins the moment we set foot into our place of work, whether that be a theatre or a studio.

Remembering that an ideal presentation of a play will be most appreciated for its ensemble acting, knowing that we are not soloists but part of a communal profession, our inclination to want to be part of the "family" is often misdirected. It is in the nature of most performers to be garrulous and outgoing. Already upon entering the workplace, there is the tendency to bring in all the "interesting" little things that have filled our day, to share them with our colleagues—before rehearsals, during rehearsals while sitting on the sidelines when others are working, before performances when we drop in on each other's dressing rooms, and, worst of all, when we feel compelled to continue gabbing, even in the wings, waiting with others for an entrance.

We also chatter excessively before the beginning of classes and between the presentation of scenes and exercises. Those who do not enter into a spirit of merriment and an exchange of personal problems about love, budgets, and agents are often viewed askance, accused of being aloof or "phoney." But socializing is not a proof of professionalism, nor is the ability to crack a joke just before making an entrance. This is merely proof of being a hack. The answer to such prevailing conditions lies not in acting techniques, but in the development of a serious work ethic and the discipline that will give our technique a chance to function. Although I may not be as prone as some to participating in the "family fun," I am certainly guilty of it and try to be on constant guard against it. I *try* always to leave my personal life outside the stage door. When rehearsing, I'm usually the first one there. When performing, I'm there at least an hour before the official call of "Half hour!" Between matinee and night, I eat lightly, nearby or in my dressing room. I *try* to limit the conversation with my colleagues to the play itself and to the problems that occur in a long run from one performance to the other. *After* a rehearsal or performance, I am free to "rap" to my heart's content without jeopardizing the work.

On arrival at the theatre, if you are lucky enough to have your own dressing room, head for it and shut the door. I'm not implying that you must put yourself into some kind of mystic trance in order to prepare your body and soul for work. Empty your mind of the outside world and fill it slowly with your character's life, even when this evolves merely through such simple actions as removing your "street" makeup and applying the powder to "your" character's face. If you share a dressing room with others, try to create your own circle of privacy and ask the others to respect it, the same as you would the members of any loving family. Occupy your mind with the upcoming performance. Instead of putting on the "costume," dress yourself in "your" clothing as a step toward transferring yourself to the character. Just as you should come early to work, be sure to arrive in the wings for your entrance with time to spare. Nothing is worse than being rushed for an entrance unless it is being too *late* for it. I was guilty of this offense to my colleagues and the audience only once in my life, at the age of eighteen. I felt so guilty and was so apologetic afterward that a reprimand was almost unnecessary, but rightfully, I was not allowed to forget it until the end of the run. Such an act is truly *unforgivable*.

Entrance nerves are familiar to all performers and can be agonizing. They may set in already in the dressing room and usually reach their peak in the wings just before you make your first entrance. They can take control of us for a variety of reasons. When the ambition to be successful supersedes the desire to fulfill the character in the play, nerves can be totally destructive. The same holds true for the performer who lacks confidence or a sense of self-worth, when the fear of failure overrides his enjoyment of playing. An acrobat will fall from the tightrope if he shows off, questions his sense of balance, or looks down instead of concentrating on his task and trusting in his acquired skills. Conversely, as an unskilled youngster, rather than being nervous, I was merely excited before performing for the simple reason that I had no conception of failure. I played my head off believing I was just great. Now, with age, experience, and a good technique, with each new role my nerves *increase* rather than diminish because my goals are always higher, and I am aware of all the areas in which I might fail to achieve the standards that I set for myself. I simply accept my nerves. They sharpen my wits and heighten my energy. The very challenge of each new performance increases my enjoyment of playing. I have long since learned that when rehearsals are thorough and bear fruit in a solid score for the actions of my role, nerves will not destroy me. Nerves can put me out of commission only when rehearsal time is short or its quality is poor, or, in the case of certain films and TV plays, when it is nonexistent, and I have been forced to resort to clichés or preconceived old "tricks."

Actors sometimes ask if there isn't a way of "talking oneself out of nerves." Yes, there is. I once succeeded in doing so on the occasion of a Broadway opening (when I was twenty-two) by telling myself that the entire event, including the audience and critics, was stupid, that it didn't matter what I did, that I didn't care. My performance was a washout. I had better have stayed at home. I know that many athletes, tennis stars in particular, consult sports psychologists to help them arrive at an ideal mental preparation for a match. I've always been curious what their methods might be. I also realize that there are many *individual* ways in which actors help themselves to achieve the right frame of mind before performing, and if they help, no matter how eccentric they may seem to others, God bless them. However, many obvious *errors* are made in preparation for the entrance, all of which I have been guilty of. They will be familiar to most young actors, as well as to seasoned professionals. After many trials and tribulations, these are the things that I eventually learned *not* to do. *Don't* try to "put yourself in the mood" while waiting in the wings by thinking general thoughts that may seem appropriate to the circumstances, such as sad, glad, or angry ones. Remember that "Mood, spelled backwards, is Doom!" A mood is the result of a sum total of actions executed under specific circumstances. *Playing* "the mood" or trying "to get into the mood" leads to mush. *Don't* try to pump yourself up into a general state of emotion. If, as in rare cases, you must enter in an overwrought state, for instance, screaming with terror because you are being pursued by a mugger who was lurking in the corridor, apply the principles of emotional recall.

When the circumstances preceding the entrance dictate that you have just rolled out of bed with a hangover and you are now entering the kitchen with a wild thirst for a glass of cold milk, it will not help to review that your character has a father fixation. Or just before running in from the barnyard to confront De Baudricourt as St. Joan, you will find it more than a little distracting to reconstruct where "you" were born or who "your" mother was. Above all, *don't* do what so many "pros" do to avoid nervousness: divert their attention to irrelevant things in their personal lives until the split second before they enter. Any of these errors result in blurred, diffused attention and are often made **because the actor has not learned** *what to concentrate on.*

In life, when *going toward* a destination, we always know where and what we are *coming from.* But think how often you have happily followed such stage directions as: "She enters the living room in her robe and slippers, picks up a pack of cigarettes from the coffee table,

lights a cigarette, and takes a deep drag when the telephone rings,"
without having made the slightest considerations for what had just
happened before you entered. As long as you retain the misconception that your character's life begins *on* stage, your entrance nerves
will be excruciating. When working on a role or an exercise, never
forget that one of the answers to "At what time does my selected life
begin?" is: "It starts in the wings." You must explore how you got
there and what you are doing there in conjunction with what you
want on stage. And whatever you eventually select for your physical
and psychological actions in the wings, they must be relevant to the
circumstances to feed your life on stage. In the above example, the
stage directions have supplied you with a destination—the cigarettes
on the coffee table. You also know that you are at present just outside
the living room. No one will tell you what this space looks like so
you must imaginatively supply it as well as its architectural connection to the living room. Does it adjoin a bedroom, kitchen, or bath,
or is it connected by a hallway to other rooms? (For the purpose of
the exercises, this task is easy because you will use the memory of the
surroundings of your own apartment.) You also don't know how
you got to this particular space outside your living room. Perhaps
you have **just come from** a brisk shower and **are now** fluffing your
hair around the edges to make sure the shower cap kept it dry, while
dreaming about the cigarette you'd been longing for, promising yourself it'll be the last one until noon. *Or,* you may have **just come from**
the bedroom where you'd carelessly put on your slippers and **are
now** adjusting the elastic at the heels while deciding that you badly
need a cigarette before showering to help dispel the bad dream that
awoke you. *Or,* you might have **just come from** brushing your teeth
and **are now** loosening the belt of your robe, worrying about the
weight you've gained, hoping that a cigarette will detract you from
the eggs and bacon you'd really like to eat. Naive as they may seem,
these examples should help for an understanding of the kinds of
psychological and physical actions that must occupy us *off* stage,
making for the continuity of a life that brings us *on.*

Beginning the character's life *on stage,* waiting for the curtain to go
up, is much easier than making an entrance. Even though similar
distractions of stagehands and other performers may exist, at least we
are surrounded by the realities that belong to the play, the furniture

and other objects that allow us to maintain our faith in the present circumstances. Even an amateur will not suspend himself in a frozen position on stage while waiting for the curtain to go up, but will connect himself with some kind of logical activity. Nevertheless, the definition of the first action must evolve out of the same three steps of preparation. If you are in the kitchen preparing coffee, you should define how you got there and what you plan to do next. If you are discovered seated at a desk, about to make a phone call, determine what you did just before, as well as what you expect from the call, etc., etc.

In summation: A correct preparation entails clearing the runway by creating an area of privacy and stillness in the wings or on stage, having arrived there in plenty of time, blocking out existing distractions and unrelated realities by concentrating on the three things essential to a smooth takeoff. We "rev up" by giving attention to: **Where did I just come from and what was I doing there? Where am I right now and what am I doing here? Where am I going and what do I want to do there?** If I follow through, I will be in flight for my journey in the play.

The actor who believes that his life begins on stage, rather than before entering, usually has a similar misconception—that it also ends there, before exiting. In order to MAKE AN EXIT truthfully, we must pursue the continuity of being alive, which hinges on the fact that we are always coming from and going toward something. Therefore, we can't omit the last moment of our acting score—our final destination. During our last action on stage, *we know* from what we have come and what we are doing now, but *we must also know* where we are going next and what we want there as we leave the stage. It must be defined so specifically and followed through with such consequential expectations about the immediate future that we will be truly en route when we leave the stage. Mechanical mental clicking off of fictional facts will be of no help. You have only to remember your own problems with making an exit or those you have observed in others to understand why I make such a point of this.

When sitting in the auditorium, you may have noticed that an exit is often predictable because of an actor's sudden self-consciously embellished behavior accompanied by a forced spurt of energy that seems to spell out *THE END*, just before he leaves. If he has seemed vain on stage, you can almost envision him in the wings, waiting for applause (with which the audience, usually eager to obey such formalistic signals, may even oblige him). You can also predict the "exit" of a modest actor who, for lack of final destination connected with his last action, simply fades into the wings. Both have simply stopped truthful acting *before* leaving the set.

At the end of a scene, if you are putting on your coat and making sure you have your keys, when your hand is on the door your attention may be on the long flight of stairs you will have to descend, or on the length of time you will have to wait for the elevator, or on the possibility of finding a cab or taking a subway. Or you may have already decided on such things and are now speculating about the confrontation with your lover who is waiting for you at a restaurant. If your last action is to tell off your mother who has been nagging at you, as you slam the door on her you should know that you are heading for the bedroom to dress for the party in spite of her having forbidden it, etc., etc. In any event, whatever your logical final destination may be, it is incomplete until you are well off in the wings, or, at least, fully out of view of the audience.

For the purpose of the exercise, your preparation will most likely include putting up your set with the help of one or more colleagues. Be considerate of your teacher's and colleagues' time by being well organized for the procedure. Know ahead of time where every piece of furniture and each object in the place will go. Make a diagram if necessary. While setting up, it helps me enormously to make myself at home, reminding myself, in the handling of each object, every lamp and table, every vase and utensil, that it is mine and of what it means to me. This can be achieved just as expeditiously as by setting up mechanically. It helps my faith to "create" the place in which I will soon be living.

The only other thing I always add to my three steps of preparation is to "psych" myself with childlike innocence into the belief that I am living now, that what has just happened is happening at the moment, and that what I think will happen next has never happened to me exactly like this before.

FOR THE PRESENTATION

Follow the basic principles that pertain to this and all of the remaining exercises: **Explore two to three minutes of your behavior in the pursuit of a simple task, taking into careful consideration all of the six steps** on page 134. For the purpose of the given technical problem, choose circumstances that necessitate an entrance from the wings into your playing area, and eventually an exit into the wings. If your main action takes place in the living room, for instance, it is inconsequential whether you enter through the front door or come from another room. The same holds true for your exit. While occupied with the task on stage, you may also choose to leave *momentarily* to get or leave something in another room before reentering the playing area. This will further test your faith in creating a continuity of life between the physical realities on stage and those that you imagine off stage.

In the examination of your selected actions, put your DESTINATIONS under a microscope to discover how many are consciously motivated, how many occur by reflex, and which of them are subconsciously instigated. An hour of actual rehearsals should be the minimum. Lying in bed to *think* about what you will do doesn't count!

12

The Second Exercise:
The Fourth Side

FOR many years I had trouble maintaining faith in the reality of my life on stage whenever I allowed the presence of the audience to intrude on my sense of privacy. While performing, enclosed on three sides by the illusionary realities of my character's life, I felt the area of the auditorium sometimes looming up like a gaping hole, filled only by countless pairs of eyes all aimed at me. THE PURPOSE OF THIS EXERCISE IS TO DISCOVER AND TEST WAYS OF CREATING THE IMAGINED FOURTH SIDE OF THE PLAYING SPACE, one that is logical to it even as it embraces the audience area. We must imaginatively surround ourselves on *all* sides, completing the environment in which our character lives, if we want to sustain uninterrupted faith in "our" existence.

Recently I decided to replace the term the *fourth wall* with the *fourth side*. I did so, first, because many students failed to understand my interpretation of the meaning of the fourth wall and, second, because it is an overused theatre term applied by actors with formalistic tendencies as a mechanical device to justify playing to the audience, and by naturalistic actors literally as a "wall" behind which to hide, often in order to indulge in irrelevant "private experiences." Long ago, I was once caught between these two stools during a dress rehearsal. Suddenly spooked by the notion of the gaping hole in the auditorium, trying to regain my confidence, I pretended that no one was or ever would be out there. When this failed, I focused first on the floor and then, gradually, I directed my attention more and more to the back wall of the set. The old-fashioned director sitting in the audience finished me off by calling out, "I can't see you! Use the fourth wall! Keep your eyes trained at balcony-rail level!" I obeyed by playing straight out front, my faith in the life on stage now totally destroyed.

Of course we must never ogle the audience. *Of course* we must never hide from the fourth side of the playing space. And, *of course* we must understand that all good directors will ensure that pertinent action will communicate. It is their responsibility. But it is *our* job to endow the fourth side with imagined realities that will complete the space in which we find ourselves, whether that be a room, park, restaurant, or landscape. No one can do it for us. Then there will be no desire to *duck from or push into* the audience.

COMMUNICATION

All artists, whether they are writers, painters, sculptors, musicians, dancers, or actors, share the fervent hope that their work will communicate, that it will be *understood*. Real artists know that both the initial *idea* for a creation and the work involved in the *process* of creating spring from a profound urge to find expression for a particular point of view. This point of view excludes any and all manipulative speculations about the effectiveness of the work and its eventual reception by the viewer and/or listener. Whether and how it is understood can only be taken into consideration *after* it is finished. This is what separates artists from their commercial counterparts who use their ideas and skills from start to finish for the sole purpose of making and marketing a consumer product. In itself, that can be an admirable goal, and I don't mean to denigrate it. However, it is not my goal. While exploring a role, I avoid speculating about how my work will be received—whether it will be understood, liked, or disliked. To do so would immediately result in formalistically shaped actions. The kind of communication I seek cannot take place when catering to an audience either by selling them "brilliant" ideas *or* effectively "dazzling" techniques. Real actions are not projected into the audience but solely toward their targets on stage.

Ideal communication between actor and audience occurs when the actor is intensely alive, physically and psychologically involved in fulfilling his character's needs, in action—*within* the magic circle of his playing area. Then, as if by a powerful magnet, the attention of the audience will be drawn into this circle, free to become involved in the life being revealed, to empathize with it, to be surprised and, hopefully, enlightened by it.

I have heard young actors express the fear that they may get so deeply involved in their roles that they will forget they are on stage. Nonsense. This could only happen if they were drunk, drugged, or crazy. When all of our five senses are sharply attuned to our character's existence, our sixth sense, the actor's "extrasensory perception," gives us a *subliminal* awareness of the audience. We know when they laugh (in the right or wrong place), when they get restless (for which *we* are usually to blame), when they cough on a crucial line or become hushed in spellbound attention, when they weep or blow their noses. We must aim for *maximum* involvement in our life on stage, mastering all the techniques that will make this possible, just *because* we are always subliminally conscious of such things. And, since one of the main distractions can be the intrusion of the gaping hole, let me deal with the solution to the problem—the creation of the imagined fourth side of the playing area.

PRIMARY USE OF
THE FOURTH SIDE

On occasion, some of the actions of a play are directorially conceived to extend beyond the proscenium arch, asking that actors focus on imagined objects in the area of the audience for a primary purpose. For instance, as the stage lights came up at the opening of the original production of *Cat on a Hot Tin Roof*, Maggie was discovered *facing the audience*, arranging her hair while looking into an imaginary mirror straight ahead of her. This device was accepted by the audience because it was established at once, then carried out by other actors throughout the performance in a variety of ways as they related to imaginary clocks, looked at pictures or out of imagined windows placed imaginatively somewhere in the auditorium. Unless they are part of the directorial scheme, an actor must never be the only one in the play to execute such actions, or the audience will mistake his intent and look back to see if someone has arrived late, or otherwise speculate about the actor's mysterious intention in looking out front.

On the other hand, making primary use of the fourth side is a common device when a scene takes place out of doors. Often a particular tree, cloud, steeple, or house on the horizon is referred to, looked at, even pointed to, in the audience area. Once the actors have decided where in the auditorium the particular object is situated, this is simple to do. Most outdoor sets are mere suggestions of the elements of nature required by the scene, and it is up to us to supply the realities through our behavior. To arrive at the behavior we must first imaginatively **visualize all aspects of it,** making everything as specific as possible. I usually transfer a landscape that is familiar to me, one that will be logical to the given place. (For example: The moors beyond my house in Montauk remind everyone of Scottish moors and could easily be transferred to the heath in *Macbeth*. The remains of World War II gunsights are similar to the outlines of Celtic castles. An actor can use such a landscape to understand his total surroundings, the swirling mists, the scents, the underbrush, the erica. The Cloisters in Fort Tryon Park in New York City, with their formal gardens high above the Hudson River, have served me well for many a medieval play.) Just as we fill out the realities of the three sides of our set, so we must extend them to include our visualization of the horizon on the fourth side. (On a thrust stage, we must imaginatively supply all *three* vistas in which the audience is seated in the same way, and on an arena stage, we must create the *four* sides surrounding us.)

Whatever landscape you use, be sure that it is specific and includes **landmark objects** such as a bush or tree, the fork of a road, the jut of a cliff, or a canoe anchored to a pier. **The objects must be so well known to you that you can see them clearly in your mind's eye,** so that any or all of them will bring about the entire vista for you. Of course they will be of little use if they remain in your mind's eye. **They must be projected onto the fourth side.** In order to do this, **anchor them to something you can actually see in the auditorium,** to an exit sign, a door, a pillar, or the outline of a lamp on the balcony rail, because **it is impossible to suspend visualized objects in midair.**

Try it. At home, project a familiar face or lamppost somewhere away from you in the space between yourself and the farthest wall. Turn your back to it, then face it again and try to relocate it. It will elude you. You may even become cross-eyed in the wild attempt to bring it into focus. However, the moment you anchor it to something you can actually see, something that is present, such as the corner of the room or the edge of the window frame—or in the case of an auditorium, the side of a loge—your fencepost will be there for you, as well as the fleecy clouds above it!

Be sure to locate the places to which you anchor your landmark objects during rehearsals, *before* you start performing, never while playing. When the curtain goes up, they should be there for you. Actors who claim that the auditorium is too dark to find points of focus in the audience when the houselights are out are mistaken. It is rare to be so blinded by stage lights that one cannot discern the outlines of aisles, exits, loges, or partitions at the back of the house. I always try to place my objects above or slightly to the sides of the dim shapes of people so that no movement will disturb my faith.

You may already have successfully applied these techniques to plays and scenes that took place out of doors. And you may have correctly followed directions in making primary use of them in interior settings such as described for *Cat on a Hot Tin Roof.* But it is in the completion of the fourth side of a *room* (in which plays are most commonly set), to make visual use of it in a *secondary way* **when *none* of our activities should be *overtly* directed out front**, that difficulties arise, presenting us with many problems and doubts about freely maintaining *privacy.*

SUBLIMINAL USE OF THE FOURTH SIDE

In life, even at the height of a confrontation with others, when they are the main target of our attention, we are subliminally aware of our surroundings. For example, when, in order to communicate something to someone, we contact an *inner* object, we are not *outwardly* blind. Our eye will land without conscious awareness on a spot on the rug, a pattern of the upholstery, a picture or window or smudge on the wall. On stage under similar circumstances, without thinking or planning, we intuitively alight on such things *inside* the room and on things on any of the three sides of the set. It is only when our eye would normally alight on such things on the *fourth* side that we have tendencies to duck or look spacelessly into the auditorium with an immediate loss of concentration. **We must want nothing from the fourth side except faith in its existence so that neither our body nor our subliminal vision will shy from it.**

I establish my fourth side at early rehearsals in exactly the same way that I would if I were to use it for a primary purpose. I complete the room by imaginatively placing at least five or six objects that are familiar to me and logically consistent with the rest of my set, projecting them onto the things that actually exist out front. As in the case of a landscape, my objects must be so particular that **I can take them directly from my mind's eye and place them where I choose.** Then, what visually exists between them takes care of itself. (**Be sure to hang your image of the picture or window at something like an exit sign; don't try to turn the exit sign into a picture or window.**) Whatever objects I use to create my reality for the fourth side are my own business, no one else's. Don't discuss them with the director because they will bore or confuse him. Don't discuss them with a colleague. He should be constructing his *own* fourth side. What is real to you may not be real to him, and vice versa.

When testing your ability to use the fourth side in a *secondary* way, remember that you are making no demands on the objects you have placed there except that your eye knows on what it might alight while your *primary* attention is focused on your task on stage. For instance, **while engrossed in a phone conversation,** your eye may be on the clock opposite you, but if you take note of the time, the clock will immediately become a primary object. Or, you may be subliminally aware that your eye has rested on the window curtain. Don't check to see whether it's hanging straight or needs to be washed or it will become an inaccurate divergence from your primary purpose on the phone. (Mirrors are almost impossible to make secondary unless they reflect only inanimate objects, so avoid using them.) At first, some actors worry about the seeming illogic of the relative distance between the imagined objects on the fourth side and the rest of the room. In a literal sense it's true they may be too far away, but this is of no consequence, since the objects serve no primary purpose, demand no actions that relate to them, and are there simply to make you believe you are in a room. Just remember that you cannot pull them closer by dangling them in midair.*

FOR THE PRESENTATION

In order to experiment with the technique of subliminal use of the fourth side, I would like you to use a telephone call as the premise of your two-minute exercise. For the next few days, whenever you are at home making a call, observe on what your eye alights while your *main* attention is solely on the content of the phone call. You may notice that your eye usually lands on the same one, two, or three objects. To test correct use of the fourth side, you must be seated or standing in such a way that it remains logical to do so. Obviously, if you are lying on your back on a bed or sofa, your vision will go to the ceiling. If you are slouched forward in a chair, elbows on knees, it will go to the floor. If you need to write or refer to papers on your desk, be careful that the activities don't prevent you from using the fourth side at all. In addition, after settling on the nature of the phone call, be sure to include all aspects of a basic exercise: time, place, circumstances, objectives, and obstacles. Whether you are discovered at the phone at the beginning of the exercise, or decide to make a call after entering, or receive a call while otherwise occupied is unimportant. Just make certain that the balance of the exercise concerns itself with a phone call. Rehearse the call; don't improvise it when you present it, or correct subliminal use of the fourth side will fail. While you shouldn't write out the dialogue, you must know exactly to whom and about what you are speaking, as well as the *content* of

---

* Exact distance, closeness, or focusing on something far away, as well as looking into an abyss or down into the street from a fifth-floor window, or looking high up at mountain peaks or skyscrapers, are all achieved by bodily adjustments. These are all dealt with in Re-creating Physical Sensations, the fifth exercise, and particularly in Bringing the Outdoors On Stage, the sixth one.

what is being said to you.* And if you rehearse this conversation at least ten times, the words will take on their own spontaneous inevitability.

When working on *any* scene or exercise while creating the place in which our life will unfold, we usually automatically determine which of the four sides of our space will represent the audience area. Now, when rehearsing at home, start to determine how you can transfer the fourth side of your room to that of your studio or workshop. When you set up the exercise there, take as much time to place your imagined objects (connecting them to what is actually there, above and to the sides of your colleagues and teacher) as you do to place the real furniture and the tangible objects that belong in it. When performing, *never* dictate at what points during the conversation you will make secondary use of the fourth side. Let your eye go there only when it wants to. Above all, don't *check* whether or not you are *really* seeing the objects that your eyes light on, because that immediately gives them primary importance. They must simply be there for you.

In order to master this exercise, you will most likely need to repeat it several times in ensuing classes, using different circumstances and different kinds of phone calls each time. You will also discover an interesting by-product of the work, one that relates to *all* of the exercises. You are establishing *habits* of self-observation. From here on, you will probably notice what your vision lands on, not just while rehearsing but every time you make a call, at home, at some other place, or outside at a public telephone. (I'm sure you have already become observant about your primary and secondary destinations during the course of an ordinary day after having completed the first exercise.) No one will have to tell you when you finally use the fourth side of your room correctly. Once it works for you, you will feel liberated from any sense of audience intrusion. In the future you will *want* to construct the fourth side of your set for every exercise, scene, and play on which you work.

---

* Remember, don't try to hear individual words. See Listening, page 113.

13

The Third Exercise:
Changes of Self

Returning to the theories of Chapter 4 about our need to expand our sense of self, **it is the purpose of this exercise to put some of these ideas into practice.** We want to explore the many aspects of seemingly different people, all of which are part of our total persona, to learn why and how we change, sometimes from one moment to the next, and how these changes manifest themselves in our behavior. Eventually we will trust that we have sufficient "selves" to feed all the characters we will play, and we will instinctively avoid the trap of illustrating preconceived character images. The exercise is divided into two parts, each one emphasizing a different aspect of bringing about changes in self-perception and consequent actions.

PART I

For this exercise, take the example I gave at the bottom of page 55 as your guide. Find circumstances under which you will make a phone call or calls during which you speak to at least three people. Make sure that your relationship to each of them is *markedly* different from the others. For instance, if you are calling home and reach your parents, they may want you to speak to a sibling, another relative or in-law who lives there, or a visiting neighbor. Or you may receive a call from a colleague who is at a party at which others are present who also want to talk with you, perhaps someone of the opposite sex who turns you on (or off), or someone of whom you are envious who often puts you down, or an agent of whom you are in awe, etc. The change in your sense of self and how differently you present yourself to each person will manifest itself while you are dealing with the content of what you are saying to each other, in your tone of voice, verbal idiom, even in bodily adjustments. And this will occur *spontaneously* when your relationships have reality, when you see the other in your mind's eye, when you truly believe you are in contact with the person on the other end of the line. When talking to your parents, for instance, you may feel like a child again, responding with obedience, love, defensiveness, or manipulations, depending on the circumstances of the call. Or, you may test a recently discovered "friendship" with them, playing the role of being their equal, and trying ways in which to prove it. Or perhaps you are at the point when you feel wiser than they are, tolerating their faults, merely paying lip service to their need to be treated as authority figures, and so on.

FOR THE PRESENTATION

For practical purposes, it is unimportant whether you talk to three people in the course of the same call, make three separate short calls, or are interrupted by incoming calls. Remember to define your circumstances, your needs, the place, and the required primary and secondary objects in it. Set aside at least one hour in which to rehearse the conversations if you want your explorations to become concrete. And, since this part of the exercise takes place on the telephone, just as it did in the second exercise, don't forget to include your newly acquired skill in making secondary use of the fourth side.

PART II

When I first became aware of the intuitive role-playing that goes on when putting on or changing clothes, I was ecstatic. I realized, almost at once, how useful this process was for the identification with other characters. I wanted to learn how to pin down and follow through on the psychological and physical results of this process, which had previously occurred without my conscious awareness. In Chapter 4, The Self, particularly on pages 56–57, and throughout Chapter 5, Transference, I have given examples of ways in which clothing influences us and brings about changes in behavior. Review these sections now. Then take a few days to observe yourself whenever you get dressed in the morning, when changing for various occasions during the day, and when preparing for bed at night. Notice the care you give even to the *choice* of garments, when readying yourself for an audition, a class, a trip to the store, the arrival of a relative, colleague, or lover, a doctor's appointment or dinner at a fancy restaurant, etc. Pay attention to the condition of the clothes to see how that feeds into role-playing. Is something tatty or new, clean or soiled, in or out of fashion, elegant, cozy, slatternly, etc.? If a crisp white shirt makes me feel like a proper suburban matron, I may begin to behave like one already in the way I use my fingers to button the Peter Pan collar. If donning a threadbare terry robe makes me feel like a downtrodden abused wife, I may slouch my shoulders while looping up the dangling belt. If, in slipping into satin pumps, I see myself as a snobbish jet-setter, I will probably rise to my full, arrogant height before dousing myself with perfume, etc. Once you have become alert to such things, be sure to remember that **these "roles" are different aspects of yourself.** *You are not illustrating someone else's behavior.*

FOR THE PRESENTATION

Select specific circumstances for a two- to three-minute event, during which you get dressed for a particular occasion. There are several things to bear in mind. In the privacy of your home, knowing that no one is watching, you are free to follow through on changes of self-perception. In performance, be sure to re-create this privacy. Don't fall into the trap of wanting to prove the differences in your actions, either to your teacher or to your colleagues. When truthfully executed, they will prove themselves. You will discover, *after the fact,* that you have presented new aspects of yourself on stage, that this is *one* of the many ways of escaping from the cliché image of yourself which is so often presented in the desire to feel "natural."

The sensorially suggestive aspect of a garment is what most often instigates the role-play, that is to say, how you consequently imagine yourself. That is what I want you to explore. Unless you are *consciously* role-playing, checking out how you look in a *mirror* can destroy this self-image. Consequently, avoid making the use of a mirror central to your event. You are also going beside the point when you judge the garment itself—whether you approve or disapprove of its outer effect. The follow-through of a changing self-image will evaporate. When I slip my foot into my thick rubber-soled sneaker, I already begin to feel myself a sporty "girl" and continue to live up to this image as I set myself into springy motion, but the mirror tells me another story. When walking down the street in a free-flowing jersey dress, I have felt and behaved like a young Isadora Duncan and have been horrified by the frumpy old lady I inadvertently caught reflected in a store window.

To reap maximum benefits, present this part of the exercise three or four times in ensuing classes. Use different clothing and accessories under varying circumstances each time you do it and avoid the attire you usually wear to class.

14

The Fourth Exercise: Moment to Moment

We rehearse a play in order to unearth and eventually to select the behavior that will most pertinently reveal each moment of the life of a particular human being caught up in the events prescribed by a playwright. In the case of the exercises, we ourselves determine the events. All possible actions logical to the circumstances must be looked for, tested, and defined before they are settled on. Once that has been accomplished, the actor faces one of his most difficult technical problems: how to repeat the selected actions at every performance **from moment to moment,** as if for the first time. Be assured that it is not a contradiction in terms to demand that every moment of this life must be precisely selected and rehearsed over and over and over again while insisting at the same time that it should be executed with spontaneity. **It is achieved by a suspension of knowledge of what is to come,** by "forgetting" everything except what is needed at the moment with the profound innocence that is part of an actor's soul.

Before tackling this exercise, study Chapter 9 once again. It deals with the influence of *expectations* on our actions and goes a long way toward solving our dangerous tendencies to *anticipate.* Remember that *in life,* what we do is always accompanied by expectations of the consequences of our actions, what we *think* will happen next. However, we never know for sure what that will be. How we receive what *actually* happens brings about our next action, which is again sent

164

with certain expectations, hopes, speculations, or assumptions about its consequences. **We never know whether we will succeed or fail in fulfilling our wishes until *after* the fact.** Obviously, **this is a totally different process from the one so often used *on stage*, when an actor, while delivering one line, is thinking ahead, anticipating his next line and action or those of his partner, already knowing what the consequences will be.** When this occurs, he is stuck in preshaped, mechanical actions and reactions, concerned only with external effects. We must **strive to be newly alive from moment to moment,** alive in every fiber of our being, surprising ourselves every time we repeat a performance.

To move from theory to practice, I ask you to choose an event for this exercise during which you must find an object you have mislaid or believe to be lost (an almost daily occurrence for many of us). For example:

Just this morning, while preparing for my return to New York after a weekend in the country, I acted out a minidrama when I discovered that my wallet was missing. My guest was refueling the car at the gas station. I had finished most of my packing. (My friends often refer to me as being over-organized.) The tote bag was in the hall, ready for the car, packed with a few books, pages of completed manuscript, mail, sundries such as pills, dog toys and leash, extra sneakers, and articles of clothing. The cooler, containing leftovers and fresh vegetables, stood next to it. I put a pack of cigarettes in my shoulder bag for the journey before checking to make sure the bag contained my makeup kit, checkbook, house keys, and wallet. . . . No wallet! It *had* to be there! At first, I fished in and around the jam-packed bag and in both side pockets in disbelief. Impatiently, I dumped the contents on the dining table, pawing through the pencils, pens, notepads, extra lipsticks, a mirror, Tic Tacs, cigarette lighters, loose tobacco—disgusting—and, disgusted, I pushed everything back inside. I looked under the table and the chair on which the bag had been slung, while my mind raced ahead to other possibilities, trying to reconstruct the events during which I'd last had the wallet. Aha! Last night I'd paid for supper at the docks. What had I worn? I rushed to the closet in my bedroom

165

and groped through the large pockets of my sport shirt, then pushed the hangers aside and searched among my shoes on the floor. I fumbled hopelessly through my white purse and in my catchall bureau drawer. Irrationally, I knelt to look under the bed while screaming, "I'm getting senile!" I even hunted for the wallet in the bathroom on top of the toilet tank and in the sink. Calm again, but still cursing, I returned to look through my shoulder bag yet another time. Then I recalled that I'd given the wallet to my guest early in the morning when he went for the newspaper. Perhaps he still had it. He certainly didn't need it for the gas because we always charge it. On a few earlier occasions he'd left it on the counter next to the phone. By now in a panic, I ran there, looking next to the phone book and the Rolodex, and, stupidly, even under it. On my way back to the bedroom for another stab at a seemingly fruitless search through my clothes closet, I passed the open tote bag in the hall. Accidentally, my glance lit on the wallet, nestled cozily in the folds of a blouse. After a classic double take, I emitted a triumphant yell.

After a few days of self-observation, when similar things happen to you, you will realize that the logic behind each of your destinations during the hunt for a missing object is based on *previous* as well as present circumstances, and especially on your expectations about where the object could possibly be.

FOR THE PRESENTATION

When you re-create behavior during such an event, it becomes clear that the attempt to do so is fraught with the dangers of anticipation. At our first rehearsal we already know where the misplaced object will be found, since we, ourselves, have put it there. During rehearsals, while discovering and defining every step of the search, we become familiar with the consequence of every action. Therefore, the final presentation of this exercise should truly test the ability **to direct one's full attention to one need at a time.** Make yourself believe in the existence of each new moment. If you are looking for a key, *really* examine the contents of your purse until you are sure it isn't there.

Really hunt on the desk and in a drawer; convince yourself that it must be there before heading for your jacket in the closet with the assumption that it could be in one of the pockets, etc. By suspending all knowledge of the key's ultimate location, you will intensify an immediate need to find it.

Be sure that the missing object has meaning to you, so that your stakes remain high when looking for it. A treasured locket, watch, or earring, a love letter, money, or a check should do the trick. The choice of circumstances can also determine the importance of an otherwise ordinary object. Simply looking from one logical place to another for a pencil when the ballpoint pen lying nearby would do just as well may be a daily occurrence but will have little technical value and be rather uninteresting to work on. *However,* the lack of writing equipment can become crucial if you are on the phone with an agent who is providing you with the address and phone number of a producer. Even a missing comb can matter if your hair is a mess on the way to an audition.

While we are involved in the actions of looking for something we *really need,* a variety of emotional responses will inevitably set in along the way. No matter how hard we try, we rarely remain cool and collected under such circumstances. Many actors mistakenly *preconceive* the development of their psychological responses, assuming that they will first be slight ones that gradually intensify during the search, rising on an upward curve until they peak at the end. (We make similar mistakes when working on a character who is in crisis.)* In actuality, our anxiety, panic, frustration, despair, rage, disappointment, elation, even a sense of the ridiculous, all manifest themselves rather like the marks on the fever chart of a patient whose temperature jumps around, rises, drops, leaps higher, and drops again, interspersed with periods of seeming normalcy. It is possible to be overcome by intense panic at the very first moment of realization that an object is missing. This may be followed by regaining control when you set about the task of looking for it, only to be undone again by frustration when you fail to find it at the first logical place. Scrounging about on the floor for the object might produce

---

* Review Chapter 7, The Psychological Senses.

gales of laughter when you are suddenly struck by the ludicrousness of your posture.

In other words, **don't prejudge where and what to feel.** Don't squelch real feelings when they do move in on you. Above all, **don't *set* what you do feel** at specific moments during the rehearsals. If you burst into tears at a certain point, don't demand that it happens the next time through. If a sudden calm settles in, don't dismiss it as being inappropriate. It may precede a storm. **Give free rein to your psychological responses; allow them to take you** in new ways each time you work on the exercise and each time you present it, always maintaining faith in the newness of your existence from moment to moment under your selected circumstances.

While searching, always remember to keep the missing object visually in mind; it dictates where and how you will look for it. When this exercise is presented to me, I always know when an actor has forgotten his object and begins to look just for the sake of looking. His behavior becomes illogical. Although we may rifle through the pages of a book to find an important piece of paper, it is only possible to look through the book for a set of *keys* in a desperate moment of *irrationality.* Resort to such an idiotic action only if it is genuinely provoked, if you are driven to it. Then it will have *human* logic.

Be sure that the object is a small one. Your belief that it has been lost will be impossible to maintain if it can't be properly concealed on your set. Even something the size of a shoe, which at home could be the very devil to locate under or behind your furnishings and usual clutter, might be spotted at once in the barer confines of a studio.

Even when your object is small enough to "lose," keep in mind that this exercise takes much longer and needs more care to set up than the previous ones when re-creating your own place in the workshop space. Your faith in reality will dissolve if you are forced to pantomime fumbling through an empty drawer which, at home, was stuffed with papers or clothing. If you had to plow through piles of litter on your coffee table at home to find a wristwatch, your moment-to-moment life will be rudely interrupted by the sight of an empty table in the studio.

Don't forget to time your exercise before you bring it to class. Be sure that all your actions are pertinent to the search. It is easy to stray into irrelevancies under these particular circumstances.

Once you have experienced the glorious sensation of being newly alive that accompanies the full involvement in each moment of playing, trusting that the next one will arise logically out of your circumstances with no need to anticipate, you will never again want to settle for anything less—certainly not for the vastly different experience of simply repeating behavior, of skimming over actions while anticipating everything that is about to happen, hanging on to the external form you had settled on—no matter how meticulously or "humanly" it may have been initially arrived at.

Repeat this exercise under differing circumstances in future classes until you have mastered the correct technique for playing from moment to moment. Use it as a yardstick against which to measure all your future work. The same principles can be applied to all the exercises and every role you will ever play, and also, of course, to the way in which you send and receive the words of the play.

15

The Fifth Exercise: Re-creating Physical Sensations

As if by magic, an actor can grow tipsy from drinking tea, enter a room in rain-soaked clothes which are actually dry, sniffle with watering eyes while chopping an apple that looks like an onion, or nick himself when shaving with a bladeless razor. However, unlike a magician or an illusionist, he does so not to fool the audience but first of all himself, to make *himself* believe in all the realities of his character's existence. **By endowing the objects and the conditions prescribed by the playwright with imagined realities, he can produce sensations at will.** The theories underlying this technique, accompanied by countless examples of sensory responses to imagined stimuli and the consequent behavior, are given in Chapter 6, The Physical Senses. Study it carefully before proceeding. I have divided this exercise into two sections, each one probing different sources and technical problems for the practice of sensory recall.

Because of my belief that sensations recur most strongly while one is dealing with them, I disagree with those who teach sensory recall isolated from its consequent behavior. When I start to imagine that my hands are sticky with perspiration, for example, I *believe* I am hot or nervous when using my handkerchief to dry them off, *not* when concentrating only on the palms of my hands, *waiting* for them to feel hot and sticky. Therefore, I ask you to practice sensory recall in both parts of this exercise within the framework of a selected two- or three-minute event, the same as in the previous ones.

PART I

Here you will learn **to test sensory responses to visible and tangible objects that have been imaginatively endowed with properties that cannot or should not be real on stage.** For example:

On a chilly autumn morning at seven-thirty, you enter the kitchen to make yourself a nice breakfast. The pilot light on the stove has gone out. You strike a match to light it, holding the match gingerly to the side to avoid getting singed when the pilot pops on. You test the kettle for water. There's enough for a cup or two of coffee so you place it over a flame. You light the oven, split an English muffin, and place it under the broiler. You reach for a jar of instant coffee and try to unscrew the lid, but it's stuck. After a few raps on the counter and a brief struggle of twisting, it loosens up. You spoon some coffee into a mug and set it by the stove. While waiting for the kettle to boil, you take a swallow of milk from a carton in the fridge, but it has soured. Your mouth puckers in disgust and you quickly spit out the milk into the sink. In disbelief, you sniff the carton to see if it's really turned that bad, then empty it in the sink and dump the carton in the garbage can. Your mouth still tastes terrible, so you wash it out with a swig of cranberry juice. Meanwhile, the water has boiled and while pouring it into the mug, you avert your face from the steam that issues from the kettle. After stirring, you puff and blow across the hot coffee, test the rim of the mug gently with your lips and, with squinting eyes, you take a sip. You manage to swallow but immediately open your mouth to exhale and then take in air to cool your tongue. A faint odor of burning sends you rushing to open the broiler. You pull back from the heat with your head and shoulders while carelessly trying to flip the hot muffin onto a plate with your fingertips, performing a clumsy juggling act in the process. Mission accomplished, you bring everything to the table for a pleasant break-fast.

Think, if you were presenting such an event on stage and wanting to support all the actions with genuine sensations, how many of the objects would have to be endowed with imagined realities? The stove would not be connected, so there would be no pilot light, burner flame, or hot broiler. There should be water in the kettle, but it will not boil or produce steam. There should be coffee in the jar, but the lid should not actually be stuck, or you might *never* get it open. The milk will not really be sour, or you might throw up. The muffin will remain cold. (Remember that objects used on stage must have suffi-cient reality to prevent any necessity for pantomimed actions—unless you are playing something like *Our Town*. For instance, when taking a drink, don't use an empty glass and then have to worry how far to tip it, or what actual swallowing is like. Drink water and endow it with whatever property is needed, whether it be liquor, something hot, or medicine, etc.)

Through self-observation, you will quickly learn to spot the cause or source of a sensation, to examine its effect on a particular part of your body and what you do to alleviate it—or in the case of a pleasant one, how to make it linger. And remember that the greatest faith in the imagined sensation occurs at the moment when you are physically adjusting to it.

If you are in doubt about what objects or elements of them must be endowed with imagined realities, use my rule of thumb: If I do not have total control over an object in using it for a needed purpose, if *it* can control *me*, it becomes *dangerous*. And whatever is actually dangerous must be exchanged for an imagined reality. *You* must dictate the sensations, *they* should not dictate you. Obvious dangers are inherent in such things as sharp knives, razors, liquor, medicines, hot irons, etc.—things that can do you physical harm. I certainly don't expect you to rehearse with such objects to see what happens when you really hurt yourself. You will *remember* what it was like. You can re-create the reality by endowing a dull knife with sharp-ness, an empty razor with a blade, water or tea with heat, bitterness, the properties of alcohol, or cloying sweetness, and a cold iron with heat, for example. I wouldn't take a real aspirin on stage for fear that it might slow me down, make me perspire, or get stuck in my throat; I would probably substitute a Tic Tac and deal with it as though it were, indeed, an aspirin.

There are other kinds of "dangerous" objects. Let's say that in an exercise or a play, you are getting ready for a heavy date and have to apply makeup. Objects such as mascara, eyeliners, eyebrow pencils, eyedrops, cold cream, lotions, hair spray or pomade, perfume, etc., can all take on a life of their own. If you use them as you do in life, with all their properties intact, you may very well end up a mess on stage. With just a tremor of nerves, you might get the mascara in your eye, smear the eyeliner, or produce a jagged eyebrow, with no time to make repairs. Gooey things like cold cream, shoe polish, toothpaste, hair cream, and lotions can get all over you or the furnishings. Use empty containers and bottles, keep eyebrow pencils and tubes capped, and, through sensory recall and accurate behavior, you will create all their needed realities. Knocking over a bottle of nail polish could create a disaster. I would use an empty bottle and smooth the imaginary polish on my nail with the little dry brush. While doing so, I would be able to smell the fumes and see the color of the polish, perhaps even getting a little on the cuticle, pausing to wipe it off. By now, by *reflex*, I would need to blow on my nails to make sure they were dry and, still by reflex, handle the next object very delicately for fear of marring the polish.

I once played Argia in Ugo Betti's *The Queen and the Rebels*. At the end of one scene, just before the lights went down, I had to remove my makeup. The next scene took place the following day, thirty seconds later, and I had to be in full makeup again. Friends swore that they had seen my face shiny, without a trace of powder, rouge, or lipstick at one minute and fully made up the next, and marveled at this miraculous feat. But I never took the makeup off. Using tissues and an empty cold-cream jar, recalling the touch, texture, and scent, I found the behavior of scooping out the imaginary fluffy cream, scraping the sides of the jar and spreading it over my face and neck with my fingertips. Then I carefully wiped it off, wadding up the tissues as I *believed* they were getting soiled and greasy, thus creating an illusion of reality.

Eating on stage can present other interesting problems. Canned peach or apricot halves must be eaten as though they were hot eggs that had just been fried, pieces of canned pears as though they were oysters, sliced bananas as if they were scalloped potatoes. In Schnitzler's *The Farewell Supper*, I had to eat an enormous gourmet meal eight performances a week. Had the management provided all the food as specified, I would have become very fat and very sick, certainly unable to continue with the one-act play that followed. What I actually ate, accompanied by gulps and slurps and smacking lips, looked accurate, although the amounts were smaller. The food was neither filling nor fattening but was endowed by me with fabulous flavors, running butter and juices, with stickiness or sweetness, smoothness or lumpiness, and with heat or cold. When I finished the meal by pouncing on the whipped cream torte, which was really a mound of strained yogurt, it elicited a joyful round of applause.

On many occasions the actor is called on to swat at imaginary flies or mosquitoes, perhaps to watch them fly and alight before the kill. Sometimes he must chase roaches or rodents. Even though such objects are not tangible or actually visible, they must be imaginatively created so that the actor can believe they exist. To do this, always *supply the path they travel* in relationship to the furnishings and walls of the set. As with your objects on the fourth side, don't try to suspend them in midair. A bug may fly from the table to a ceiling fixture to a spot on the wall, or it might land on your body. When performing, if you retrace whatever path you have settled on, you can easily imagine the size and color of the insect and its buzz, as well as its psychological effect on you. A roach can be spotted on the floor next to the stove or on a dish in the sink and be seen to scurry from there to a particular corner of the room. Follow its imagined path until you *need* to squash it.

FOR THE PRESENTATION

Select an event during which you must deal with three or more objects that have been endowed with needed realities. See to it that your senses are truthfully involved when contacting them and that all of them are logical to the circumstances. Try to vary the objects you choose so they aren't all connected with tasting, for instance, or only have to do with textures, or with "hurting" yourself. Once you have mastered each endowment in rehearsals, don't forget to include the principle of playing from MOMENT TO MOMENT. Pursue your goal: In the first example of this exercise, it was to prepare an enjoyable breakfast; and in the second, to doll yourself up for an important date. Don't just head from one endowment to the next while checking the accuracy of your behavior, or your actions will become mechanized and defeat the purpose of bringing about a spontaneous sensory life. Trust that your endowments will serve you. They should simply be there for you.

Of course, the term *endowment* goes far beyond its application to tangible objects. Almost nothing in our character's life *is* what it *is*, "but we must make it so!" We endow our character, his circumstances, and his relationship to others, the time and place and each object in it, even the clothes he wears, not only with the physical, but with the *psychological* properties necessary to the play. When we make an event, each moment in it, an object, or a person *particular*, we are, at least partially, *endowing* them with needed realities. To give you a simple example: A rose on stage would most likely be made of silk or plastic and must be endowed with texture, scent, and thorns to be handled with reality. It will *also* be dealt with quite differently if it was a gift from a lover, an apology from a colleague, or a sad memento from the funeral of a relative. The example I made earlier of turning an apple into an onion is just a first step in learning how one thing can be turned into another. By supplying missing realities, we can re-create physical and psychological sensations at will. When this technique is successful, our actions become more sharply defined, and we bring about a heightened reality, a distillation of the truth.

PART II

In Chapter 6, I described how to wake from a deep sleep, how to produce a yawn, different kinds of headaches, head colds and coughs, fatigue, nausea, sensations of stifling heat and bitter cold, etc. **Such sense memories are imaginatively stimulated by the conditions** that are a part of the playwright's given circumstances rather than being initiated by tangible objects as in Part I of this exercise. We want genuine responses to such conditions to be at our beck and call so that we can avoid having to show or illustrate them. Keep in mind that they are indeed *conditions* of the event and not the primary function of a scene. (When Blanche DuBois makes her first entrance, she is hot, dirty, and physically and emotionally exhausted by her journey. These things condition her behavior in pursuing her main objective, which is to find a haven in her sister's home. They are *not* what the scene is *about*.)

There are several other kinds of circumstantial conditions that influence our behavior that occur with frequency in play after play. They also involve the senses. Let me start with A TIME ELEMENT, a sudden AWARENESS OF BEING LATE. If I am supposed to be in a hurry, I must **first know what my ultimate destination will be and what my expectancy is about the amount of time it will take to get there. And I must have a specific idea about how much time it *usually* takes to accomplish the task I am presently engaged in.** Here are three instances to prove what a difference only a few minutes can make in my behavior:

1. I am at home finishing my coffee and the crossword puzzle before going to a 9:30 rehearsal at the Studio. I check my watch. It is 9:20. The Studio is about ten blocks away, but it is still possible to make it on time. I spring into action, every muscle alert to my needs. I quickly put down the pencil, push the coffee aside, and run for my script and purse. Snatching my coat from its hook, I run to the elevator, praying a taxi will be available in the street below.

2. The circumstances are the same as before, only this time when I look at my watch, it is 9:25. Totally rattled, with the puzzle still in hand, I grab for my purse, upsetting it in the process so that some of the contents spill out. I scurry about, first going for my coat, then back to the purse. I retrieve only a few of the items that had fallen out, take along my puzzle instead of the script, put on my coat and catch a sleeve on the door, tearing it when I yank it loose. I will undoubtedly be late and am already thinking up plausible excuses.

3. Again the circumstances are the same except that my watch now reads 9:30. I stare at it in disbelief. I am *late*. My very soul feels rushed, but, overcome with rage, I *slowly* put down the pencil on the puzzle, take a last drink of coffee, and rise with great deliberation. I put on my coat and fasten the last button with a dramatic flourish, pick up my purse firmly by the handle, and put the script under my arm. I stomp out of the room and slam the door shut behind me.

Or consider how the behavior that results from THE NEED TO BE QUIET almost takes care of itself **once you know how far away the person is whom you don't want to disturb and when you have an expectancy about what you think he might hear at the specified distance.** Experiment with this condition at home. Put a willing friend in another room. If you have only one room, ask him to stay in the bathroom and to occupy himself by washing his hands or fixing his hair. You will immediately have assumptions, accurate or not, as to what sounds could penetrate your particular walls, sounds you might make while wrapping a surprise birthday present, for example. Also try putting someone in your bed. Assume the person is sleeping and try to get dressed in the same room or to retrieve something you've misplaced without waking the person. When an actor must remind himself of someone in another room or of the fact that the person is sleeping by continuously looking in that direction, I always know he has no faith in the circumstances. When he *does* believe in them, when his behavior has been correctly arrived at, the sensations accompanying his need to be quiet are usually so suggestive that he may continue to move on tiptoe even after his exercise is finished. The quiet is in his bones and has set up reflexes in his ensuing actions. Be sure that the need to accomplish a task (to wrap the present or find a missing object) *supersedes* the need to be quiet, or you may never fulfill your goal. You might not even be able to enter the set because the squeak of the door opening makes you too fearful of disturbing the other person.

Sometimes a play requires that you enter a room IN THE DARK, that you grope your way to a light switch and bump into the furniture en route. Or the lights are supposed to go off in the middle of a scene, staying off for a protracted length of time while the action continues.

In most instances, the director will have arranged for enough light on stage for you to be seen by everyone in the auditorium. It is up to you to find believable actions to convey the darkness.

Once, when heading down the hall to go to the john in the middle of the night, not having turned on a light, I discovered that my eyes were wide open. At first I believed that I was staring in order to penetrate the darkness, to be able to see better. Then I realized that the opposite was true. I *knew* I couldn't see. **The act of wide-eyed gaping actually deadened my sight even more, allowing my full attention to be given to a heightened sense of touch and hearing.** I was able to concentrate on my hands and feet and ears to orientate myself to the place, to help me find my way. Experiment with this technique, first with the lights off, then with them on. Soon you will really be able to bump into a chair in your path, even though, with the light on, it is clearly in your line of vision. *You will believe that you can't see when you rely on the senses of sound and touch instead.* This is another example of the actor dictating his needed realities. (The same principle holds for a state of blindness, except that in such a case, the person would be in the *habit* of using the other senses to accomplish his actions, executing them with relative ease. An actor would learn to direct his *ear* rather than his eye toward the person speaking to him.)

A condition of DRUNKENNESS crops up in endless tragedies and comedies. It seems to remain a trap even for some of our finest actors, leading to a series of clichés. Of course, when we are drunk, it is difficult to remember how we behave, or perhaps we have never been drunk and have observed its consequences only in others. Drunkenness also affects people in different ways, and exists in many forms, which can range from slight tipsiness to the point of losing physical and verbal coordination. Most people are affected psychologically and become loud, argumentative, and openly hostile, or foolish, silly, and giggly. Some are overcome by depression, getting weepy, sentimental, or maudlin. In a play such variations are specified by the writer in the stage directions, in the descriptions of the particular character, and, of course, in the words that are spoken. No matter how unfamiliar various kinds of inebriation may be to you, any of them can be made real.

Let me begin by making operative a few *psychological* responses to alcohol. For instance, by endowing a harmless remark with a venomous intent, it becomes easy to take offense, since you've supplied a reason for taking out the resentment on the perpetrator. Similarly, by imagining that someone's lipstick or hat is askew, even when it's not true, or when someone suddenly reminds you of a rhesus monkey, or when you, yourself, seem to look peculiar in the mirror, you can be taken by a fit of giggling. When drunk or tipsy, if we talk too much and are inattentive to others, if we believe that we are misunderstood by them as well as by the rest of the world, it is often because concentration is deeply centered on ourselves. When we get maudlin and wallow in self-pity, our problems are disproportionately important to us—and we can make them so. Such illogical responses to the surroundings and the things that occur to someone when he is drunk can all be made specific by the actor, using other sources to transfer to the given circumstances.

If you have never been intoxicated, *physical sensations* can also be taken from other events and transferred to the conditions that are required in a play. Dizziness is a familiar sensation, whether it has been induced by fever, cough syrup with codeine, or just by rising too quickly. How you adjust to the need to overcome it depends on what you are doing when it strikes you and on the part of the body most strongly affected. **When seated,** allow your head to feel heavy. Imagine that it's spinning and let it pull you forward until you need to support it with your hand or with your elbow on the table or the arm of a chair. Sensations of sleepiness or loginess and a lack of eye focus may follow until you have to fight to stay alert. When you imagine that an ashtray next to you seems dimly blurred, you will have to bead in on it, overextending the normal action of extinguishing your cigarette. **When standing,** or trying to get from one place to another, allow your knees to feel wobbly. Momentarily give in to the sensation until you need to straighten them, to strengthen the muscles to prevent yourself from falling over. If you are supposed to have **trouble articulating,** imagine that your tongue is fat or swollen, or that your lips feel very loose, then try to speak clearly and distinctly. As liquor begins to affect us, when getting a little tiddly, something in our behavior usually loosens up; we get a little careless. Experiment with some or all of these examples. Also look for your own sources, finally settling on those which are sensorially most suggestive to *you*. It is possible that only *one* accurate psychological response, added to *one* specific physical sensation, will create such a feeling of reality that other accompanying sensations will recur by reflex.

A HANGOVER can be achieved in the identical way. Even though you may never have had one, you need only know that it usually includes sensations of nausea or queasiness in the stomach, a bad taste in your mouth, a headache or sense of loginess, hypersensitivity to light and noise, and a wild thirst for water, juice, or milk due to dehydration. Because we have experienced each of these things singly or in combination under other circumstances, we can transfer them to the condition of a hangover. (Altitude sickness has identical physical manifestations.)

You will quickly learn that no condition is static, that any state varies in intensity. Something else can take precedence so that it is temporarily forgotten until a specific action again reminds you of it. For instance, if you are looking for your checkbook in the bureau next to a sleeping person, the need to find it might make you yank open the drawer although you know that it sticks and makes a horrible scraping noise when it opens. The sound will be a sharp reminder that you must be quiet. If you are fixing your hair to get ready for a date but you have a headache, while thinking of the marvelous person you are going to meet you may forget the headache until sensitivity to the comb pulling through a snarl painfully reminds you of it. You may become conscious of it again when leaning down to pick up the brush that had fallen from the dresser, etc. In other words, don't demand that the conditions stay constantly with you or have the same degree of intensity during the accomplishment of a task.

FOR THE PRESENTATION

If the practice of sensory recall is new to you or the technique seems particularly difficult, prepare this exercise in the following way. Start by determining an event the same as you would for any exercise. Let's suppose that you want to create an intimate atmosphere for dinner at home with someone for whom you care deeply. You might need to arrange flowers, set a beautiful candle-lit table, check what's cooking, and cool the wine, for example. You will rehearse, as always, making sure that everything has been particularized. When it is all real to you and can be repeated with spontaneity, rework it **by adding one condition.** Perhaps you will begin by being **in a hurry:** You arrived at home half an hour later than expected, your guest will be arriving in twenty minutes, you still have to get yourself gorgeous and perfumed. Explore how this time element influences all the actions. When such a condition truly affects you and has become truthfully incorporated, present the exercise in your studio for evaluation. *The next time* you work on the exercise using the same event or a different one, add more than one condition to your circumstances. If you are already experienced in the use of sensory recall, add more than one condition the first time you work on it. During the event I just described, you might be **in a hurry, have a headache or a stiff neck,** *and* **be hot** because it is mid-July and you have no air conditioner.

If you think the incorporation of several coexisting conditions is an unreasonable demand resembling a difficult juggling act, remember that things like drunkenness, hangovers, and colds usually include *many* sensations such as headaches, nausea, dizziness, blurred vision, aching bones, coughs, and running eyes and noses. Also consider all the plays in which you are expected to deal simultaneously with many different sensory responses. At the opening of Sean O'Casey's *A Bedtime Story,* the young man has risen from bed after "sinning" with a lady of questionable repute. She has asked him to find her lipstick, insisting that she cannot leave without putting some on. He is terrified that she may be discovered by his roommate who is due to return soon and that her presence will be heard by the landlady on the floor below. The room is without heat. It is dark because he refuses to put on a light. In his hunt for the lipstick, he knocks over a vase, spilling water over the table and into his shoes and socks. Without anticipating, playing from moment to moment, the actor must look for the lipstick, *conditioned by* **his hurry** to get rid of the lady. It is **dark.** He is shivering with **cold,** is soon soaking **wet,** and needs to be **quiet.** I decided long ago that limbering up my technique by practicing sensory recall in exercises was infinitely preferable to waiting until I'd been hired for a role to learn in rehearsals how to work on such problems.

Let me stress that if dealing with more than one condition at a time frightens you, stagger them in rehearsals in the following way: Start with the easiest one, the one most suggestive to you—perhaps the need to be quiet. Rehearse your task, exploring its influence on your actions until the sensation stays with you by reflex, until it is in your bones and no longer needs conscious attention. Then repeat the task, and to the quiet add the condition of a dark room or the necessity to hurry. When the actions can be accomplished with ingrained faith in the existence of both conditions, add a third—for instance, a feeling of nausea. For this example I have deliberately taken nausea as the last condition to work on because it is difficult to make subconscious or reflex, usually demanding a concerted effort to control.

Obviously this exercise should be repeated in ensuing classwork again and again, using different events and many combinations of conditioning forces, so that when such problems arise in plays you will be ready to solve them.

16

The Sixth Exercise: Bringing the Outdoors On Stage

Even without the help of a set designer, an actor can create an entire landscape on a bare stage. He can watch a sun rising over the ocean or setting over a prairie, look high up at a towering mountain or down into a valley below. He can teeter at the edge of an abyss or across the rocks in a rushing stream. He can turn the floor into sand, gravel, mud, or grass. He can make it rain or snow, be buffeted by a gale or caressed by a gentle breeze, be blinded by a glaring sun or toasted by it on a beach: all **through the sensory recall and physical adjustments he makes to the imagined elements.**

By starting with your **physical relationship to space,** you will learn that a mere shift of the body can make you believe that something is near or far away, that it looms above you or is down below. Strangely enough, I came upon this miraculous discovery *indoors*. You, too, can practice this technique in your own apartment, afterward applying the same principles to the outdoors. If your room is a few floors above street level, go to the window to see if a tardy guest is in sight on the street below. **Observe what your body is doing:** If you are standing at an angle, note how your weight shifts to the foot nearest the window, how your upper body leans forward, how your neck cranes so that you can see down and your head turns right or left in the direction from which your friend might be seen to be arriving. Now step away from the window and, using the back of a chair as your windowsill, immediately repeat the physical action, not mechanically, but with the same intention of locating your guest, retaining the visualization of the street and the appearance of your friend. From the same window, discover what your body does when you want to see why a helicopter is hovering high above, or why smoke is coming from the top of the tall building across the street.

See what happens when you check your face in the mirror, what your body does when you lean in closely to see if a blemish is properly concealed. Then turn around and imagine that the top part of the door frame across the room is your mirror. Without going any closer, *still needing to check the blemish*, repeat the prior physical adjustments; shoulders slightly hunched, neck stretched forward, head tilted to the side to catch a better view, dabbing lightly at the imagined blemish. You will believe that the mirror is right in front of you, even that your face is reflected in it. Find a different spatial relationship to it by stepping several feet back until the hem of your skirt is visible in the mirror to make sure it's hanging straight (or, if you are a man, to see that your trousers don't bag at the knees). Notice that you may stretch or stand on tiptoes to get it in your line of vision, turning back and forth as you check it. With the muscular adjustments and sensations still in your bones, repeat the action, again using the door frame for your imagined mirror. The actual distance to your mirror will seem to exist.

Self-observation is at the heart of discovering the physical adjustments to distance, height, and depth. You don't need to set aside special time to rehearse this technique. Make it a part of your daily life. Take it into the streets and parks, on outings to the country, the seaside, and the mountains, testing all aspects of your response to nature. You will soon learn that **when your body tells the truth, *you* will believe, and that when it tells a lie, your faith will crumble.**

Apply the principles of establishing your relationship to space through the re-creation of bodily adjustments to all scenes that take place outdoors. As a young actor, I had no trouble finding my physical behavior in a room that had doors and was furnished with tables, chairs, sofas, and desks but I was usually stymied by stage directions that dictated that the action take place outside, in the backyard, or in a garden. I often found myself glued to the spot, seemingly surrounded by a vacuum, or when I tried desperately to visualize the place, I didn't have the slightest idea how to go about it. First I had to learn how to create a specific landscape on stage by applying the procedure described for establishing the fourth side* except that, for this purpose, I projected my landmark objects on *all* four sides of the set.

Let me use a simple example from James Hagan's *One Sunday Afternoon*. It takes place in 1930, and this particular scene occurs "in a park." There is also "a rustic bench" on stage. A young girl and her friend are awaiting the arrival of a young man who will be bringing along a blind date for the friend. They are terribly excited by their daring adventure. The friend is also terrified that her mother may get wind of such goings-on, often threatening to leave. They look in all directions for the arrival of the boys, eventually spotting them in the distance. To lay the proper groundwork for this scene, take a section of a particular park that is familiar to you and transfer it to your set. Or better still, if your partner is willing and the weather permits, have an early rehearsal outdoors in an available park. Either way will immediately provide you with your surroundings (the kinds of trees and shrubs, fences, flower beds, perhaps a fountain, and the specific paths that give access to this spot) to project on the perimeter of your set, your clearing in the park. It will determine many of your destinations. You will know from where you have come, what you do when seated on the bench, in what direction you would head when threatening to go home, and where and how you would look for the young men, among other things. If you also particularize the weather, perhaps even the insects, squirrels, and birds that might be there, and certainly what's underfoot (grass, sandy earth, gravel?), endless possibilities for your behavior will arise to be explored.

FOR THE PRESENTATION

As a further test of our sensory skills and powers of imagination, this exercise is devised to **explore what we *do* about our responses to nature, not just how we *feel* about all its wonders.** Begin with an

* See pages 154–156 in Chapter 12.

event that takes place in a specific area of the outdoors. If you choose an experience at the beach, first determine your objective—to take a sunbath, for example. That you may also be there to enjoy the view and the fresh air should not be the *primary* factor. Select all the things you might need for such an occasion, including your attire: a towel or blanket, a beach hat, sunglasses, tanning lotion, and other paraphernalia like books and crossword puzzles. Re-create your landscape. If a sparkling sea spreads out before you (on the fourth side), note how you stretch in order to make out a tiny white sail bobbing on the horizon. If the waves lap at your feet, stick a toe in the water to test the icy temperature of the water. Jump back when the tide surges toward you. Even if the completed landscape on your right and left does not affect your behavior, it will surely add to your faith in the place. In the distance on the right, there might be a family kicking a beach ball back and forth and, on the left, a pair of lovers nestled in each other's arms on the sand. On arrival, you may have just stepped onto the hot sand from a boardwalk or, when coming from a refreshment stand in the background, you may have added a hot dog and diet soda to the load you are toting. How do you walk in the soft sand, especially when it's hot, as you hunt for the best place to settle? How do you spread out the blanket, pinning down the corners with your belongings so the wind won't catch them? How do you brush the sand off your feet to keep the blanket free of it? How do you orient yourself to the sun to find protection from the worst of the glare before snuggling your behind into a nice soft groove? How do you unpack your things, oil your body, eat your hot dog, and chew with sand in your mouth? Nature will storm in on you when you *deal with its realities* as it affects your activities.

If you choose a landscape in the woods or fields, on a hillside or high up in mountains, in order to find your physical adjustments to the space and your psychological responses to the elements always remember that they hinge on **a purposeful task**—perhaps to make camp, or to take a brief rest during a hike.

Begin your rehearsals with the appropriate clothing and the objects you would have with you, such as a picnic basket or backpack. Explore where and how you settle, unpack, take a swig from the canteen, take off a shoe to remove a stone or bandage a blister, eat a sandwich, deal with gnats or chiggers, look down a trail or over a precipice to the path below to see if a companion is catching up with you, etc.

Even when your conscious objective is simply to go out into the yard for a breath of fresh air, or into the garden to enjoy the flowers, notice that you are never physically suspended when doing so, but are occupied with a task. You may come out with a cup of coffee and sit down on the stoop while sipping it. Or you may bring along the trash to dump in the bin and then take a peek over the neighbors' fence to see if they finally cleared up their yard, or you will examine the rhododendron to consider if it needs pruning this year, all the while "taking in the fresh air." When I stroll through the garden, I always have a tined fork in hand to remove any little weed that offends my eye and *that* is what adds to my "enjoyment."

Because of my firm conviction that when my *feet* know where they are and what they are doing there, I will believe where I am, I ask you always to examine **what's underfoot** in this exercise. It often has specific relevance to your physical life in the place. As in the case of the beach, the sand will materialize for you when you deal with its condition, when it is very soft and hot, becoming damp, cool, and harder at the water's edge, for instance. If you are walking along a dirt path which is hard and smooth, it is unlikely to be influential. If, on the other hand, the path is uneven or rutted, or muddy with occasional puddles, or the dust can be kicked up, or if it is gravelly and the pebbles can get into your open sandals, or poison ivy sprawls along its borders, *then* all possible adjustments to it can be found and re-created. If the grass is just grass, it won't have importance (and in some cases it needn't have any), but when it is newly mown and covered with clippings, or moist with dew, mushy after a rain, has bumps and bare spots, is dotted with anthills, or, as in a public park, is littered with dog or bird droppings, it will certainly demand specific physical adjustments when you are walking or sitting on it.

The **weather,** too, conditions what is underfoot. You already know how strongly it can influence you psychologically: how a gloomy day can put you in the dumps and a beautiful one can make for feelings of exuberance. You have already learned how to work on conditions such as heat and humidity, of cold or chilling dampness when indoors. Now, by applying the same technique of sensory recall and what you do about it, you can supply a rain that teems or drizzles down, that floods the walks or gutters, a snow that whirls around producing drifts, or one that falls in soft flakes that melt on the cheeks or on an outstretched tongue, a sleet that glazes the street and stings the face, the gales that buffet you, into which you lean while hanging on to a hat, or a breeze that strokes your skin, barely ruffling your hair, which you give in to with pleasure. Whenever you are actually outside, *be self-observant*. Always alert yourself to the areas of your body most susceptible to weather sensations and the physical adjustments made to protect yourself from them or to bask in them. Note how important your clothing becomes, how you handle it, and how, for example, you deal with an umbrella, a paper shopping bag, or a new purse or briefcase in bad weather. Soon you will not have to rely on special effects to make yourself or the audience believe in the elements of nature.

When you have presented the exercise many times in successive classes, selecting different landscapes and a variety of conditions, you will begin to understand how to approach Shakespearean scenes that occur on a street, on the ramparts, or in the palace garden. You will know what to do there with no anxiety about falling back into frozen, artificial positioning, and, when you speak, your words will spring from an animated body. If you were to play King Lear, you would eventually be able to challenge the elements with complete faith in the storm that rages around you, providing the sources for:

> Blow, winds, and crack your cheeks! rage! blow!
> You cataracts and hurricanoes, spout
> Till you have drench'd our steeples, drown'd the cocks!
> (*King Lear* III.2.)

A last warning for the presentation: If you repeat the actions without sensory cause, or if you become intent on showing an *audience* what missing realities you are providing, no matter how accurately or impressively you execute your task, it will at best become a slick, mechanical illustration.

17

The Seventh Exercise:
Finding Occupation
While Waiting

In all of the previous exercises I have asked that you particularize the furnishings of interior sets and the landmarks of exteriors in order to determine logical physical destinations. I have stressed the use of *tangible objects* as one of the primary means of furthering the actions and how their use can *intensify* the sensory life and faith in imagined realities. In the previous exercise I tackled the problem of re-creating the outdoors on stage and finding a physical task that requires the handling of various objects (such as the beach gear or the backpack and its contents). However, the actor must also address himself to the difficulties that arise on a bare stage **when nothing in the action of a scene allows for an obvious *physical* task or the many tangible objects that are central to it,** when the playwright, director, and designer provide him, at best, with an archway or a pillar, a platform or a tree stump. Even after creating a physical relationship to the imagined space, the actor is often left with a feeling of emptiness that compels him into posing or finding artificial "arrangements" because he doesn't **know what his body is doing there while trying to pursue a psychological objective.**

In order to solve this dilemma, I looked for parallel circumstances in my own life: When was I ever on my feet, temporarily arrested in one place, not occupied with an obvious physical task, outwardly seemingly inactive? It was usually when I was alone, away from home, outside, waiting for someone or looking for a taxi, bus, or subway. I began to examine what it *was* that was occupying me physically and psychologically while waiting. I would like you to do the same whenever you are in a similar situation. Through self-observation you will begin to understand the things that bring about your behavior and what you will need in order to re-create it.

FOR THE PRESENTATION

Find what you actually do while waiting when you mistakenly think you do nothing. Find true inner and outer occupation with a minimum of dependence on tangible objects. When selecting a particular event and the time and place in which it will occur, **strip yourself of all but the essential objects,** such as your clothing, a handbag, or briefcase. Avoid circumstances that demand a variety of "interesting" activities such as a return from a trip, when you might be carrying books and suitcases, or from a shopping spree, loaded down with bundles and bags. Don't include extreme weather conditions because the actions and objects needed to protect yourself from the elements will do away with the problem posed here. Also, if in your choice of place there is somewhere to sit comfortably, you will be bypassing the technical difficulties of this exercise.

Here are the things you *do* need to determine: Once again **know your place** in detail, whether it be a park, a street corner, or a subway platform, before transferring it to your playing area and anchoring each landmark to the four sides. **Find your bodily relationship to the space** as you did in the last exercise. **Know your purpose for waiting.** It is at the center of all your actions. **Know where you have come from and where you are planning to go,** as well as **what has previously happened and what you expect will happen later on.** You will draw on this knowledge of the past and expectations about the future for your *inner occupation*. **Know the direction from which the vehicle or person will probably be arriving.** Pinpoint **where to look for him,** the exact area in which he may first be spotted, by using such things as an imagined street sign or trash basket a few blocks away as your landmark; use the little light at the curve of the tunnel around which the subway first becomes visible. **Establish your bodily adjustment to the specified distances.**

Know what you are wearing, and in which way your clothing influences you. To understand why I continually emphasize the importance of clothing, in this exercise, while waiting, you only have to discover the contrast in behavior between being dressed for the opera or a trip to the gym, dressed for an audition or for a sale at Bloomingdale's. And everything you put on your body, no matter for what occasion, has a personal history. Without conscious attention, you *know* whether you like or dislike something, are proud or ashamed of it, whether it is old or new, enhances or spoils your self-image, is clean or soiled, is comfortable or fits badly—and all these elements intuitively condition **what you do about them, how you adjust to them physically and psychologically.** Once you have unearthed this powerful source for your state of being, you will realize that one of the difficulties when you are walking from Olivia's house in *Twelfth Night,* for instance, arises when you are dressed in Renaissance garb and have put on the "costume," rather than her clothing, for which you have supplied no personal history.

Having provided you with an outline of the steps on which to base your own exercise, let me offer a specific example of my own:

It is eight o'clock on a pleasant Monday morning in October. I'm on my way to the doctor for my annual checkup, lucky to have landed the first appointment. I'm wearing my natty blue jersey slacks and jacket, black jazz shoes, and black purse. After a few minutes of fruitless waiting in front of my building on Washington Square, I have walked to the corner of Waverly Place and Sixth Avenue for a better chance of getting a cab. I stop at the curb and look down the street. Traffic is very light. A few cars have been stopped by the red light near Lamston's store two blocks away, and there is no taxi among them. Since my right knee is slightly arthritic, I shift my weight to the left leg and adjust the shoulder strap of my bag for greater comfort. I speculate about the state of my underarms: Should I have shaved them to look nicer for the doctor's examination? But there was no hot water in the apartment. I wonder if it will be turned on in time for my husband's bath. I look for a taxi again. No luck. I walk a few steps to the subway entrance next to the bank behind me and consider taking the train. I change my mind, stop to check my neat appearance in the reflection of the bank window, fluff up my hair, and, after a quick look down Waverly to see if a cab might be coming from that direction, I make myself comfortable at the curb again. I see the coffee shop across the street and dream about the breakfast I wasn't allowed to eat. I speculate about the doctor's reaction to the weight I've gained and look to see if my tummy bulges. I suck it in. I check my shoes to see if they are properly laced. They are, but I decide I need new ones. I notice a crack in the sidewalk and try to walk along it without teetering. I recall how the last cabbie yelled at me when I'd handed him a twenty-dollar bill, so I open my bag to make sure I have smaller denominations. I have a ten. I close the bag and readjust it on my shoulder. The traffic is getting heavier so I step off the curb for a better view, crane my neck, and spot one taxi. It's occupied. After stepping back up on the sidewalk, I notice a gray hair on the sleeve of my jacket. I pick it off gingerly and let it float into the air from my fingertips. I consider my plans for the afternoon. Etc., etc., etc.

In order to record this example, I have had to give the event a particular sequence. If I were to repeat the above in an exercise, the order in which I gave attention to the inner and outer objects would vary, even *what* I gave attention to and what I did *about* it would differ— except for my arrival at the street corner and the actions of looking for a cab. *Never* blueprint or regiment at which point you become aware of and deal with such things as a crack in the sidewalk, a store across the street, a shoelace, or lint on your clothes. If, by *chance*, a certain order does repeat itself, it should result only from logical needs, not because it has been "set." Everything must spring from your *presence* in the circumstances on that particular day, from complete understanding of yourself in that place and what you want there, and from your knowledge of the past and expectations about the future.

I should also warn you not to attempt re-creating imaginary *animated* objects such as people, animals, cars. Remember that I chose an *early* hour in Greenwich Village for my example, a time when the streets are almost empty. I visualize the traffic stopped at a red light. Choose a bus stop or subway platform that is nearly deserted, or an isolated corner of a park if you are waiting for someone. Trying to produce responses to moving vehicles whizzing past or imaginary passersby is a deadly trap for indicating and illustrating and, in any event, is rarely required in a legitimate play. Such problems are also unrelated to the one I'm asking you to solve in this exercise.

When you have succeeded in FINDING OCCUPATION WHILE WAITING, you will be able to find an *existence* on a bare stage to sustain you for a minute or two without any need to perform little "entertaining" tasks, without actor's tension or anxiety about being boring. You will be **as interesting and as interested as a cat** who waits for its playmate to move, allowing for **a free flow of attention between inner and outer objects, between primary and secondary objects and your adjustments to them** as they arise from your past, present, and future circumstances in this place which you have made real to yourself.

18

The Eighth Exercise: Talking to Yourself

W ORK on a MONOLOGUE has taken on an importance totally out of proportion to the essentials of an acting technique, all in the name of pursuing a "career." As a guest teacher in colleges, universities, and workshops from coast to coast, even in high schools for the performing arts, I am continuously presented with monologues in lieu of scenes between two or more actors. When I question the teachers at these institutions about their reasons for this peculiar emphasis on a type of expression which occurs so infrequently in plays, one that is almost always peripheral to the main action, they insist that unless the actors learn how to use them for *auditions,* they won't get jobs. They shrug off my response that even if the actor does on occasion attain enough proficiency in his monologue to *land* a job, it is unlikely that he will *keep* it when he hasn't learned how to *inter*act with the other characters in the play. Emphasis on monologues is a total evasion of acquiring an acting technique, in my opinion.

The term itself is usually misunderstood. A monologue, or soliloquy, is defined by Webster as "the act of talking to oneself." Greedy publishers and editors eager to exploit the unskilled actor's thirst for self-promotion have compiled entire books for actors, inaccurately called *Monologues,* which are filled with long *speeches* lifted from scenes of plays—speeches that were originally intended to be addressed to another character or characters. As long as someone is in earshot, a single word can elicit a response. Such a speech constitutes a *dialogue*! The person being addressed can silently interrupt or *talk back* with a snort, a look of disdain, or a smile of approval, with a yawn or grunt of disgust, or by a turn away. The *continuity* of verbal action is dependent on this kind of dialogue. It is true even when the other character is merely a sounding board for a personal problem. When, because of ignorance, old-fashioned tradition, or for *any* idiotic reason, an actor removes the prescribed presence of another character and talks into space or to an empty chair, he violates the truth. He immediately manifests aspects of worn-out theatrical conventions. An interesting by-product of such a mistake is that at a future date, should the opportunity arise to play the role from which he has lifted the speech, the actor will have ruined this section for himself. It will be stuck in the artificial shape he had once given it, compounded by the felony of repeated use for auditions.

Now that I have given my reasons for the negative aspects of work on monologues—an overemphasis on "solo" acting, a confusion about the meaning of the term itself, and its resulting misuse—let me deal with the historical development of monologues and with a truthful approach to preparing you in this exercise for the rare occasions when you may be called on to execute them in a play.

In dramatic literature, actual monologues—not to be confused with stage "asides," or words to be addressed directly to the audience—have undergone many changes in form. The serious actor may want to study their origins. Based on the Aristotelian concept of the "catharsis," they arose with such dramatists as Aeschylus, Euripides, and Sophocles. The written play re-emerged after the Dark Ages in the sixteenth century, flowering through the seventeenth and eighteenth centuries in the comedies and dramas of Shakespeare, Marlowe, Sheridan, Wycherley, Goethe, Schiller, Racine, Molière, and their contemporaries, presenting us with many kinds of monologues. Monologues are also provided by nineteenth-century Russian writers like Turgenev, Ostrovsky, Gogol, Chekhov, and their European, Scandinavian, and American contemporaries.

From one epoch to the next, playwrights have devised new usages for monologues or adjusted them to fit a current fashion in the theatre. Whether their emphasis is on the poetic, on selective realities, or on the naturalistic, whether their monologues deal with plot development or with the psychological problem of a specific character, they usually **represent a part of the character's thoughts.** (In rare cases such as in O'Neill's *Strange Interlude* the words are meant to be the character's *unspoken* thoughts.) As a rule, they are **the words that arise audibly though involuntarily from a human being who is in crisis!** "To be, or not to be, that is the question."

But before tackling the classical writers and their overpowering poetic realities or even the realistic monologues of our own time, we should learn through self-observation **why, when, and how we talk to ourselves aloud.** I have purposely placed this problem near the end of the exercises, so it can be put into proper perspective within the broad range of the human experience and, above all, because all of the principles that have been practiced in the previous exercises must be applied to it.

Because **talking to oneself out loud is involuntary,** the actor sometimes has trouble pinning it down in his personal life. Some people are unaware that they do it at all. An auditor in class once interrupted to disagree with me, claiming that only madmen talk to themselves. When, preferring not to argue, I reminded him that "to audit" meant to listen, not to speak, he demurred. But within a minute, he began muttering loudly at the back of the room, "She's nuts! Nobody does that. Just drunks on the street. Doesn't know what she's talking about!" And on and on he went, oblivious to the fact that he was indeed talking to himself.

On my initial hunt for an understanding of this process, I went to Dr. Palaci, the psychologist, who explained that **the underlying reason for verbalizing when alone is a need to gain control over one's circumstances.** This made sense to me when I related it to the words I was frequently aware of uttering aloud, which were EXPLETIVES. When I cursed aloud, emitting a *damn!* or any or all of the other, more meaty, four-letter words, I knew they were evoked by *frustration* about something that had happened, was happening, or would probably happen. I soon discovered that frustration could also lead to an extension of an expletive, to whole or broken sentences: "God damn it, how could he *do* that?" "Oh hell, she's full of . . . !"

But I didn't understand how the common kind of chatter of which I am capable, something I call LIST MAKING, would fit into the psychologist's explanation. Before leaving for the store or an appointment, I often verbalize things like, "I need my checkbook," "Where are my gloves?" "Keys? Aha!" "Don't forget yellow onions," etc. I finally realized that I *did* need **control over a fear of forgetting**, that I verbalized **to help retain information, and to keep my thoughts organized.** The more rattled I was, the more I talked aloud.

Still another kind of verbal utterance occurs when we are occupied with something like an ordinary household task, when we COMMENT ON OUR BEHAVIOR: "Dumbo, now look what you did," "Ooooh, you're doing this nicely," "What's the matter with you?" "Let's chop this up. Real fine. . . . Chop, chop, chop," "You're a good person," etc. My stream of vocalized approval and disapproval of my activities has often been interrupted by someone coming in to ask "Who are you talking to?" And, sheepishly, I have had to admit "To myself." It took me a while to realize that the reason for such words came from **a need to gain control over the boredom** of the routine itself.

Boredom can also cause PLAYING GAMES. When applying makeup in the morning, for instance, after a fat kiss on my image in the mirror, I might finish off with "You're so cute!" or "Yup! You're gorgeous." Or I make a grimace and snarl "You look like an old hag!" Or I take a closer look and bellow dramatically, "Dear God, *more* gray hairs!"

While busy with something like sorting soiled laundry, I sometimes combine all four kinds of talking: expletives, list making, commenting on my activities, and playing games. "This needs bleach. Christ, these socks could walk by themselves. White, colored, colored, white . . . Why am I keeping this shmatte? Oh, well . . . And this shirt! Into the ragbag with you"—with which I drape the offending garment over my head like a Spanish mantilla and stamp my feet like a flamenco dancer while dealing with the next few items of clothing. When making a bed or doing dishes, we sometimes play out our fantasies, such as pretending to be a movie star and imitating her speech and mannerisms: "I vant to be alohn."

And then of course, there is the **fifth kind of talking to yourself** which is at the heart of most monologues in plays, **when a person is IN CRISIS and looks desperately for control over his frustrations by trying to solve the problem.** We don't have to look for a major event in our lives to exercise this need. A humiliating experience with a producer or director can elicit an outburst the moment we've slammed the door behind us, knowing we're in the privacy of our home: "Jesus! Who does he think I am? An amateur? Read it again? With more emotion! No siree, Buster, you don't treat me like that! Stick to vaudeville. That's what you're fit for. Bastard. Son-of-a-bitch!" all the while ripping off one's coat, throwing down the script, and heading for the bar or the refrigerator. We also talk out the things we *wished* we had said or *should* have done under the circumstances. Slamming down the phone after a lovers' quarrel or a spat with friends or relatives, even with the super when he has refused to fix a leak, can produce lengthy private verbal eruptions—or monologues.

Before starting actual work on this exercise, spend a few days or more on self-observation and "self-listening." Take note of the times when you sigh, grunt or groan, ooh or aah, or voice expletives. **Pin down what you are doing at these moments. Pin down which particular inner and outer objects have elicited these seemingly involuntary utterances.** Discover how the contact with the smelly T-shirt you were putting in the hamper brought about "Peeyew, this stinks!" and how a sigh of rebellion sprang from an inner image of the aunt who'd given you such a hard time at lunch. In other words, **take note of the way in which your utterances come from contact with tangible outer objects or visualized inner ones.**

When you rehearse or present the work, these objects must always be psychologically fed and contacted anew when you execute the actions in order to arrive at "involuntary" spontaneity each time you deal with the problem that has just occurred, is occurring, or looms ahead.

If you are among those who believe they don't talk to themselves, you may be surprised to discover that words *do* sometimes follow an expletive or a groan; if they don't, they *could*. And, if you sense that they *could*, try them, voice them, let them fly. You might also want to review Chapter 8 on the subject of the animated body and mind to remind yourself of the necessity of determining your destinations. Remember that **we don't sit, rise, stand, or walk in order to think, but rather to reach the next destination, because this is equally true for talking aloud.** We are *always* thinking. You will soon become aware that **the thoughts you voice are only a part of your thought process,** that while uttering one thing, your mind is racing with other *nonverbal* thoughts related to the circumstances.

FOR THE PRESENTATION

After lengthy periods of self-observation, when you feel ready to work on this exercise, I suggest that you **choose an event that can provoke one or more of the first four kinds of talking to yourself.** When you have explored and answered the questions posed in the Six Steps (see page 134), begin to rehearse your task without *any* obligation to spoken words. Only when the physical actions have become reflex or habitual should you give fuller attention to the psychological springboards for the words, those that will allow them to pop. Avoid a rigid order of "scripted" words. If the need for certain words or sentences abates during a repetition of your task, leave them out. If new needs arise, go with them. Only after you have successfully presented an event during which you were honestly compelled into audible expletives, listed reminders, comments on your behavior, or game playing should you tackle the fifth kind of talking aloud—during a "crisis" situation. When you have thoroughly digested and correctly presented that particular problem more than once, you will have understood the physical and psychological realities of this aspect of human behavior and be ready to work on realistic monologues.

There are a few don'ts I'd like to alert you to. A common error is caused by a mistaken desire to let your audience in on your problem, to tell them the story. If I am reading at my desk at home, while turning the last page of a script in disgust, flailing it in the air or pushing it onto the floor, I might explode with "Don't do this to me. I don't need this kind of junk in my life. Uh-uh! I won't go!" I would never verbalize something like "I realize you're my agent and that I'm supposed to do what you want, but I don't like acting in the trashy plays you keep sending me. And I refuse to go to that audition you set up for me." Our words and sentences are not "arranged," they have little *external* logic or sequence. They have *inner* logic arising from their connection with the circumstances. We ourselves *know* what the story is and need only the words we believe will help us to understand or solve our problem, to gain psychological control over what's bugging us. Remember that no one else is present, that no one is listening to your "monologue." The humanness of your behavior will reveal what's important.

Actors seem to enjoy selecting circumstances under which they are preparing a verbal confrontation with someone at an upcoming meeting or before a phone call, practicing aloud what they plan to say. Although this is a rare occurrence, if it seems a valid subject for an exercise, don't forget that this kind of verbalizing is *also* not outwardly logical or consistent, that it has no syntax or precise phrasing. You are not *writing* a speech, but testing possibilities for making an impression, getting the upper hand, or settling a score. The words connected with the plan may be interspersed with comments of approval or rejection, even with some that are quite off the subject, those connected with your routine activities.

The most typical mistake, which has its origins in old-fashioned stage tradition, can also be blamed on a desire to inform the audience. It is to illustrate the "story" by physically acting out what we are talking about. Let me use the preceding outburst provoked by the terrible script as an example: **I must not outwardly place** the imagined agent who is the target of my onslaught anywhere in the room, on the sofa or in a chair or standing at the other side of my desk, and address him as though he were actually **there.** But **I must keep him in my mind's eye,** addressing him as if he would be seated at his own desk in his office, or opposite me in the restaurant where we last had lunch. My physical actions *while talking to myself* are connected with my immediate, reflex destinations, to tidy up my desk before making a phone call, for instance. If I threaten the agent by waving the script in the air, it is not directed *outwardly* at his imagined presence here in my room, but into the air en route to something like replacing it in its envelope. To take a different example, I may look heavenward for a *second* when addressing God with a "Please, God, let me do it better," or a "God, don't be mad at me," but I *don't* place God on a particular spot on the ceiling and talk to him as though he were visibly present there. Or, when Juliet looks at a star from her balcony while dreaming of Romeo, Romeo is *not* in the star, but *in her mind's eye* at the ball or on the street.

The practical application of this exercise to monologues from plays, contemporary or otherwise, should be delayed until you have understood and mastered the technique that truthfully evokes audible words when you are alone. Even so, I would like to review the principles that will eventually make it possible.*

Avoid the mistake of building a monologue only on the words. I myself make it a rule, after a careful study of the text, to *begin* the work by asking and looking for answers to **what "I" would do in the given place under the particular circumstances if "I"** *didn't* **talk,** because I have learned that words can only spring spontaneously from an orientated, occupied body. Once I have found identification with the character's psychological problem and *taken care of the physical life,* it is relatively easy to contact the inner and outer objects that propel me into the words. I try **never to complete the thought or find the answer to a problem** *before* **speaking,** as is so often done, **but rather to let the words travel toward a possible solution,** using them to arrive at answers to the problem. Otherwise, they will remain inactive, mere statements of fact or illustrations of feelings and attitudes. Even when talking about a past event, we are re-examining it in the present.

When you are experienced and limber in the execution of contemporary monologues, those in which you use a familiar idiom, you will be ready to tackle CLASSICAL AND POETIC MONOLOGUES. **Be assured that all of the above tenets remain true for them.** There are, however, several additional considerations to make. The young actor seems to be continuously caught between two stools when faced with the expression of unfamiliar, special, or magnificent language. In addition to being lazy about attaining perfect standard American speech, he either falls into the trap of traditional bombast, singsong intonation, and the "grand" vocal manner, believing that it is the only way to pay tribute to famous authors, or he rebels, remembering that this kind of performing had put him to sleep as a child when taken to see the "classics." Then he is often mistakenly lured into the opposite camp of tedious, naturalistic articulation and casual verbal attitudinizing.

The fine line on which the actor must find his balance lies not in between these two stools but far apart from both, *when the words*

---

* I will *not* deal with this again as a separate problem in Part Four, The Role.

have a powerful reality and are uttered by a human being. If, at first, the language seems alien, the answer to dealing with it is neither to intone or sound "grand," nor to sound "natural" or look for a "normal" tone or for the way the character "usually" talks. The playwright has provided *crisis* circumstances that are not usual, natural, or normal, and it helps me to know that, because of this, **I *need* the extraordinary language and must assume that "I" have never spoken like this until this moment.** To make the words real, study their *content,* look for their *meaning,* not their tone.

This brings me to the necessity for **providing the particular inner objects that must be selected for the phenomenal imagery of classical writers** and for contacting them as sources for the words. Gliding over them, supporting them only with general ideas or emotions, or landing on them to make sure the audience gets their meaning is not the answer. Let me use a few lines from a short monologue as a simple example. They are from *The Two Gentlemen of Verona,* when Julia tries desperately to piece together the love letter from Proteus after having spitefully shredded it.

> O hateful hands, to tear such loving words!
> Injurious wasps, to feed on such sweet honey
> And kill the bees that yield it with your stings!
> (I.2.)

The vision of stinging wasps attacking the bees in their hive connected with the "hateful hands" must be specific and inwardly contacted in order to feed these words of self-abuse. But, as previously stated, such problems lie in your future development. Don't put the cart before the horse.

Use this exercise to come to grips with the human process of talking to yourself when you are alone at home now, at the end of the twentieth century. Explore and present it many times under a variety of different circumstances.

19

The Ninth Exercise: Talking to the Audience

THROUGHOUT the centuries right up to the present day, playwrights have on occasion asked that a character introduce, interrupt, or conclude the action of a play by talking to the audience. This can pose momentous technical difficulties for the actor who, like myself, is hell-bent on finding a believable existence on stage, an impregnable reality for the world in which his character lives. When the goal is to perform, without a conscious awareness of being observed by creating a "magic circle" of action into which the attention of the audience will be drawn as if by a magnet, it may seem a complete contradiction in terms to be asked by an author to pierce this circle deliberately by making direct contact with the audience by talking to them. It has taken me many years to discover how to reconcile these seemingly conflicting demands.

First I had to remember that **when the writer asks a character to address himself to the people in the auditorium, he is *not* asking him to step out of character,** although he may ask him momentarily to suspend and step out of the circumstances within the play. Even when the device of a narrator is used, the narrator is defined as a specific character who is peripherally or centrally linked to the time and place of the play's circumstances, whether it be Chorus in the prologue of Shakespeare's *Henry V* or the Stage Manager in Wilder's *Our Town,* whether it is Tom setting the stage for *The Glass Menagerie* or Rosalind delivering the epilogue for *As You Like It.* It seemed impossible to keep faith with a character's life when, for example, as Rosalind I was asked to step from the forest of Arden in the sixteenth century directly into the twentieth century in New York, Chicago, or Los Angeles to confront the audience seated there. On the occasion of an opening night, was I supposed to address the critics, columnists, friends, and enemies all decked out in today's high fashion? How could I reconcile talking in Shakespeare's prose to a party of chintzy club women at a matinee, or to a group of corporate executives and their wives in the evening? How could I sustain a sense of truth when affected by a handful of drab tourists speckling an empty auditorium at the end of a run—or by my colleagues facing me in a studio, lolling about in their jeans?

The imaginary world we have created for a character's existence will instantly collapse when it collides with the reality of the world confronting us in the auditorium. To bridge this gap, we must **imaginatively make the world out front at one with the world on stage.** My own way of achieving this may be very personal, but I have passed it on with a large measure of success. If you find other ways that work for you, by all means stick to them. On page 154–156, when describing how to make primary use of the fourth side, I provided some of the tools that make it possible for me. And let me repeat that in every aspect of our work on a role, "Nothing is what it is, but we must make it so!"

Just as we have learned to project an imagined landscape onto the fourth side of the playing space in order to complete our faith in its reality and its connection to the life on stage, so we can create an imagined auditorium and audience out there, one that is in harmony with our character's needs and actions. If I were to deliver Rosalind's epilogue, I could well imagine that I was addressing the gentry seated in boxes around the periphery of the commoners standing in the pit of the Globe Theatre in the latter years of the sixteenth century. Or, I might decide that I was performing the play in a great hall at Windsor Castle or at Hampton Court for Elizabeth I, her courtiers and attendants. Once I have a clear visualization of the structure of the Globe auditorium, or of the great hall, I can project the landmarks of that interior onto the fourth side of the theatre in which I am playing, just as I placed them there to create a specific exterior landscape. This visualization need not be historically accurate. It serves its purpose as long as I *believe* in it.

A more difficult problem arises for particularizing the imagined *people* whom we must address. Since we already know that when we talk to someone he becomes our partner, it is logical to assume that **when we talk to the audience, they become our partners,** albeit silent ones. "Our" relationship to them must be constructed as precisely as that to any other character in the play; we must make them belong to the world of the play. Are they friends or foes, social peers or otherwise, familiar acquaintances or strangers, etc.? Before we can talk to them we must know what we want from them—to gain their sympathy, to win them over, to bully them into submission, to enlighten them—always taking into consideration the time and circumstances of this moment in the play.

Of course the very term *audience* can seem so all-encompassing that it becomes vague and general. But, if you think of any audience you have personally addressed in the past—at a high school or college assembly, at a union or club meeting, or at a session with your acting colleagues—you will remember that you usually contacted *one member of the audience at a time,* one whom you used to give you confidence, wanted to convince, to entertain, to appeal to, or to sway. Even when you were so frightened that you looked at the floor or over their heads at a pillar, exit sign, window, or house light, you felt as though you were talking to one known individual who seemingly represented the group as a whole.

Taking such facts into consideration, I always make selections of one, two, or three people, four at the most, for the partners of my character. I determine the psychological relationship to each one, "my" assumptions about him and what "I" want from him, even what "I" think he expects from "me." Finally, I clothe him in the appropriate period and transfer him to his seat in the auditorium. Once I know who my partners are, where they are, how they look, and what I want from them, it now only remains for me to know *where* to direct my attention when "I" talk to them to be able to believe in their presence among the rest of the imagined audience.

Essential to the retention of faith in our imagined partners is **to**

place them just above, to the sides, or in between the members of the existing audience, making it impossible to contact anyone actually seated there.

In total disagreement with those directors and actors who insist that direct eye contact should be made with people in the audience, I always begin by asking how they feel when they, themselves, sit out front and a performer looks them straight in the eye. They must have shared my own experience of discomfort and self-consciousness, of ignorance of what was expected, of a feeling of being abused by this act, which is in fact an act of aggression. If people are good-natured about being put on the spot in this manner, they often play back to the performer with exaggerated facial grimaces. If they are shy, they sink down into their seat or begin to adjust their hair and clothing, convinced that the entire audience is now looking only at *them*. If they resent being "used," they may yawn into the performer's face, stare him down, or challenge him with a sneer. Sometimes they even talk back, loudly and obnoxiously, to vent their resentment. If such reactions seem familiar, ask yourself what possible use they could be to the actor on stage for the furtherance of his character's life and verbal actions. If he looks someone in the eye, he must want to see him. So awareness of responses such as I have described can only stop the actor cold and make him wish he'd never looked there in the first place. In a night club or revue, eye contact might be a prerequisite for a stand-up comic when he uses (or abuses) a member of the audience, making him the butt of a joke for the sake of the rest of the audience. But when doing so, he deals with that person *improvisatorially* in conjunction with the person's spontaneous response. He is not obligated to an author's concept or text. An *actor* cannot change or improvise on the playwright's circumstances, the character's intentions, or a syllable of the text. He must justify them, identify with them, and bring them about anew at each performance.

In most theatres, the spill of light from the stage will illuminate only the first few rows of the auditorium. Behind them the rest of the audience is shrouded in a kind of darkness in which only vague outlines of bodies are visible. As long as it is impossible to make eye contact with them, these shapes are not dangerous. Rather than using any of them for my partners or trying to place my imagined partners *among* them, **I apply the technique of projecting objects on the fourth side to seat them near an exit sign, right next to an existing loge, at the base of the balcony rail, or at the top of an aisle.** Then my visualizations can stay precise without interference of conflicting realities presented by particular bodies in the actual audience.

To my joy, I learned that when I address my imagined people, the existing audience always feels included and drawn into the illusionary life which I am sharing with them. Without fear of being put on the spot as individuals, they are free to believe that "I," the character, am indeed talking to *them*. In different roles, with a change of circumstances and milieu, I always use the identical technique—for instance, when making "an aside" to an imagined courtier, lady-in-waiting, or duke seated in the King's loge during a performance of Molière's *Tartuffe* or *The Misanthrope,* or when letting an imagined lackey or coachman at the back of a rural playhouse in on a secret of the plot in a play by Sheridan or Wycherley.

It is not always necessary to assume that a character is talking to an audience per se or that their partners are actually seated in an auditorium. Within a playwright's circumstances we might imagine instead that our partners consist of one or more friends or neighbors or strangers, even enemies, who are observers of the action, whom we ask to participate in it. We can suppose that they have gathered across the street or are present at the far end of the garden. They may be seated at the other end of the room. They may even be someone peering in through the window. Let me take an example from Thornton Wilder's *The Matchmaker.* Near the end of Act IV, Dolly Levi is left alone in Miss Van Huysen's living room while the others, including Horace Vandergelder, are having coffee in the kitchen. Dolly is trying to make up her mind to marry Horace, to justify this intention. She begins with a monologue, talking out her problem with her deceased husband, Ephraim. The stage directions ask that "she comes to the front, addressing an imaginary Ephraim." Since Ephraim is not present in the room *or* the auditorium but rather *in her mind's eye, she is actually talking to herself.* Therefore, it follows that her physical behavior must remain connected to the circumstances of waiting in the room, and, even if a director demands that she come "to the front," the actress can establish a normal destination there (such as to get a glimpse of herself in a mirror on the fourth side). While talking, she might be taking off her gloves or arranging her hair for the upcoming meeting with Horace. Perhaps she doesn't come up front at all but readies herself on the sofa. When her "monologue" is finished, Wilder indicates that "she is now addressing the audience." If she is already seated, she needn't necessarily rise to talk to them, but she must become aware of their sudden presence and know what draws her attention to them. She must also know who her partners are and what they are doing there: Possibly they are friends from Yonkers who have been pestering her to stay faithful to Ephraim's memory or nosy neighbors who have been gossiping about her goings on. Perhaps they, too, are guests of Miss Van Huysen who had been standing by the window at the far side of the room, eavesdropping on her monologue. When all these questions have been answered, Dolly will know how to share her views with them about "rejoining the human race" and her beliefs in the value of money and how to put it to use.

In contemporary plays such as Peter Nichol's *A Day in the Death of Joe Egg,* similar circumstances exist. The characters are momentarily arrested from their behavior inside a room by the awareness of observers whom, in this case, they use as sounding boards to help them grapple with guilt about their handicapped child, Joe.

At the opening of *The Glass Menagerie,* Williams provides a stage direction for the narrator, Tom: "The narrator is an undisguised convention of the play. He takes whatever license with dramatic convention as is convenient to his purposes." This leaves the actor truly free to create whatever partner or partners will best serve his character, free to put them into whatever imaginary place will most actively stimulate his memories and his compulsion to share them.

Let me conclude with the problem posed in the plays of Bertolt Brecht by the very reason he gives—not in stage directions but in essays—for asking his characters to talk to the audience. In his theory about audience "alienation" (*Entfremdung,* in German), he states that when his characters interrupt the action of the play by addressing the audience with a speech, poem, parable, or a song, he wants the audience to stop to think, to examine the causes for the dilemma in which the characters find themselves, to draw parallels between these dilemmas and those of their own society. He wants the audience to be *dis*illusioned rather than so emotionally caught up in the illusion created on stage that it becomes fogged by it.

This theory and how to make it function in a production has been endlessly expounded upon by scholars and critics and has been confusing to many directors and actors. In my opinion, it is most often misinterpreted. I knew Brecht and his wife, Helene Weigel, personally, saw a number of productions of his plays in Germany and Austria, and was *not* confused by them. I also talked to many performers who worked with Brecht. The famous actress Therese Giehse played the title role in the original production of *Mother Courage*, which was directed by Brecht himself. When I wanted to know what he had asked for, she told me in detail how he had led her single-mindedly to an exploration of the character's subjective, psychological reality, to substantiate the very human behavior, *including* that entailed in all her addresses to the audience. There was never a question about breaking faith with the character's existence.

So, when I played Shen Te in *The Good Woman of Setzuan*, whenever I had to talk to the audience, I chose to imagine addressing my Chinese neighbors squatting on the curb across the street (at the back of the auditorium) or standing in the doorway of their shops (to one side of an exit sign), or other villagers who had congregated (at the top of an aisle) to watch what was happening, who needed information or understanding about my problems. As Shen Te, I asked them to beware, or to have compassion, or to draw the parallel between my struggles and theirs. In this way, Brecht's theories can be fulfilled by the very act of interrupting the play to clarify the character's position *and* the position that the audience should take to the problem posed.

This is my personal solution and answer to an approach not only to audience address in the plays of Brecht but to the content of the plays themselves. It is also my answer to audience address in the productions of plays that were *not* written by Brecht, which are nevertheless often conceived to be presented willy-nilly in a "Brechtian manner." Directors and actors should beware of misunderstood, intellectualized "concepts" that will lead them right back to the old-fashioned theatrical traditions that Brecht was rebelling against.

FOR THE PRESENTATION

When addressing an audience, before tackling a play's problems of character identification, historic distance, and unfamiliar idiom, I once again ask you to make use of your own life experience. When practicing this technique, you will learn **how to talk to one or more acquaintances who are present on the fourth side of the stage only in your imagination.**

First, you must provide an occasion during which you relate **a personal experience, one that does not demand verbal responses or interruptions** but that requires more than just a few sentences. The subject matter can be something as simple as the plot of a film you have just seen. It can be about a remembered event from your child-hood, or about a run-in with a loved one, a colleague, or an em-ployer, or about a recent dream that scared or puzzled you.

I suggest that in your first attempt at the exercise you talk to only one person. Save an event at which you address several people for later efforts, until you have mastered this one. As always, it is crucial to cover the work given in the Six Steps to establish precise circum-stances for the occasion. Explore your relationship to the imaginary partner or partners, your objective for talking to them and, in par-ticular, **where they are, why they are there, even how they got there.** Be sure to determine whether your address is in answer to something just said, an interruption to it, a change of subject, or something instigated by you. *Know what occupies you physically while talking. Include the principle of eye contact with your listener.* * Remember that when telling a story we look at our partner *intermit-tently* to ascertain whether he understands, approves or disapproves, shares our point of view, etc., and that, if we look at him continu-ously, we lose our inner objects, the very sources we need for the re-creation of the event we are trying to recall. And remember that even one minute of stage life is a long time, so don't strain your need to talk by demanding a lengthy tale. Send the words only as long as they can be substantiated by their content with a continuity that does not require a verbal response.

* See pages 118–119, in Chapter 8.

20

The Tenth Exercise: Historical Imagination

Ask yourself how often you have attended a performance of a classical play, or, for that matter, any play set in a historical period, and truly believed that the costumed characters on stage were human beings with whom you could identify? If you are as lucky as I am, you may be able to count them on the fingers of one hand. You may have been interested, occasionally even exhilarated by the brilliance of the pyrotechnics exhibited on stage, but rarely were you allowed to forget that you were the spectator at a performance. When the power of the play itself moved and stimulated you in spite of a deadening performance, you may have rushed home to read or reread it, to savor its meaningfulness while imagining what an experience it would have been if the performance had brought the play to life instead of burying it under the dust of convention. Classical and historical plays are continually performed with the identical sound and shape no matter what their meaning and intent, in what period and place they are set, whether the characters speak prose or poetry. And when they are done in the current fashion adopted by directors who, in their attempt to overcome the tedium of predictable, traditional productions, merely superimpose a historical period on the play other than the one in which the dramatist has put it, the acting usually remains as stilted and artificial as ever.

Unfortunately, the actor himself too often accepts such representations. Exposed to them since childhood, he gradually becomes convinced that this is *the* way to do these plays, that this "style" is the appropriate one. He has seen it copied in high school, college, regional theatre, Off-Broadway, and Broadway productions, whose differences hinged only on the degree of the external skills of their particular directors, designers, and actors and on the extent of the available budget. He is also confused by the critical acclaim often bestowed on the flashier ones. He rarely questions the current fashion of "updating the material." He ought to. It certainly didn't enhance my faith in Chekhov's world when, in a "modern" version of *The Sea Gull*, Masha chewed gum instead of taking snuff.

The use of regional dialects can also be disconcerting. For example, in *Julius Caesar*, members of the senate sometimes speak in a mishmash of Southern drawls, Brooklynese, and Midwest twangs while the imported British star intones Brutus's words in affected Oxonian. Or in *Othello*, in order to alert the audience to Iago's lowly origins, the actor might be asked to speak the verse in an East End cockney.

Sometimes the very actor who is convinced that both the traditional approach and the imposition of "modern" gimmickry on classical plays fall short of vitally communicating the meaning of a play finds himself in the worst kind of dilemma because he doesn't know what to do about it. Many an experienced player who works from the inside out and is able to identify with *contemporary* characters with all their human complexities stumbles when approaching characters whose milieu, speech, and clothing are unfamiliar to him. Confronted by historic distance, his faith crumbles, and he fails to understand how his prior training can be of service to him.

If you share my desire to make a real revolution in the theatre, to bring the classics to audiences in all their glory, newly and vibrantly alive, we must unearth the real roots of the existing problems. The first lies in a terrible **misconception of the meaning and use of the word** *style;* the second arises from a **lack of historical imagination;** and the third, which I have already addressed in Chapter 3, rests in **the actor's poorly developed voice, speech, and body.** In this chapter I want to deal with a theoretical understanding of "style," as well as with historical imagination. Finally, I want to illustrate ways of developing this kind of imagination and how to put it to use in an exercise.

STYLE

What *is* style? According to my dictionary, it is a designation, title, "distinctive manner of expression," and its synonym is *fashion*. And what is *to create*? It is "To bring into being; to cause to exist." By now we must know that if we want to bring a character (or a baby) into existence we cannot predetermine its form, shape, or sound—its style. **Style is a label given to a finished work by critics, scholars, and viewers.** It does not belong in the vocabulary of a creator. If you give stereotypical consideration to the form or sound of a character before or during your exploration of it, you will box yourself in, cut off a flow of creative imagination, and place yourself on the wrong side of the footlights. You will also be sitting in the formalist's seat, no matter how much you may pretend that you're not. I have continually stressed that such things as tempo, rhythm, mood, timing, energy, "louder-faster-funnier," are all the *results* of human needs, intentions, and their consequent actions. It should be obvious that the same holds true for style, and that we should therefore avoid any preconception of the style or "manner" of a character's behavior. THE SOUND AND SHAPE OF A FINISHED WORK IS THE PRODUCT OF THE *DIRECTOR'S CONCEPT* OF THE *PLAYWRIGHT'S CONTENT* EXPRESSED BY THE *LIFE OF THE ACTOR*. **It is our job to explore the content of the playwright's world,** his vision of it, and to find identification with it. Then we will be able to give cause and substance to our selected actions—and a style will be *the result.** The tendency to categorize the plays they are going to work on, to label them with a ready-made idea of presentation (as farce, satire, tragi-comedy, neoclassicism, avant-garde, neorealism, surrealism, absurd, black comedy, epic, à la Brecht, etc., etc.), is deeply ingrained in most performers. They continually at-

---

* Ben Shahn's book *The Shape of Content* (Cambridge: Harvard University Press, 1957) and Paul Klee's *On Modern Art* (London: Faber and Faber, 1948) were particularly illuminating to me on this matter, even though they are both about painting.

213

tempt to justify this notion, failing to see how it enchains them. Recently, after a long discussion of the matter in a class, when everyone finally seemed convinced by my point of view—that working from the inside out bears the freshest fruit—one of the actors threw in almost as an afterthought, "Yes, but what about Noel Coward? You *do* have to do *him* with a certain style, don't you?" The other actors groaned, but I patiently asked him what he meant by "certain style." After much hemming and hawing, he had to admit that he meant a swift delivery of lines and an even swifter "picking up of cues." His opinion was based on the manner of representation he had seen applied to Coward's plays, to which he had become accustomed. Even sadder, when I asked if he enjoyed watching this kind of performing, he replied, "Not particularly."

As long as we stand outside of the play, or sit in the director's chair, or view our work from a seat in the audience, *and* as long as we misuse our education to arrive at academic editorializing and intellectualized commenting while working on a role, we will continue to be trapped into clichés, into stale predictability, into playing "in the manner of. . . ." If we aspire to bringing to life the people we are going to portray, if we demand of ourselves that they walk and talk, see and hear, touch and are touched as they interact with the other characters in the play, **we must find our way into a playwright's particular world by exploring its content and meaning, by looking for identification with the human struggles in that world.** When we succeed in doing so, we may shamelessly accept a critical judgment that *we have arrived at a perfect style for the play.* If, on the other hand, in a mistaken hunt for reality or for lack of skill, **we fail to identify with the dramatist's vision of reality,** or if we willfully ignore it or simply bend it to suit our own limited vision of reality, **we may rightfully be accused by the viewer of having no style.**

The first barrier on a journey into a previously unfamiliar world is often thrown up by the actor's sense of historic distance.

HISTORICAL IMAGINATION

Many actors never fully shake off the childish notion that the real world came into existence only on the day of their own birth, that everything preceding it was a kind of fiction in which a strange breed of one-dimensional, costumed figures moved about and posed, amidst scenic illustrations of palaces, battlefields, formal gardens, or period drawing rooms while speaking in measured, mellifluous tones. Some of the blame for this can be put on traditional theatre and trashy historical films, but much of it lies in the miserable, dry, and impersonal way that history is usually taught, increasing the feeling that history is fiction, and boring fiction at that. But before we can persuade an audience that our character—from ancient Greece or medieval Denmark or Victorian England—is alive and kicking, we must believe it ourselves. We have to understand, not just with our heads, but in our hearts and souls that, since the beginning of time, human beings have been *human* beings! They have *always* eaten, slept, made love, washed and dressed, worked and played, been born and died. They have always been capable of love, hate, jealousy, greed, generosity, compassion, and cruelty. They have prospered or suffered, sought power, were enslaved by it, accepted it or fought against it, whether they were kings or corporate executives lording it over their subjects, ladies-in-waiting or secretaries currying favor, whether they were soldiers resting in the fields of Runnymede or Vietnam, girls dressing for presentation at court or for a prom. What separates them and brings about differences in their *external behavior* is caused not only by the differing landscapes, clothing, and objects they handle, but by the influence of the particular *social order*, its culture, values, fashion, and manners. These are the things we must explore.

Both the purpose and the nature of our research into history differ completely from those of an academician. Chronological dates and facts about wars and treaties, succession of reigns, shifting global empires, crusades and revolutions, and critical evaluations of these events are not the issue. Our aim is to open the doors of the imagination, to make the past come to *life*, to find identification with the differing social mores, to be able **to convince ourselves that we exist in the given world of a dramatist,** the world into which he has put the play. Unlike the scholar's, it is a totally subjective approach in which literal-mindedness or pedantic accuracy can become a dangerous deterrent. We can take a lesson from Shaw, who insisted that he was not interested in history literally as recorded, only in the way he perceived it. He made imaginative use of it with relevance to his own society from the artist's, not the scholar's, point of view.

When we think how much today's society changes even within a decade and how quickly we adapt to shifting values, fashion, manners, and idiomatic expressions, consciously or otherwise—even when we rebel against those that exist—we will see how readily we can adopt those of another time. In order to substantiate the human realities of a particular period in history and to find relevant transferences we can re-educate ourselves. When we tap the available sources in literature, historical biographies, paintings, sculpture, music, pottery and artifacts, and those we contact as tourists, **we must experience everything personally,** imaginatively identifying with it, putting ourselves into it as though *we* were walking on those floors, drinking from that goblet, climbing into the canopied bed in that ruffled nightshirt, extinguishing the taper on the little table at the bedside, listening to the horses clopping on the cobblestones below our window—whether we are reading about it in a novel or biography, looking at it in a painting, or traveling through a historic house in Boston or in Europe. Our job is **to make ourselves participants in other worlds** until we can see, hear, touch, taste, and smell them. The fact that contact with such sources may also broaden one's education and be esthetically edifying is a wonderful by-product. Sometimes a particular artist succeeds in sucking us into another time, doing the work for us even while we think we are merely fulfilling a scholastic requirement. Tolstoy's *War and Peace* convinced me that *I* was Natasha, that Tolstoy was writing about me. I still have memories as real as my own about those years in nineteenth-century Russia. These memories served me well, together with other sources and biographies, when I played in Turgenev's *A Month in the Country.*

Some actors intuitively exercise their imagination in the various ways I've described, but if the idea is new, you may be unsure where to begin. Start with a classical play or role that interests you. An easy, direct way to substantiate the realities of the period in which the play is set is to look for a good biography of the dramatist. Michael Meyers's book, *Ibsen,** vividly draws you into the world that shaped

* *Ibsen: A Biography* (Garden City, N.Y.: Doubleday, 1971).

Ibsen's themes. When, for example, as a young man he first arrived in Oslo, he was appalled by the sight and stench of raw sewage running in open conduits through the streets. *An Enemy of the People* immediately comes to mind, making it easy to identify with Stockmann's fight to destroy the polluted water system. Nora Helmer was inspired by one of Ibsen's actual acquaintances whose struggle for self-liberation was even more terrifying than the one in *A Doll's House*, but reading about the real person's struggle gives a strong sense of the social and sexist values of those days, illuminating the causes of Nora's oppression, the seeds of which are still in existence. Ibsen's personal terror of heights lends credence to that of Solness in *The Master Builder* and Rubek's in *When We Dead Awaken*, relieving the actor from an obligation to mere symbolism when dealing with the tortuous self-justification of ruthless behavior in the creative artist. In the case of the latter play, if you also read about Auguste Rodin and his relationship to his disciple Camille Claudel, who served as models for Rubek and Irene, you will come upon so many realities that the characters will pop from the pages as potentially fully dimensional human beings. Among the many biographies of Shaw, Margot Peters's *Bernard Shaw and the Actresses*** is still my favorite. It personalizes his daily life and point of view about his world so vibrantly that you can truly believe you are a part of it. Consequently, his characters begin to breathe in a way that makes it easy to shake off preconceived notions of a "style" for playing them.

Many *auto*biographies and diaries are available by people who weren't particularly noted for special achievement in their fields, but who have been published because of their insight, wit, and charm in reflecting their societies. These books are wonderful sources for details of daily living in historical times. A helpful librarian will steer you to those relating to the period on which you are working. There are also many written by the geniuses of their eras. The life of the Renaissance, which began to pulse in my veins when I visited Florence and the neighboring Siena and San Gimignano, opened up even more when I read *The Autobiography of Benvenuto Cellini*. Suddenly I had a sense of the prevailing spirit of bravado and derring-do, the individual's sense of destiny which bordered on egomania, coupled

---

* Garden City, N.Y.: Doubleday, 1980.

with the awareness that death was always lurking around the corner. I could identify with an artist's complex relationship to his patrons in the nobility, his enslavement by them as well as his need of that patronage—not psychologically unlike today's struggle between the artist and his producer or manager. Of course, I also learned about their eating, drinking, and lovemaking, how they brawled and caroused and worked *and worked*. All during the reading I pretended to do so in the same way.

My memoir, *Sources,** is filled with examples of the games I play when traveling, always imagining that I live at another time in the place I am visiting. I have played them since childhood and still engage in them whenever possible, sometimes for months at a time, fourteen hours a day, until I fall asleep exhausted, continuing these fantasies in my dreams. (My husband once remarked that I should have married a millionaire able to indulge my never-ending thirst for this kind of tourism.) Everything I see and touch, taste and smell and hear in the countryside or streets and gardens of the cities, in the palaces and cottages, churches and fortresses, museums and galleries, even restaurants and wayside inns, provides me with proof positive of the realities of history. In Rome I can transfer myself to the era of my choice within a range of more than two thousand years. When walking on the ancient pavement of the Forum, it is easy to imagine being Calpurnia accompanying Caesar on his way to the senate one day, and a Vestal Virgin—or her slave—about to be interred alive in one of the tombs the next. On another day, one can stand in the Piazza Venezia to imagine being addressed from a balcony by Mussolini.

In England, abetted by all the biographies I have devoured about their kings and queens, leaders of uprisings, religious zealots, and "heretics," I have often played out my transferences. At such landmarks as the Tower of London, I have become one of the people, perhaps Elizabeth the First herself, being brought as a prisoner through Traitor's Gate. I have read the messages scratched into the stones of the cells as though I had written them, knelt at the prayer stands, and peered through the slits of windows for a last, desperate look at the sky. Walking past the eerily peeling trunks of the beech trees toward the actual block where Anne Boleyn and so

---

* New York: Performing Arts Journal Publications, 1983.

many others lost their heads, I've shivered with fear that I might be next. At other times, I've imagined that I was a lady in attendance to a royal prisoner, or the mistress of a courtier in residence in the Tower's palace. Such transferences are usable for the bloodiest of Elizabethan plays.

I am always wildly impatient with colleagues who, when accompanying me, ignore these paths to historical identification, who look *at* everything as though they had to fulfill an educational chore. (By the way, I never take the *prescribed* tour of a landmark, following behind guides, who pander to the average visitor, because they ruin my fantasies with their memorized prattle.)

If you need further prodding of the imagination, read one of the exciting travel books filled with personal anecdotes to point the way. Those of H. V. Morton are very stimulating, even though they're not recent. If you haven't yet been lucky enough to travel abroad, begin at home. Explore your own city and those you visit. Take the walking tours recommended and described in personal detail in travel books and imagine how you would participate in the life connected with the various landmarks. In them you will find realities to substantiate daily life in the United States for the past three centuries. I sometimes wonder how many actors have imagined what it must have been like to sit next to Eugene O'Neill at a rehearsal of one of his plays when walking past the Provincetown Playhouse on MacDougal Street in New York? How many have gone to the Players' Club on Gramercy Park, the home of Edwin Booth, or to The Little Church Around the Corner where he was buried, and pretended to be his colleague? Once you have learned how to make yourself belong to one period of history, you will know how to apply the same principle to *any* time.

Let me take Oscar Wilde's *The Importance of Being Earnest* as an example, since so many young actors seem to enjoy working on Jack, Algernon, Gwendolen, or Cecily while continuing to fall into the trap of playing in the tedious "style" they think is required. Begin by asking what it is about these upper-middle-class people in London during the time when Edward, Prince of Wales, was setting the tone of frivolity and excess, that makes you care about them, even though their life-style was so different from your own? What makes you laugh? **We laugh and care when we recognize something about *our-***

selves in the behavior of *others.* **It is this recognition which must be brought to the characters** rather than our historical distance from them. We don't have to be scholars to see that Wilde is spoofing slavish needs to belong and shine in society. Much of his world is available to us on the printed page of the play itself. Without further research, the eccentricities of behavior, the assumed elegance, the flowery language, even the fanciful recurring non sequiturs reveal the etiquette and the hilarious social mores of high society in those days. What makes us laugh, even when we are not consciously aware of the reason while reading the play, is that the characters *impose* these fashionable affectations on such basic human instincts as to pursue adventure, fall in love, court and woo, use one-upmanship in competing with rivals, to gain acceptance and be in the swing of things. Language, clothes, landscape, interior furnishings, customs, and the nature of etiquette are different from our own—but that's all. We must remember that adherence to a prevailing fashion exists *now* as idiotically as it has always done. As with our instincts this need has remained unchanged. Today, as young people strive for the opposite of contrived artificiality, and the "natural look" is "the in thing," hours are spent on deliberately mussing, tangling, and spiking the hair so it won't look combed or brushed. Men go to beauty salons to "sun-bleach" their hair or to have permanent waves for a curly, tousled appearance. T-shirts and designer jeans are torn at the seams, holes are made in them, knees dirtied, elbows patched, fabrics bleached to look old, all to conform to the carefree look. Sometimes the manufacturer supplies jeans already in these conditions. Slouches are cultivated, feet in dirtied sneakers are flung on polished furniture, and the latest slang, punctuated by as many four-letter words as possible, is studiously practiced—as self-consciously as the characters in *The Importance* cultivate and imitate *their* fashion's vanguard.

We must recognize a very important fact that conditions the behavior of the characters in this play, which at first may also seem to separate us from them: They don't have to work for a living. To find a transferable situation, one that is psychologically comparable, that brings about the same need to wrestle with boredom by manufacturing dramatic conflicts, a desire for mischief-making, one in which cockeyed values become meaningful and irrelevant things take on weight, you have only to think of how you respond to people and events when on a vacation. Think how feverishly you look for excitement, for change, and especially for self-gratification, on days that stretch out before you without responsibilities or feelings of genuine accomplishment. Think of the emphasis you put on your appearance and manners when visiting a resort, for instance, how you try to conform to what is expected of the elite, not only when socializing with other guests in the salons, restaurants, and recreational areas, but even in your own room when dealing with hotel employees. (This comparison to a vacation is equally useful in finding psychological realities and needs for countless other plays that deal with the idle rich.)

After reading the play, in the search for identification, you will probably want further substantiations for the realities of your character's life. Do as I have already described by reading novels, diaries, letters, and biographies of the time. Look at paintings and listen to music of the time. Often a film about the period is helpful in filling out interesting details. When exploring daily behavior, social customs, and rituals, remember always to imagine how *you* would participate in them. Never file away academic facts about them in order to imitate how and what *they* used to do.

Our aim is not to make historically accurate replicas as dusty as the shelves from which we borrowed them, but to bring our characters to life with relevance to our own world. Backed up by the psyche and our physical senses, everything we say and do, down to the smallest object we handle, must become our own. In this case, the airs we assume must impress the others in our life on stage and are not to be used as illustrations to show the audience how affected Algernon or Gwendolen are supposed to be. Explore simple things such as what was expected of you in those days when making a social call, pursuing a courtship, taking a carriage ride, hanging out at your "club," or participating in the ritual of teatime. (Today we call it "happy hour.") Discover how important it can become to pour tea without leaving a smudge on the silver, ivory, or ebony handle of the pot, to pour from the proper height without splashing. Assume that the way you hold the fragile cup and saucer, the daintiness with which you sip, is proof of your gentility—moreover, that it is your *custom* to perform these actions with elegance. Adjusting to such differences is no more mysterious than to those in your own manners when you are eating from fine tableware and drinking from crystal glasses at an elegant restaurant or at the table of a rich friend or relative, compared with your behavior when, seated on pillows on the floor of a friend's "pad," you drink from soda cans, mugs, or jelly glasses and eat with plastic forks from paper plates.

We should not be intimidated by the differences in a period's clothing when we become aware of our personal chameleon-like ability to adjust to fancy evening dress, to a business outfit, and to the accepted "casual" wear of our time. Throughout this book I have stressed the importance of the clothing we put on our bodies, how profoundly it conditions our state of being, sense of self, reflex behavior, and, at times, our primary actions. We now know that, in life, everything we have on has a personal history: where and when each article of clothing was procured, whether we like or dislike it, are proud or ashamed of it, whether it is comfortable or not, in good or bad condition, right or wrong for the occasion, etc. We know that even our underwear has relevance in particular circumstances. We have learned that how we walk or run, sit, stand, or pursue any activity is influenced by what we are wearing. We understand how to apply this principle to contemporary characters by giving everything we wear in the play a pertinent history and endowing it with our character's realities. Since most of the apparel is familiar and similar to our own, this isn't difficult to do. However, many actors fling this training to the winds when confronted with a different period in time, hoisting instead a red flag signaling: "*Achtung!* Costume play!" (The very word *costume* still has connotations of something worn by mannequins, people on parade or at a masquerade, or by other actors, rather than by human beings.) They carry this notion into rehearsals, into fitting rooms where they pose before the mirror in imitation of photos, historical drawings, or famous stars, finally bringing their struttings to the finished performance, stuck in the mold of the old-fashioned actor from which they thought they had escaped. Even a few noted designers make the same mistake when devising costumes that are merely beautiful or historically accurate replicas, that serve neither to clothe a human character nor as an illumination of the meaning of the play. We mustn't compound the felony by serving as models to show off these costumes. When actors uncover the *similarities* between putting on and wearing the clothing of another period and those of their own, they will find the way to satisfy the expectations of those designers who know how to provide us with **garments that create the very essence of the characters** we want to bring to life in another time and place, as they reflect and reveal our own.

Let me point to some of the ways in which the dictates of our *present* fashion determine logical physical adjustments to them (just as they always have in the past). When you put on a cinch belt or new jeans, or lace up the inside of a wasp-waisted gown or button a cummerbund, you will suck in your gut, not only in order to close the garment, but to retain and enhance the nice flat look of the stomach. If the jeans produce a sharp outline of your buttocks and you are proud of them, you will intuitively push out your behind a little, possibly swinging your hips as you walk, especially when in the company of a sexy partner. A man who is vain about his rippling chest and leaves his shirt unbuttoned will draw back his shoulders in such a way as to guarantee that it stays open. A lady's head position is influenced by a turtleneck when she is wearing makeup and doesn't want to stain the collar. The importance of the shoes on our feet (to which I continuously harken back because they are so basic to our physical life and state of being) should by now be self-evident. As I have said, it is hard to get Mrs. Warren's words out of my mouth at a first reading when wearing beat-up sneakers, and equally difficult to find the language of Mother Courage in high-heeled pumps—although they might serve me at rehearsals in reverse order.

The fashions of other times all have special aspects that dictate their physical adjustments. When a tightly fitting sleeve is made of silk taffeta rather than Lycra or stretchy Spandex, it will burst at the seam if the elbow is sharply bent. In order to eat or drink or pour tea, the arm must curve, and wrist action is needed for mobility. When a loose sleeve is finished off with an elegant flounce of drooping lace, the elbow will also steer clear of the body and the wrist will bend upward to keep the flounce out of a cup or plate while similarly occupied. If you wear large, jeweled rings on every finger and want the assembled guests to notice them, you will extend your fingers and raise your pinky whether you are playing cards or taking a walk in a formal garden. You will no longer raise your pinky, with or without a ring, merely because you believe it to be a stylistic requirement when playing Molière. You will sit or stand with a very straight back, not in imitation of period drawings, but because your character's tightly laced corset makes it impossible to slouch. You will avoid crossing your legs not only because it was considered impolite, but also because your two cotton petticoats make it impossible to do so without getting tangled in them. A gentleman may refrain from crossing his legs because he wants to retain and show off the perfect creases of his trousers (which were *not* made of permanent press fabric) and to avoid ruining the work of his valet in pressing them. When seated, he may stretch his legs and cross his ankles to reveal the latest natty spats. A lady wearing a bustle will *have* to sit sidewise on the edge of a chair to avoid squashing it, etc., etc.

In summation: When we explore what was worn, what was in *or out* of fashion, what adjustments were needed to something brand-new and to those that had become habitual, we must always examine the psychological relevance to the present and *wear the clothes* that we have endowed with all the physical and psychological properties that put our character in action.

How to begin living in the characters' clothes, when to begin dealing with the physical objects of the period, depends on the working conditions—whether they entail rehearsals for a full-scale production, for a workshop, for the presentation of a scene in class, or for the purpose of the tenth exercise. With the exception of a production, all of the research and consequent selections are up to you. When you have been hired for a role, the explorations will be led by the director and designer. If the management is generous, the director and designer, who should understand the importance of such things, will be persuaded to provide you with mock-ups of the costumes and semblances of the furnishings at the first rehearsals. If not, as regards your character's clothing and the objects he handles, I suggest that you consult with the director, and, after a careful study of the costume sketches, devise your own mock-ups. Put them together out of your personal wardrobe and belongings to use during rehearsals until the actual costumes and props are available. In any event, this is what you must do on your own when working in a studio in the absence of directors and designers, researching and devising all the essentials you need to put your character in motion in another period.

Most actors are pack rats and, no matter how poor, have a variety of useful things in a closet at home, or they have friends from whom they can borrow them. Women have one or more long "rehearsal" skirts, petticoats, nighties that have a Victorian or Elizabethan air, an evening dress to which they've attached a train, blouses with a peasant air or a frilly Edwardian look, a tailored shirt to befit one of Shaw's liberated females, for instance. They have amassed shoes, sandals, pumps, even bedroom slippers, that give a sense of other periods. Men have belongings like leotards and sweat suits from dance classes and gyms which serve the Middle Ages and the Renaissance, a vest or two, an old silk lounging robe or jacket, scarves or fancy hankies to use as flowing ties or ascots, capes borrowed from lady friends, belts to which they have attached a sheath for a sword, and so forth. Old sheets have been draped, sewn, or pinned to become togas, robes, or billowing skirts. You don't have to be rich to find access to items—such as gloves, walking sticks, umbrellas to serve as parasols, a beaded bag, or a cloth bag with a drawstring, and costume jewelry—to be transformed into the accessories of other times.

In class I have seen candelabra, a kerosene or hurricane lamp, snuff boxes, antimacassars, washbowls, quill pens, and ink pots turn up in various scenes, not so as to "dress a set," but to help genuine manifestations of behavior at a given time. Everything I have described has one thing in common. None of it looks outwardly like the real thing—nor need it do so. The visual *effects* and the accuracy of scenery, costumes, and furnishings are the responsibility of the director and designer who prove themselves at the opening night of a public performance. Our responsibility, up to that point, lies in using the rehearsals and classroom presentations as a testing ground for our explorations, making subjective, sensory use of all the elements needed to bring us to the actions of the life of another time.

Allow me to hammer home my point about using the imagination *creatively* when applying it to history just one more time. All the realities we hoard from travels, books, and the other arts to substantiate our faith in the existence of history should be kept *flexible* in order to adapt them imaginatively and selectively to the dramatist's vision of the world we are about to enter when we work on his plays. Shakespeare's point of view about ancient Rome and Egypt, for example, which reflects the violence and intrigues of his Elizabethan era, finds expression in a world totally different from the one perceived by the Victorian rebel and freethinker George Bernard Shaw when each of them deals with the lives of Caesar and Cleopatra. We, in turn, must envision their worlds from the standpoint of our own society. Then we too can call ourselves artists.

FOR THE PRESENTATION

In the nine preceding exercises, you have dealt with the technical problems that often arise to derail, short-circuit, or detract us from a continuity of life on stage, no matter what the play or the character may be. Until now, you have worked on these various problems from the vantage of *your personal life experience*, thereby developing habits of self-observation which, among other things, lead to a discovery of differing aspects of yourself as sources for the characters with whom you need to identify. You have also been applying the principles entailed in these exercises to scenes from the contemporary plays you present in class, as well as incorporating them in the roles that some of you are performing in professional or community theatres concurrently with your workouts in a studio.

For the first time, I ask you now to base an exercise on a character from a play. Since most of you already make use of the lessons learned from the earlier exercises when working on scenes in which the character's background and milieu are familiar to you, I want you to take a further step by exploring and substantiating the life of someone in a distant time, a time you consider to be history. (World War II, the McCarthy era, the dissident 1960s, which are very much a part of *my* life, even the events of the 1970s, may seem like history to *you*.) Go on a hunt for the roots of the characters in plays that interest you, for the environment that helps to shape them, for the things that will allow you to believe in their existence, and try to find personal transferences that enable you to step into their shoes and put them in motion. Every time I see a newborn baby yawn, sneeze, burp, screw up its face and turn purple with rage or frustration, or smile for the first time, I'm amazed that this tiny being is *so* human. Similarly, a light of recognition flashes on when, during my research into her past, I suddenly grasp that my character is also capable of such behavioral manifestations, *not* because they are necessarily relevant to *any* of her actions in the play itself, but because they are proof that she is alive for me. (Did it ever occur to you that Juliet might have burped after gulping a glass of water too quickly; that Hedda Gabler could at one time have caught a cold and sneezed; that Horatio might very well yawn when cramming for an exam at the university in Wittenberg?)

After deciding on a character, for the purpose of the exercise, **remove him from his conflicts in the play.** (Don't become bad writers or rewriters by filling out or expanding on the author's dramatic events.) **Put him into normal circumstances, giving him a habitual task** in order to discover how "you," as this person from another time, will eat, drink, rise in the morning or go to bed at night, spend a leisure moment, prepare for work or for a social event, etc., **finding identification with the fundamental life and behavior of the person** before you come to grips with the problems he faces in the play. In order to accomplish this, after studying the play, you will need to learn more about the time and place in which your character lives, what was worn and the kinds of objects that were used. Make use of the sources which have already been discussed in this chapter, remembering to approach the research subjectively, *not* so as to be able to give a dissertation on the period you are exploring.

Here is an example:

Let us suppose that Varya, Lyuba's adopted daughter in *The Cherry Orchard*, interests you. You know that the play is set on Lyuba Ranevskaya's country estate in Russia at the end of the 1800s. You have decided to explore Varya's early morning rituals in preparation for the day. You imagine it is a blustery day in March. The embroidered curtains at the window are drawn, and the small bedroom is dimly lit. The bare, scrubbed wooden floor is cold when you put your feet down as you get out of bed and you reach hastily for your felt slippers and put a robe over your long nightshirt. Early sunlight streams in as you pull back the curtains. You say a silent daily prayer before the icon on the wall. You consider making up the bed, but decide instead to let Dunyasha do it because there's so much to get done before the family returns from Paris the next day. You head for the washstand and fill the blue and white china bowl with icy water from the matching pitcher and splash your face with it, shivering all the while.

Holding back the collar of the robe and nightie, you use a cloth to wash your neck. With a little bar of brown soap, you wash your hands and wrists, then dry them with a heavy linen towel, which you then fold and replace on the washstand before heading for the wooden cupboard in which your clothes are kept. Etc., etc.

The value of taking such a simple journey through another time should be self-evident when you start to believe that you are living then, when **the past becomes your present.** Of course, this kind of an exercise is also excellent preparation for further work on the role for a scene in a class or for a full-scale production. If you think that the extensive research needed to find the realities of the environment and habits of the times is too much to justify such a short exercise, remember how many other magnificent plays are set in this period in Russia. If you explore the daily habits of just one character living at the beginning or end of the sixteenth century in England, you will also open the doors of reality to countless other plays.

Suppose you decide on an event during which your character is writing a message to a lover, a letter home, an answer to a formal invitation, or a thesis for the university. Depending on the historical time, you must find out what kinds of pens or quills, what kinds of ink or graphite sticks were used instead of today's typewriters, ballpoint or fountain pens, and those nice Eberhard pencils with soft erasers at the other end. On what kind of paper—pulp, linen, or parchment—did they write? How were notebooks or diaries bound? Did the ink flow smoothly or did it clot? How was it blotted? With a cloth? Or was it dusted with blotting powder which was then blown off the page? (When working on Wycherley's *The Country Wife*, you can have an inventive field day when writing Margery's famous letter to Mr. Horner, once you discover the proper writing materials and the problems they pose for her.) Whenever you have difficulty in answering questions about specific daily habits, clothing, or objects needed to fulfill your chosen task through the usual channels, consult a kind librarian. Those of you who live in New York City might use the fabulous services provided by the Lincoln Center Library to attain detailed descriptions, photos, and drawings of anything you might ever need: cosmetics, toilet articles, pots, pans, crockery, and personal accessories that were used at different times in history. It is delicious to discover amusing things like the gold or ivory needles used to scratch at lice crawling under one's powdered wig—and that it was *fashionable* to use them just as it was to paste interestingly shaped beauty marks on one's face to conceal large and small pimples.

As further examples for this exercise, you might take:

From *The Three Sisters*
> *Irina* preparing tea and a snack after her Italian lesson
> *Olga* correcting school papers late at night
> *Andrei* getting ready to practice his violin after an argument with Natasha

From *The Misanthrope*
> *Arsinoé* or *Célimène* doing her toilette before going visiting
> *Alceste* or *Philinte* preparing for a social call or a trip to the theater

From *Hamlet*
> *Laertes* coming home after carousing
> *Ophelia* preparing to retire

From *Hedda Gabler*
> *Thea Elvsted* coming from the market to prepare a meal for her husband
> *Eilert Løvborg* playing solitaire and drinking to avoid working on his manuscript.

21
Combinations

I have constantly emphasized that the exercises should be rehearsed and presented many times using differing events and circumstances until the application of their techniques to your roles when rehearsing or performing becomes a reflexive habit. After numerous presentations of the tenth one, you can only assume that you are now finished with the exercises *if* you fail to equate them with the pianist's or violinist's finger or bowing exercises, with the stretches and barre work of the dancer, or with those exercises of any other performing artist, all of whom understand the necessity of practicing until the day of their farewell performance. However, if you feel you have exhausted all the possible variations of each exercise and are no longer challenged by them (ha, ha), you can experiment with combinations of their individual problems. For instance:

> While shaving or putting on makeup, when most of the objects you use must be endowed with missing realities, you could be talking to yourself.

> While making or receiving a series of phone calls, you might have a bad cold or be drunk, simultaneously trying to find a misplaced object.

> You can place a historical character outdoors, waiting for a lover at the edge of a forest on a hot, muggy, mosquito-ridden day— or in the middle of a snowstorm.

And so forth and so forth. Every moment of work on an exercise will limber you up and act as sustenance for your work on the roles you develop and for their performance on stage. Good luck!

Part Four:
The Role

22

The Play

WHAT is the first thing to do to prepare for a role? You may have chosen a particular character for the purpose of personal exploration because you love it or have hopes of playing it in the future. It may have been assigned in a scene for presentation in a class or workshop, or you may have been engaged to play it in a full-scale production or film. Unless the circumstances are unusual, you will have been given a script or found out where to obtain one. Now—before doing anything else—READ THE PLAY in its entirety. This obvious advice is aimed at the numerous actors who fail to do so. Such an omission can be blamed on inexperience, poor training, a "show-biz" mentality, or on simple arrogance and laziness, with the assumption that whatever information or exploration is needed can be "picked up" at rehearsals. Some performers are so eager to start "acting" that they start reading their lines aloud "with emotion" before knowing what the first scene is all about, let alone the whole play.

The need to READ THE PLAY from beginning to end may also be news to those actors who have omitted or skimmed over the previous sections of this book and jumped straight to this one, determined "to get down to business." Unless they have read Part One, digested Part Two, and begun to practice the exercises in Part Three, Part Four will have little meaning for them.

The reasons for my insistence that the play be read, not only once

233

but again and again, are given in the dictionary under the verb *to read* and its synonyms:

To read:	to receive or take in the sense of
	to learn from what one has found in writing
	to become acquainted with
	to attribute meaning to
To peruse:	to make a study of
To understand:	to interpret the meaning or significance of
To foretell:	to learn the nature of by observing outward signs
To read between the lines:	
	to understand more than is directly stated

If you truly incorporate these definitions, the reading of a play will tell you much more than "the story." It will supply much needed information about your character and the world in which he lives. More importantly, it will provide you with the *specific* questions entailed in each of the Six Steps in Chapter Ten, page 134, as they now pertain to your role, those six guideposts that you have been using to bring a human experience on stage in the exercises. (Remember that we can only find *answers* to our problems when we know how to ask the right *questions*!) Intensive reading will point the arrows to the paths we will explore on the journey into the playwright's world.

Theoretically, when we turn to the very first page of a script we should read with *innocence*, with a wide open mind. However, unless both the play and its author are completely unknown to us, this is difficult to do. Even when one of their plays is brand-new to you, if the title page bears a name like Shakespeare, Chekhov, Brecht, Williams, Coward, or Neil Simon, you will most likely conjure up a manner of presentation before having read the first page of the text. In Chapter 20, in my discussion of style, I have stressed the dangers that lie in conceptual preshaping, how stultifying it can be to the creative imagination, to the interpretation of a play and a role. Be on guard against it.

In any case, your response to the first reading of the play will be similar to that of an audience. It will, of course, inform you about the time and place in which it is set and about the society that shapes and influences the characters' lives. You will know whether the play deals with its subject in poetic or prosaic terms. You will also visualize it and hear its tone. Instinctively, you will take sides, with feelings of empathy for the "good guys" and antipathy for the "bad" ones. You will know whether the play is funny, sad, or both, whether it is outrageously comic or fatefully tragic. And you will laugh *at* the characters' antics—usually when they are unaware that they are being funny—and weep *at* their travails, often when the character is *not* crying. You will laugh the most at the character you are going to play and cry the hardest when the character suffers or is being victimized. All of this can be expected.

There's nothing wrong with it, as long as you don't confuse these early responses with those of the characters while they are in action, struggling with their problems, caught up in their life in the play; as long as you realize that you are still on the other side of the footlights, not yet on stage. The first images you have and the sounds you imagine—how your character looks, walks and talks, with what delicacy or crudeness, how down-to-earth or flighty he appears, how plainly or fancily he speaks, in harsh or melodious tones—are destructive only when they are retained or in any way used as a guide to the future work. Such visualizations of your own and the other characters in motion should be discarded and forgotten as quickly as possible if you truly mean to part company with formalistic techniques and strive to create a role from the inside out—until you are at one with it.

While reading the play you may also have all kinds of intuitive sensory impressions about it and about your character. It may evoke feelings of robustness or of fragility, of clarity and crispness or of shadowy gloom, of harshness or ephemeral dreaminess, of gentleness or brutality. It may suggest particular colors, textures, music, paintings, and aspects of nature. It may sound or feel like Mozart or jazz, red velvet or olive tweed, a sapphire blue mountain lake or a puddle of muddy water, like a cut crystal tumbler or a crude terra-cotta bowl, a field of poppies and cornflowers or a forest of birches. Such totally *personal*, intangible responses to the material can be of value later in the work as long as you realize that they are *qualifying sources* not only for the play but for a state of being and for the behavior of a character in action; as long as you remember that *no* quality, feeling, or mood is playable by itself, that only actions have meaning and can communicate. Furthermore, unless we keep these subjective responses to ourselves, they become a hindrance. They are a private matter! While working on *Saint Joan,* I once eagerly shared my use of a Bach cantata for a specific section of the cathedral scene with a colleague. I was appalled to discover that the very thing that sent shivers through me and evoked feelings of nearness to a higher Being induced a spontaneous yawn in my fellow actor, to whom the mere name of Bach spelled unbearable boredom. A vast, cactus-covered desert suggests to me the epitome of desolation and loneliness, whereas it may represent something exhilarating and awe-inspiring to someone else. Discussions about the psychological or hidden meanings of such sensory "essences" are usually pointless, and attempts to reach an agreement about their applicability can lead into a swamp of generalities. I once heard a director complain to his cast: "You're playing in November tones. I asked for *October* tones! Let's try it again." Art and creativity are mysterious enough without any efforts to make them more so!

Once you have READ the play and PERUSED it, you will begin to *understand* it—that is, "to interpret its meaning or significance." Since it should always be our aim to serve the playwright, we must try to understand the intent of the dramatist, to define his theme, by asking WHAT IS THE PLAY ABOUT? When that has been answered, we will understand what place our character has in it.

Let me stress that an *intellectual* approach to the play, *a thorough analysis of it,* is and always has been the director's responsibility, *not* the actor's. However, if we want to claim the right to be creative participants in bringing it to life, we must be armed with more than our technical skills. We should be able to **make an *intelligent* evaluation of the play's purpose:** first, in order to be able to follow the director's analysis when he shares his intentions with us, and, perhaps more importantly, so that we **don't go interpretively astray in the initial stages of our homework on the role.**

Such preparation should also assure directors that there are no grounds for treating us like "pawns" or as "putty" in their hands—or like willful, uneducated, immature "children." Directors who pattern themselves after Gordon Craig will simply have to look elsewhere to find the "super-marionettes" they sometimes long for. *Most* directors are relieved when they don't have to do our work for us and grateful when we know how to translate their definitions and analyses of the play's through line or motif into personal layouts for our character.

Let me add, emphatically, that if a working relationship between director and actors is to bear fruit, the actor must never usurp the authority, nor court *dis*agreement, no matter how passionately he may want to defend his own findings. He should always remain flexible and look for the things that will bring his view into line with that of the director. The director is the captain and navigator of the ship; we are members of the crew. Every one of the officers and able-bodied seamen should have a degree of knowledge about the currents, the weather conditions, the dangers of sandbars, reefs, and icebergs, about the maps that are used and the routes to be taken. But they must put their trust in the captain's decisions and assume responsibility for each task he assigns to them. If just one member of the crew pulls in a different direction, the ship will founder and have difficulty not only during the journey, but in arriving at its destined port.

In order to earn the right to be considered a useful participant in the re-creation of the play before he begins to rehearse, the actor should know how to examine the play for something more than its plot or story line, to approach it from a different perspective. First, you must **explore what the play is about to define it thematically.** Don't be intimidated by this proposal. It's not as difficult as it may sound. Above all, don't turn it into an intellectual exercise. Follow your intuition; use your actor's intelligence. Harold Clurman's advice to the director is just as useful for the actor: "Let the play work on you before you work on it." Don't be confused by the many variations in *terminology* used by directors, teachers, and experienced actors when, in rehearsals, classroom sessions, or in textbooks, they discuss the play's THEME, SUBJECT, MEANING, MESSAGE, LESSON, INTENT, CONTENT, or POINT OF VIEW. These terms are all more or less synonymous, and the use of one rather than another is based solely on the individual's semantic preference. Any or all of them are summary **expressions of the playwright's view of the human condition within the particular society he has selected.**

The play's theme is sometimes suggested by its very title. *The Prisoner of Second Avenue* has immediate connotations, for anyone living in New York City today, of someone trapped in an urban environment. An actor has little trouble in grasping the play's meaning or in identifying with the problems facing Mel and his wife as they **struggle to survive*** the bureaucracy, the noise, the crime and pollution, the breakdown of toilets and air conditioners and transportation systems, as they come to grips with the fear of failing in the corporate world. Neil Simon's comedic point of view sharpens and highlights the idiocies of our own behavior when confronted with such devastating and frustrating circumstances.

George Bernard Shaw's title, *Mrs. Warren's Profession*, is also revealing of the play's content once it is known that the profession is prostitution. The message of this very dark comedy becomes apparent when we understand that Shaw almost makes a case for prostitution by exposing its causes and by proving that the arranged marriages of Victorian England were just another way of selling women into bondage. When the heroine, Vivie, discovers that her education and well-being have been procured through the profits of her mother's brothels, her **fight for integrity and self-determination** leads her not only to a rejection of her mother's offer of luxury and security, but to the decision to support herself by becoming a simple office accountant *and* to accept the state of spinsterhood as the only way "to get away from it all." To be able to identify with its problems and fully appreciate the play's meaning, the actor must familiarize himself more deeply with the particular world of which Shaw is speaking, a time when women literally perished of starvation in workhouses or gutters unless they became prostitutes, had rich relatives or married, for convenience. As one woman wrote, the only option was to "render up your body, or die." A reprint from the journal *The Lancet* states that "in 1885 one out of every sixty houses in London was a brothel, and one out of sixteen females was a whore." It may be even more interesting to read in *The Observer* that "in 1985 prostitution in London is sharply on the rise, as women are forced into it to pay the bills." Such circumstances obviously have their counterpart in American society. Just recently in New York the "Mayflower Madam" insisted in her self-defense while on trial that

---

* All main objectives of the play or a particular character will appear in boldface.

she was providing a safe and honorable livelihood for the indigent call girls she supplied to her "clients." We may even draw psychological parallels to our own profession when we consider to what extent we, too, let ourselves be bought and sold in the marketplace of the commercial theatre, while our souls, if not our bodies, wither away in our commercial "workhouses."

If you are not accustomed to looking for thematic definitions of plays and their relevance to your own life, you can acquire the ability through practice. The meaning in most of them is not obscure or difficult to find. Once you have looked beyond the plot of Ibsen's *A Doll's House,* for instance, you will recognize its theme as the spiritual enslavement of women and that the male chauvinist Scandinavian society, which patterned itself after that of Central Europe, is the villain that has made Nora into a perpetual child-bride, into the toy and ultimate victim of her husband. When, cornered by circumstances, she finally finds the strength to assume personal responsibility for her dilemma and is able to fulfill her desire **to break the locks,** to walk out of the house, she, not unlike Vivie, is able to face the world alone. In spite of today's gains in women's rights, Nora's psychological problems and her battle for self-liberation are easily recognizable.

Since conflict is at the heart of dramatic expression, whether that be tragic or comic, because it demands *action,* we must pay attention to THE NATURE OF THE CONFLICT which the writer has selected to reveal his point of view, when we explore the play's content. To exist, a conflict needs *adversaries,* and the playwright will have taken sides. In most cases the conflict is self-evident, and you can once again rely on your instincts and intelligence to guide you in making logical decisions about who's for and who's against what, who's in the right and who's in the wrong, who is the victim and who is the predator, who's the hero and who the villain—in other words, WHO IS THE PROTAGONIST and WHO IS THE ANTAGONIST of the theme.

Once this is done, you will know how your own character is positioned in the play and his consequent basic relation to the other characters in it. For the conflict to surface or erupt, there need be no visible hand-to-hand battles; the resolution or denouement of a play does not necessarily hinge on actual winners or losers. The play that ends with a question, one that provides no precise answers, or one in which the *wrong* side wins, is presumably intended to raise the audience's awareness of the problem, as a warning or a lesson.

As in the case of *Mrs. Warren's Profession, A Doll's House,* and other works of Shaw and Ibsen, many late nineteenth- and early twentieth-century plays take the prevailing social order as the underlying villain of their theme, as the subject of their attack. However, in many of Chekhov's plays of the same period, the leading characters are victims of their *past,* which has left them ill prepared to face the *changes* taking place in their society. In *The Three Sisters,* the protagonists "want to go to Moscow," **to return to what they used to have.** In *The Cherry Orchard,* the family members are their own worst enemies as they **struggle to evade the present, to hang on to the old** values and ways. The characters are defeated by the crumbling away of their familiar world and by the axe that ruthlessly chops a path into the future. We may draw a parallel to the impotence of our own shrinking middle class; and though the forces that are devouring it are vastly different, they are just as ruthless.

Social comedies which continue to thrive as expressions of contemporary playwrights and those exemplified by classics such as *The Importance of Being Earnest* (which I discussed at length in the previous chapter) usually have as their aim to hold a mirror up to their audience, to offer a reflection of their own slavish adherence to fashionable artifice, of their own vanities and stupidities. The characters' **efforts to outshine** each other, **to fit in,** or **to climb the social ladder** come in conflict with *nature,* with their basic human urges. In the more penetrating seventeenth-century satires of Molière, the characters' hypocrisies are devastating indictments of corruption in the prevailing society. In *The Misanthrope,* the cynical Alceste, who is portrayed as the last protagonist of perfectionism, is finally disrobed by his own fanaticism.

The last years of the Hapsburg empire provided the climate for many notable plays, such as Arthur Schnitzler's *La Ronde* and *The Affairs of Anatol.* The main characters in them are often undone by the hollowness of their **striving for self-gratification** which was a reflection of their society as a whole.

In one of our own American classics of the 1930s, Thornton Wilder's *Our Town,* the conflict may seem difficult to define until we discover that the relatively minor clashes of will between neighbors, family members, and the young lovers result in the heightened action of its characters who have such an appetite **to achieve a simple, loving life.** The nearness and finality of death are clearly dramatized as the ultimate antagonists.

We certainly don't need to hunt for the conflict in the countless plays that dramatize the battle of the sexes. However, we have to explore and interpret THE NATURE OF THE CONFLICT and the purpose for which it has been used, before we can put our character into the fray. Aristophanes, the father of comedy, made it his subject, already touching on "women's lib" more than two thousand years ago, when, in *Lysistrata*, the women wrest power from the men by denying them sex in order **to prevent them from making war.** Shakespeare's Petruchio tames his Shrew, Kate, who wants so desperately **to test his strength.** Shaw, the ultimate feminist, pitches his ladies into crusades against the male adversaries, and the heroines usually triumph. On the other hand, August Strindberg's women are often the villains who, in a **struggle for dominance,** destroy their hapless victims on the bloody battlefield of marriage. On a much lighter note, in Neil Simon's *The Odd Couple,* the problems between the newly divorced men in their **struggle to coexist** arise from the same causes that had broken up their equally mismatched marriages.

How our evaluation of a play's theme, its conflicts, and its adversaries influences the work on our role will be minimal or stay theoretical unless it includes our interpretation of THE PLAY'S MAIN ACTION or, as you may otherwise have heard it referred to, the play's SPINE, THROUGH LINE, MAIN OBJECTIVE, SUPER-OBJECTIVE, OVER-ALL ACTION, AXIS, or HUB. These synonymous terms all fairly describe the thing that supports the central theme, binds the play together, and provides its driving force. In most of the brief summaries beginning on page 237, I have stressed my own interpretation of each play's main action: Mel's struggle to survive; Vivie's fight for integrity; Lysistrata's campaign to prevent war; etc. If you refer back to them, you will see that the ideas are an integral part of each play, that this driving force or main action is usually in the hands of the protagonist and that it is the *antagonist* who provides the conflict. (If it is Nora's need to break the locks of her gilded cage, for example, it is her husband Torvald's need to keep her confined in it.)

The play's through line is always stated in the form of **an active** verb, which need not be the case with its theme, usually defined by a noun. And it is from the standpoint of the *play's* main action or through line that we must explore our *character's* main action to see how it relates to the "driving force" of the play.

Finally, we should never take for granted or lose sight of the fact that when the characters in the play pursue their goal, when they "struggle" or "fight," "strive" or "hunt" to achieve it, they must obviously *want* or *desire*, have a *need* or a *wish* or a *will* to fulfill it. **Such basic human emotions are the causes and the catalysts that precipitate our actions.**

In summation: When studying the play in preparation for a role, we must explore and give special attention to the play's theme, conflict, the alignment of its adversaries and our character's relation to them, its main action, and its motivating causes.

The interpretive *considerations* you make for each of the above remain *your* responsibility as long as you use them as guides for a role you hope to play in the future or when preparing for the presentation of your work in a classroom or studio—in other words, *in the absence of a director*. In such cases your teacher or peers will, hopefully, help to solve any problems that may have resulted from your failure to grasp the playwright's intent, to help you find what in the play's content you may have omitted, misunderstood, or wrongly emphasized.

For instance: Christopher Fry's delightful play *A Phoenix Too Frequent* takes place in ancient Greece in the tomb of a recently deceased town clerk. His widow has moved there with her maid, hoping to starve herself to death to join him in the other world. The actress who stops there to look for the truth of a grief profound enough to generate a death wish may be ready to work on a Sophoclean tragedy but will have a hard time reconciling it with Fry's comedy. She must follow through on the author's premise that the phoenix, which rises from the ashes, is **a desire for life, sex, and procreation.** She must incorporate *all* of the play's realities in order to be ready to fall in love again, to be susceptible to the charms of the guard who soon enters the tomb. She cannot ignore the information that the husband was obviously a colossal bore who "made Homer sound like balance sheets" and only "in his more perceptive moments" took note of her. She will realize that her tears spring more from frustration than mourning when she wails, "Why did you insult me by dying?" and that her conception of dying is to glide gently across a river into Hades in a boat steered by Charon. Her hunger and thirst and the appetite for sex and for the wonderful world outside the tomb come into continuous conflict with her middle-class, wildly romantic notions of self-sacrifice.

Similarly, in Murray Schisgal's one-act comedy, *The Tiger,* the actors often sink into a morass of heavy-handed, illogical actions when they fail to examine the whole truth of the material. The actress will only be able to justify that being abducted and dragged to a man's apartment can be an exciting adventure if she remembers that her character is a bored, suburban housewife whose sole entertainment is a weekly trip to town to shop and play bridge and, more importantly, when she considers that her abductor is a *sheep* in tiger's clothing, who is rather like Woody Allen. And the actor must not forget that his character is desperately *trying* to fulfill his fantasy of being a tiger. If he behaves instead like a sadistic Jack Palance, the play will become ugly, illogical, and pointlessly frightening.

It is possible, though rare, to arrive at two totally differing perceptions of a play which radically alter its meaning. *A Streetcar Named Desire* is a case in point. Which of its two initial productions had the "correct" meaning was hotly disputed by critics, theatre historians, and members of the profession for several years, although both productions were critically acclaimed and commercially successful. Neither interpretation was overtly questioned by its author, Tennessee Williams. One director took sides with Kowalski, seeing him as the animalistically healthy protagonist who defends his masculine independence, his territorial rights, and his sensually sound marriage from a parasitic predator, the decadent, neurotic antagonist Blanche, who must be exorcised. Stanley's lack of education and crude manners as a member of the working class were treated with compassion for the disadvantaged. One of the few negative reviews of this production noted that "the play becomes the triumph of Stanley with the collusion of the audience which is no longer on the side of the angels." The other director saw the play as a plea for the highly sensitized aspirant to beauty, epitomized by Blanche DuBois as the protagonist who seeks a haven and an understanding of her dreams and who is ultimately destroyed by the brutality of Stanley's "real" world. In response to this version, the critic Eric Bentley wrote, "Then which of us is safe?"—which in my view is a noble theme and a worthy challenge to an audience. In the case of *either* interpretation, it is easy to define on which side the other characters—Stella, Mitch, the poker players, the neighbor, the collector—are aligned, or when they are caught between Blanche and Stanley.

An example of the influence of *the times* on the interpretation of a play can be found in the two known films of Shakespeare's *Henry V*. The historic 1415 battle of Agincourt, in which 6,000 English soldiers were pitched against 25,000 Frenchmen, is central to the play's action. Olivier directed his film masterpiece of the play during World War II, when the national spirit of England was at a low ebb. He wanted to infuse his countrymen with a new patriotic purpose. His "Once more unto the breach!" became an honorable battle cry, and the pomp and splendor of the charging armies heartened and gave courage to every member of its audience. In this interpretation he fulfilled his artist's vision and moral purpose. In contrast, Kenneth Branagh's film, made forty-four years later, is the reflection of a post-Vietnam/Cambodia/Afghanistan era, in which the unheroic, bloody carnage of war is laid bare on the killing field of Agincourt.

Learning to explore the basic elements that support your character's position in the play should become an integral part of your approach to a role. And to study the play from this perspective should become habitual when working on a part which you hope to play at some time in the future or when preparing a scene from it for classroom participation. It is the teacher or moderator's function to help you develop the techniques that make you believe in your existence on stage, that animate your senses, that make you walk and talk, and consequently make you believable. The teacher is *not* there to act as an interpreter or as a director or to "fix up" your performance for public consumption.

However, in allowing you the freedom to arrive at your own interpretation and to find your own way into a role, there can be a dangerous side effect, which must be guarded against when becoming a member of a full-scale production. Since **there is no such thing as a definitive interpretation** of any play or part, else there would be only *one* Hamlet, *one* Saint Joan, *one* Oedipus, or *one* Medea, and all productions would be library-like stencils in which the actors would

truly be super-marionettes, you should always remember that whatever your own interpretations may be, they are only your *opinions*.
No matter how passionately you may feel about them, they do not
give you the license to engage in a contest of wills, in which you
egomaniacally test your interpretation against that of the director.
The director is the interpreter, and it remains the actor's obligation,
as well as a test of his technical skills, to make *the director's* vision
come into being. The actor's understanding of the process of play
evaluation should, ideally, pave the way to a deeper understanding of
the director's needs, facilitating an informed and fruitful dialogue
between them during the rehearsals.

I have chosen to make examples of plays that I believe are *familiar* to
you to demonstrate the dramatic elements of THEME, CONFLICT, AND
ACTION. I have deliberately left the classic examples on which these
principles are founded to the last. I would like to prod you into the
desire to arm yourself with a humanistic education, one which I
cannot provide for you. If your goal is to be a serious and informed
artist who is as convinced as I am that the theatre *could* be a noble
calling, you will want to study the works of Aeschylus, Sophocles,
Euripides, and Aristophanes, who are the progenitors of tragedy and
comedy, whose works and those of their contemporaries have served
as inspiration and structural models not only for the Elizabethan
writers but also for most of the great dramatists of history. The size
of their themes of man's struggle against fate, his challenge to the
gods and the forces of nature, his greed for power and his misuse of
it, his betrayals and falls from grace, his desire for vengeance, and his
lust for life may at first be overwhelming but should prove ultimately
enlightening as you find their relationship to your own world and
man's eternal hunt to understand himself. The conceptual difference
between the Greek masterpieces and those of later centuries, beginning with the Elizabethans, is brilliantly defined in an essay by W. H.
Auden. Here is a paragraph I would like to share with you.

> First, Greek tragedy is the tragedy of necessity: i.e., the feeling aroused
> in the spectator is "What a pity it had to be this way." Christian
> tragedy is the tragedy of possibility: "What a pity it was this way when
> it might have been otherwise." Secondly, the hubris which is the flaw
> in the Greek hero's character is the illusion of a man who knows

himself strong and believes that nothing can shake that strength, while the corresponding Christian sin of Pride is the illusion of a man who knows himself weak but believes he can by his own efforts transcend that weakness and become strong.*

Until we have shaken off the influence of today's theatre, so much of which seems suspended in a state of mediocrity bent on presenting witless diversions, I don't believe our feet are big enough to fit into the titan shoes designed by the Greeks. I think we should recognize our shortcomings and the necessity to develop all aspects of our artistry until we have grown sufficiently to fit into those shoes. Meanwhile, we must accept the fact that neither traditional histrionics and operatic delivery nor the contemporary tendency to naturalistic detail are the means of communicating these masterpieces truthfully.

And so, with infinite care and patience, we will learn to plant the seeds of our role in the soil of the more accessible plays when exploring each step of the work on their characters, circumstances, relationships, objectives, obstacles, and actions.

* From *The New York Times Book Review*, December 16, 1945.

23

Homework and the Rehearsal

As a child, I often vacationed with my aunt on an island in the North Sea. During the course of several summers, I became enraptured by a very tall, beautiful, and mysterious daily visitor to the beach who walked in solitude at the edge of the tides, her gaze cast down except when pausing to look off into infinity. As I watched from afar, she seemed always shrouded in a mist or in filmy robes. On balmy days she let her shawl drop to her shoulders, revealing white-blond hair loosely coiled at the nape of her neck. I imagined that her eyes must be intensely blue. On occasion, she sat motionless far back in the dunes, knees pulled up and enfolded by her arms, deep in thought. Since I had been warned never to approach or disturb her because she was "preparing for a role" for the upcoming season at the Staats-Theater in Berlin, I walked or sat at a proper distance to observe her. Sometimes I tested my own ability for lengthy concentration against hers.

Years later, at the age of sixteen, I saw her play the wife in *Stella,* Goethe's lovely play about fidelity, and was overwhelmed by her performance. I imagined that I myself had been witness to her discovery of the essence of her character during her lonely walks there by the sea. To this day that wildly romantic image and notion of creative solitude sweeps over me whenever I'm about to embark on a new role. However, even when I manage to be near the ocean during a period of my "homework," there is nothing glamorous about it. There are, of course, moments of uplift and excitement when the imagination soars, when a light goes on and I'm one step closer to the part, but much of it is just plain hard work, tedious and frustrating at times, feeling more like a chore than a creative act.

The real lesson I learned by watching "the lady from the sea" was the need for undistracted solitude. I realize that few people are lucky enough to manage this for months at a time, but privacy must be arranged for and respected by those with whom we share our lives. In point of fact, when it seems difficult to achieve, the circumstances are rarely to blame. It is usually the actor himself who lacks the discipline to ensure total concentration on the work at hand, to take off the head-set, turn off the stereo and TV, muffle the phone and close the door. After listening to the *silence* we can give our full attention to the play and the role. (If you *must* have sound, put on music that is appropriate to the play.)

The HOMEWORK, the work we do when alone, **begins the moment we pick up the script** to read and evaluate it* and continues with research about the specified society which is historically distanced from our own,† or when the locale and milieu of the play, its country, region, landscape, and culture, even when contemporary, may be unfamiliar to us. **It does not stop until the curtain comes down on the final performance of a run.** It is the work we do before, in between, and after rehearsals, covering **all the areas of our character's development, which will be the subject of the next chapter.** How to set about this solitary task should no longer be a mystery, especially after having practiced the exercises, which, aside from solving many technical problems, are training for intensive private work.

Whether the script is on the desk in front of me, or in my lap if I'm sprawled on a sofa or propped up in bed to begin the homework on a new role, close at hand a brand-new notebook and freshly sharpened pencils lie in readiness. The blank pages are inviting as I imagine how they will be filled with information, research, ideas, questions, answers, and personal substitutions, anything and everything that

* See Chapter 22.
† See Chapter 20.

will lead to the goal of becoming the character, of identifying with her so that *I* will be able to feel and do as she does, from moment to moment as the play unfolds. Although I have never lost or mislaid such a notebook, I put my name, address, and phone number on the cover as well as a large, printed warning: PRIVATE! Its contents are solely for my eyes and personal use. The first page will be labeled with the name of my character. From then on, as I start reading the script, I will make random notes, without objective logic or sequence, about anything I might need to remember, question, or explore. The only order given to the notations is dictated by the dates on which they are entered, as though in a log or diary. Since nothing in this workbook is for publication, not even grammar, spelling, or word order is of any consequence. *Subjective* logic is needed, which is quite different from the kind of reasoning necessary to explain something to someone else. In the event that later on in rehearsals, when referring to my notes, a nosy colleague peeks over my shoulder, I use nicknames and initials to designate my transferences for someone or something from my past.

In the early stages of the homework, apart from the obvious exploration of the character, the past, the relationships, and the events, all sorts of imaginative games can help in the hunt for identification with the new "you." Remember that what may seem foolish or idiosyncratic to someone else might be extremely stimulating and fruitful for you, just like the suggestiveness of specific paintings, music, aspects of nature, color, and texture.* I sometimes look for "my" new handwriting, practicing different kinds until I find what seems the right one. I even use it to write letters and notes under imagined circumstances to different characters in the play.

To give you another example of my personal work habits, I jot down imagined events from the character's past or from the circumstances that occur between scenes and acts in the first person, as though they had happened to me. (Further examples of this nature will be reserved for the ensuing chapters.)

Obviously, the workbook will stay close to you for reference and further entries all through the rehearsals, and the pages will probably be filled only after you have completed previews and the formal

---

* See pages 235–236.

opening performance. In the next chapter you will discover all the important areas in which different kinds of homework are needed as well as how the homework will interact with your rehearsals.

Under special circumstances, **"learning the lines"** is quite definitely a part of the homework: when the play's language is not colloquial or is idiomatically unfamiliar to you; when it is poetic; when it is intellectually complicated or difficult; when speeches are long and deal with past experiences; and certainly whenever the rehearsal period is short, as in the case of summer stock, or nonexistent, as for films or television; when the role is a long one and the three- to four-week rehearsal time allotted to a Broadway or Off-Broadway production is insufficient to make the character's words inevitable and one's own.

In any event, I ask you to stick to the principles and procedures outlined in animated talking, on pages 116–118, which you would do well to review at this point. As it relates to the homework, let me paraphrase what I already have discussed on page 117, where I state that we must particularize and make real to ourselves every person, thing, event, and landscape, even the weather, about which we talk in the play. This will give substance to the words and bring them to life truthfully. *When followed up in rehearsals* by the discovery of verbal intents, they will be further validated. Stick to the procedure of **learning the content,** of solidifying the particularizations that will bring about the words when you prepare scenes for classroom presentation (five- to ten-minute scenes to which you will have devoted many hours of rehearsal) until you have understood and can execute spontaneous verbal action. Stick to it **until you have shaken previously acquired bad habits of mechanized, preconceived, set line readings, and the slightest tendency to listen to yourself.**

Then you can tackle the plays in which it is a challenge to make magnificent, complicated, or unusual language your own, words you will learn as a part of your homework before, between, and after rehearsals, always testing their meaning, trying different sources and intentions. The reasons for sending them should remain flexible, becoming definitive only when the interpretive work has been exhausted in the final rehearsals.

At a certain stage you will need a friend who is not necessarily an actor to help by cueing you, reading the lines of the other characters as well as correcting your mistakes. It is a pleasure to realize how many lines we already know simply because they are logical responses to what has been said to us. When being assisted by a friend, avoid the temptation of performing for him. Never *shape* your words; always let them spring from their *content. Test* the verbal intentions; don't *settle* on them. How the verbal actions land on the other characters and how, in turn, their responses influence your replies can only be discovered during rehearsals.

THE REHEARSAL

When rehearsing becomes as exciting and rewarding as performing, you will have understood what it's all about. Even under the luxurious conditions of a workshop production when no opening-night deadline pressures us into hasty decisions, and the rehearsals continue until the play is ready to be viewed, I have never felt I had fully exhausted the exploration of my role, always longing for more. I have inwardly rebelled and wished that rehearsals would end *only* on the occasions when they were conducted in an external or mechanical fashion, when the director's search was for a formalistic, illustrative, ready-made product, *or* when my colleagues were undisciplined and lacked a serious purpose.

Since the latter problem is within our control and one about which I have passionate convictions, I feel no hesitation in reiterating the ethical behavior which I have stressed throughout the book, the kinds of disciplines that were drummed into me by my early mentors and role models, Eva Le Gallienne, Alfred Lunt, and Lynn Fontanne. They are essential to making fruitful rehearsals possible. *Numero uno* is the matter of punctuality. If the rehearsal is scheduled for 10 A.M., be there at 9:30. Head for the chair and area designated for you by the stage manager and appropriately arrange your belongings—coat, carrying case, script, notebook, and pencils. Put on your rehearsal clothes if you are using them, put your mind on the play, and be ready to start work on the dot of ten. If no one else does it, do it anyway! (In the case of scene work for class, when the rehearsal takes place in your own home, have everything ready before your partner arrives, including coffee or soda, should you feel it necessary to serve them. When rehearsing in your partner's home, arrive early and behave as for any professional rehearsal.) Before, during, and after rehearsals, limit your conversation to the subject of the play, and resist and keep to yourself all comments about the weather, your or other people's state of health, past and up-coming jobs or auditions, opinions about the latest TV series or the state of the world. Get to know your colleagues through the *work*, not by *socializing*. Jokes are sometimes inevitable to break the tension caused by concentrated, difficult work, but habitual clowning is totally destructive to the *serious innocence* we should maintain about the imaginary world we are trying to create. Always make yourself responsible for service to the play, to the director, and to your fellow actors: Don't make them responsible for being at *your* service. Don't expect the others to do your job for you.

Come to the **first rehearsal** (whether it be for a scene for studio presentation or for a full-scale production of a play) prepared with all the homework that has been previously outlined. Most likely this rehearsal will begin with a reading of the play or scene. At this *initial* reading aloud, two kinds of errors are most frequently made that can do enormous damage to future work on the role. The first usually springs from a normal desire to perform or from a mistaken need to impress the director and the other actors with artificial, "effective" line readings, forced emotions, character illustration, and false projection—that is, to overshoot your target rather than sending the words to those for whom they are intended. Any of the above will also lead to listening to *yourself* instead of to the other characters. The opposite mistake, also a common one, is to mumble almost inaudibly while listening for a "natural tone," to glide over the words while concentrating on general feelings and moods. (It is interesting to note that a gently mumbling actor usually indicates and colors his lines as much as if he were overprojecting, except that he thinks if it is done softly, neither he nor anyone else will notice.)

In either case, *the real issue* is being avoided. The real issue **is to reach the ears of your partner with words that are substantiated by their content** without yet having made interpretive decisions, always **giving concentrated attention to what is said to you and by whom.** The discussion following the first reading will probably concern itself with the meaning and through line of the play and its scenes and, depending on the play's difficulty, may be followed up by further explorative readings.

When the director puts you on your feet and defines the physical and psychological needs of each scene, it is a measure of your technical skills to be able to justify and make real to yourself everything he asks for. If something seems impossible to execute, question him or, possibly, suggest an alternative solution. (I often hear an actor complain, "That doesn't feel right," or "I'm not comfortable with that," and when the director generously responds with "What would you rather do?," the actor shrugs, "I don't know." Then I'm tempted to say, "If you don't *know,* shut up.") We must never forget that directions are not impositions, but essential requirements for any professional production, just as a teacher's criticism should be valued rather than feared. (You always have your lovers and parents to tell you how wonderful you are, though they won't be of much help in bettering your technique or your performance.) Good directors are rarely dictatorial and will be sensitive to an actor's needs, leaving room for a fruitful dialogue and the actor's participation in the creation of his role. Particularly the devout students of Stanislavsky sometimes forget that when he himself was directing he often demonstrated physical actions and gave precise line readings, expecting the actors to be technically limber enough to make them their own.

Here is an example from my own experience when working with the legendary George Abbott who, during the first week of rehearsal, showed me every single gesture and gave me each inflection for my character's words. I tried to obey, suffering in silence. At the end of one especially trying day, I finally rebelled by imitating him exactly. He frowned in puzzlement. "Don't *copy* me. Don't you know what I *mean* when I show you something?" I sighed with relief, "Oooh— *now* I understand. You're giving me my *intentions.*" From then on we worked together harmoniously, and I couldn't wait for him to "Show me more!"

When rehearsing for scene study, **in the absence of a director, *never* usurp his position.** Don't direct the scene or make editorial decisions. Such things as sight lines, covering another actor, or being upstaged are of no matter. They are the director's, not the actor's, business. They are also the easiest thing in the world to correct by an *outside* eye. Remember that no one is paying to see this work and that it will be evaluated for its reality and how well you have put yourself *subjectively* into the character's shoes, place, and circumstances.

Never tell your partner what to do. "It would help if you looked at me on that line," "You should be more threatening so I can . . ." "If you start to leave so quickly, I can't get in my line to stop you," "You have to reach for my hand. Otherwise I can't . . ." If it is important that the other actor look at you, make him do so by your own actions. If his threatening seems imperative to justify your action, *endow* his behavior with the threat, or open yourself to what you *do* receive from him, and you may be surprised by finding a better, more truthful response to him. Rather than voicing a complaint that your partner is exiting too fast, let him leave. He will soon slow down in order to fulfill his next line. On the other hand, obligate yourself to your partner's needs wherever the script requires it. For example, if he must ask "Why are you laughing?" you'd better find the cause and oblige! Don't squabble. If something goes awry, let your teacher clarify the problem after the presentation of the scene. (If, during a rehearsal or the run of a play, you come into conflict with a colleague, take the problem to the stage manager.)

Whenever you make a judgment on the other actor's work, you immediately become his audience instead of his partner, destroying all the innocence you need to receive what he is doing, to *interact* with him.

After finishing the first reading or readings with your scene partner, keep your discussions to a minimum. Don't intellectualize or theorize. If the information or facts in the scene are unclear, you should obviously come to an agreement about them, but **if you verbalize your moment-to-moment wishes, their obstacles, or your actions, you will make a truthful confrontation with each other in the scene impossible.** Get on your feet as soon as possible and make it a rule to **do something rather than talk about it** whenever you can. Instead of discussing the place, start to set it up—not definitively but exploratively. If the scene occurs in your character's room, explore its specifics together with your partner, whose character may be visiting, by discovering not just the placement of the furniture and the tangible objects in it such as books, magazines, pictures, rugs, vases, etc., but the nature of these objects right down to their texture. Walk to and around them, handle them, sit down, and discover what's comfortable or otherwise, what can be seen out of the window, or what might be heard through the walls. And so on and so on.

Make all *endowments* that will turn your apartment into the appropriate setting for the scene. Avoid making *decisions* about the use of the objects or about your physical destinations until further work on the scene progresses, when they will become logical and inevitable. When you have mutually arrived at considerations about the circumstances such as time, weather, and a state of being, **do something about it.** If the room is supposed to be cold or overheated, apply sense memory to see how it influences your behavior when serving tea to your visitor, for instance. **Improvise** on the previous circumstances until they are meaningful to you. If it is established in the play that your relationship to the other character is a highly competitive one, you will discover more about it by improvising a hand of gin rummy during which you really try to beat him than by hours of discussion. These kinds of early rehearsals can be extensive and will bear rich fruit when you eventually put the first beat of the scene into motion.

You should now be free of all concepts of "blocking," "staging," or choreographed "positioning" which always result in outmoded clichés, free to create a new life in an imagined world. The ensuing work will be tackled step by step in the next chapter.

One last warning: beware of "run-throughs," save them for the last few rehearsals. Don't finish rehearsing *just* because the run-through "felt good." If, during it, the inner and outer sources were vague or unspecific, pin them down, otherwise whatever may have momentarily inspired you will evaporate the next time you work on it or present it.

Our English term *rehearsal* derives from the word *rehearing.* In France, the rehearsal is *la répétition* which means just what it looks like—"repetition." I love the German designation, *die Probe,* because it implies everything a rehearsal should be about: PROBING, TESTING, TRYING, AND EXPLORING—A DISCOVERY.

24

Scoring the Role

WE are often overwhelmed by the thousands of ideas, thoughts, and images that storm in on us during the early readings of the play on which we are about to embark and, consequently, we may be at a loss about where to begin the actual work on the role. The need to make order out of chaos is strong in most of us, so we must be on guard against the "quick fix" provided by latching on to the character's lines as a starting point. I continue to work with actors who, in spite of proper training, still begin by mechanically memorizing their words, feeling rewarded by a sense of diligence. They may even be tempted to follow this up by testing colorful phrasings aloud. Long ago, I went a step further, trying out preconceptions of the character's physical attitudes, sometimes checking them out in the mirror! Impatiently, I awaited the rehearsals that would give me my blocking and fixed stage positions, convinced that later on I would fill them in with appropriate emotions.

Such arbitrary structuring can provide a false sense of security, which some actors are reluctant to relinquish. They should realize that it is similar to the mechanical erection of a prefabricated house, to the assemblage of precut walls, window and door frames, flooring and roofing, which results in the same kind of predictable, borrowed, trite shapes. They will be as reassured as I was when they discover that an organic transference of oneself to the role, the development of a new "I" who is alive in the world of the play, involves a creative process which is not a willy-nilly, loose way of working that depends solely on intuitive or illusive inspiration. On the contrary, it is a process which, however slow and painstaking, can be structured in an orderly way over which the actor has control, although no part of it is mechanical. On rare occasions it even leads to inspiration. It is a *true* challenge of one's diligence and of one's talent. This process is to me like the drafting of a musical score in which the actor composes the character's theme, orchestrates it, defines the phrases, individual beats, and the arrangement of the notes he will eventually play with spontaneity at each performance, putting to use his finely honed inner and outer techniques.

Scoring the role, which I now propose, **is founded on the exploration of all the whos, whens, wheres, whys, whats, and hows that are inherent in the Six Steps as they now relate to the role,** always remembering that, just as in the exercises, none of them is "finished" in itself, that they overlap, backtrack, and interweave until the last rehearsals, when they should have resulted in such inevitable human actions that we will have forgotten how they were put together.

1. WHO AM "I"?

If you have absorbed the content of Part Two of this book, nothing in this particular section will seem unfamiliar to you. You might want to refresh your memory by reviewing Chapters Four, Five, Six, and Seven—THE SELF, TRANSFERENCE, THE PHYSICAL SENSES, and THE PSYCHOLOGICAL SENSES—keeping in mind how they now relate directly to a character in a play. If you worked on the ten EXERCISES, you will have expanded the understanding of your own persona, the many changes in self-perception and ways of presenting yourself to others, all the varying aspects of yourself that have shattered your earlier, *limited, cliché self-image,* which can now be put to use in work on a "character." You will also have developed a growing recognition of the *similarities* between your own behavior, personal problems, drives, needs, virtues, and frailties and those of other human beings. Your ability to span the bridge of identification with others will have increased. In fact, alerting yourself to these things should have become habitual both in the course of your daily life and through the observation of your colleagues in class or on stage.

Of course, feelings of empathy, particularly for those in trouble or in pain, are very much a part of the actor's nature. It is no accident that performers are so ready to lend support to causes that help the needy, the ill, the neglected, or those who are discriminated against. However, when presented with a CHARACTER on the printed pages of a play, they often forget this important part of their talent and the techniques they've acquired. Reverting to old habits, they look only for the *differences* between themselves and their role, falling right back into the trap of illustrating a preconceived character who, no matter how brilliantly executed, will lack a soul and any aspect of a sensory life.

My two favorite definitions in the dictionary for the word CHAR- ACTER as it pertains to acting are (1) "an individual's pattern of be- havior, personality, and moral constitution" and (2) "the aggregate of distinctive qualities belonging to an individual, impressed by na- ture, education, and habit." After having studied the play, once it is our goal to step into the shoes of our character, it becomes our task to explore and evaluate his patterns of behavior, the personality, moral constitution, and distinctive qualities, and to examine how nature, education, and habits have shaped them. **To an *objective* exploration of these elements we must bring *subjective* identification at every step of the way.**

In order to develop a character who will move into the play with a soul and all senses alive, we must create a new *auto*biography. A *biography* may be interesting to write or talk about but will merely widen the gap between ourselves and the character rather than closing it. Based on a study of the play, after examining everything our character says and does, as well as everything that others say about us, we will **go on a hunt for new roots;** we will give ourselves a new date and place of birth, new parents and relatives, playmates, and friends, a new childhood and upbringing, schooling and religion, a different adolescence and early adulthood, whenever necessary *trans- ferring* our own landscape or a comparable, familiar one, our per- sonal experiences and relationships to the ones of the character, until the elements that substantiate this new life become believable to us and can be identified with.

Always remember that as long as you are thinking in terms of "he" or "she" rather than "I," you will be distancing yourself from the character. The creative imagination can only flow when, for instance, you ask, "Where and when was 'I' born?" Then, when the answer is "In St. Louis, in 1920" (Tom in *The Glass Menagerie*), or "In London, in 1875" (Gwendolen or Algernon in *The Importance of Being Earnest*), or "In the province of Lorraine, in 1412" (Joan in *Saint Joan*), or "In New York, in 1940" (Corie in *Barefoot in the Park*), you will no longer be tempted to file away interesting facts about a fictitious person which, at best, will result in some academic research about the time and place, but will instead force your imagination into identification with **what it must have been like *if you* had been born then and there.**

The examples I have given all through the chapter on TRANSFERENCE for the character of Blanche DuBois should suffice to clarify how substitutions from one's own life experience interweave with the imagined circumstances we conjure up. When the character is your contemporary, and the milieu of the play is familiar to you, this procedure is relatively simple to pursue. When not, Chapter 20 should help you find the ways of putting yourself into a distant time and place.

In summation: You must **look for imaginative identification with all the facts and circumstances about the character's past that can be gleaned from the play and from relevant research.** When the play does *not* provide answers to any of your questions, as is so often true in the case of subsidiary characters, use your creative imagination to supply logical answers so that, no matter how small the role, you will bring a whole human being on stage.

To the scoffers who want to know, "What good does it do to know who your grandmother is?" I reply, "It can't hurt; it might help!" Or I quote the genius who once said that "All tedious research is worth one moment of inspiration." In any event, the ways in which I establish roots for the character, providing myself with a past in which I can believe and the faith that allows me to enter the stage convinced that "I AM, therefore I DO," need never be discussed with the playwright, the director, or my fellow actors. It remains my creative secret and, above all, my essential homework! Of course, *all* the answers to "Who Am 'I'?" will not have been found until I incorporate the explorations of the next five steps.

2. WHAT ARE "MY" CIRCUMSTANCES?

You will, of course, have studied WHAT HAPPENS in the play, the EVENTS that occur in each scene that drive the play forward to its dénouement. (In case these events are complicated, I make a short list of them, including those in which my character does not participate. In *Who's Afraid of Virginia Woolf?*, for example, during the last scene of the second act, when Martha is offstage in the kitchen with Nick, I imaginatively re-created "my" sexual seduction of Nick, while making note that meanwhile on stage "George confronts Honey with her false pregnancies and formulates his plan to 'get' Martha.") It is also important to explore what must have occurred *between* each act and each scene, even when they are separated by a matter of minutes, let alone when the stage direction reads "Two years later." When the sequence of events in the play is crystal clear, the exploratory work begins on the circumstances: Where and when do these events occur and what surrounds them to condition "my" needs, behavior, and actions?

My old friend Webster gives us several pertinent definitions for CIRCUMSTANCES: "essential conditions; primary qualifications of a fact or event, or the conditions environing and affecting a person". An abridged edition simply refers to them as "a state of affairs." This "state of affairs" obviously includes the all-encompassing ideas of TIME (when?), PLACE (where?), and THE SURROUNDINGS or, better yet, THE ENVIRONS (what?). TIME includes the century in which the play occurs, the decade, year, season, month, week, day, hour, and minutes during which the life unfolds. PLACE includes the continent, country, city or village, neighborhood, house or apartment, and rooms in which the characters live. The SURROUNDINGS or ENVIRONS include the landscape, the architecture, the furnishings, the weather, the social conditions, the class structure of the community, the religious climate, the school systems, the fashion, appetites, and tastes—all of which influence and shape our own character and those of the others in the play.

Exploring the circumstances that immediately precede an event, those that condition the event itself, and those that dictate our expectations of what is to come has been an integral part of each and every exercise as we have discovered how they motivate much of our behavior and specify many of our actions. **Defining the circum-**

stances should have become an ingrained work habit since we have learned how strongly they involve our psychological and physical senses, as well as their relevance to the re-creation of a few minutes of a *personal* experience.

Now, based on our evaluation of the play, we must **learn to explore and define the dramatist's circumstances in greater depth** *from the perspective of our character,* to discover how they are perceived by our character and how our character responds to them—always remembering to look for identification with these perceptions and responses until they selectively become our own.

The steps involved in scoring the role have clearly begun to overlap. Many pages of your workbook will already be filled with information and transferences for the circumstances that have determined your character's past, that have given you "your" new roots. You will have explored the influence of the place and the society in which "you" were raised, the places, indoors and out, where "you" lived, played, studied, dated, got into mischief, achieved "your" goals, lost and won, etc., etc. You will know whether, in the play, "you" still live in the same place or have moved or fled elsewhere. You may have improvised on games "you" played, preparations for parties and special events, written letters to friends or lovers, and experimented with the sensory effect of appropriate clothing and relevant objects.

Even when the character is your contemporary and the background is not too dissimilar from your own, you must make the environs of the past as *particular* as possible, so that you can respond to these influences intuitively later on in the course of the play. When, on the other hand, the play presents problems of historic distance, HISTORICAL IMAGINATION* must be applied to your research as you put yourself into another time, place, and environment.

Examples for circumstances that condition a life on stage (and off) are given throughout the book. It might be useful to review the one of Blanche's entrance into the tawdry Kowalski apartment on pages 66–67. The exercises also have great relevance to this section, and your work on them will be repaid when you apply their principles to the exploration of the *play's* time, place, and surroundings, helping you to establish "your" physical and psychological state of being, as well as

---

* See Chapter 20.

logical destinations when you get on your feet. Such things as the completion of your playing area will no longer be difficult when you define your horizons or the fourth side of a room. Always remember that assessing and particularizing time, place, and surroundings subjectively, from the character's point of view, has to be pursued tenaciously in order to bring about inevitable, pertinent, and intuitive actions.

3. WHAT ARE "MY" RELATIONSHIPS?

My dictionary states that a *relationship* is: "A connection or the mode in which one person stands to another." That seems clear and simple enough, until we consider the phenomenal complexity of each individual and the infinite possibilities for his interaction with other, equally many-faceted human beings. We already know that, in our own way, we must pursue the hunt for an understanding of the human condition as diligently as philosophers, writers, dramatists, and psychologists do. Although we may tremble at the hugeness of the task ahead of us in exploring the relationships between our character and those of the others in the play *and* in finding relevant substitutions that will allow us to identify with the character, we can achieve our goal if we undertake our explorations patiently, in separate stages.

You have already taken the first step when, in your evaluation of the play, you defined the character's basic connection to the theme and its dramatic conflict: who the protagonist is and who the antagonist is, on which side your character stands—who is with, and who is against you. You may have begun work on the next step by using the example of the hunt for the fundamental relationships between Blanche and the other characters in *A Streetcar Named Desire*.*

Before proceeding with the ensuing stages in the exploration of "your" relationships in the play, I want to deal with certain human aspects that pertain in general to all of us, whose principles, once you grasp them, can be applied to those of the relationships in most plays. Let me remind you of those which you have already tested in the exercises, although the other people were not physically present. While

* See pages 67–69.

engaged in a simple task, you thought about others in your life, discovering that contact with these "inner objects" produced specific psychological and physical responses that conditioned your actions. Among other things, you learned that the very way you enter a room can hinge on the person from whom you just parted; that how you prepare for an occasion or fix a meal depends on those with whom you will share the event; that self-perceptions change when the doorbell rings depending on who you believe rang it; that changes take place in your behavior because of your feelings about the person on the other end of a phone call, etc. However, because the exercises are designed to be practiced alone, many elements of a relationship have not yet been fully examined or put to use. Even though you may understand these elements intuitively, conscious awareness will help make them operative for a character's positioning to others.

THE SUBJECT OF AGE has a great deal to do with the nature of a relationship. **At a given time, observe what your perception of your own age is and whether you believe that the person with whom you are dealing in the present circumstances is older or younger than you.** Your consequent assumptions, right or wrong, are essential in determining "your" actions. When working on the *character's* past, you will have established "your" present age, which, in most cases, will be close to your own and therefore easy to identify with. The days of high school, college, and amateur productions are behind you, times when you were asked to play very old or very young people, when your portrayals were also based on the misconceptions about age which we sometimes continue to carry with us: for example, that all old people are bent over, have wobbling heads, white hair and quavering voices, or that the very young are all awkward, pigeon-toed, naive or a little stupid, only sit on the floor or on furniture with their feet tucked under them, that they never walk—only run—and speak in a soprano treble with a slight lisp.

An aside: In the rare cases when, during your early years, you may be asked to play someone over sixty, or, when you have reached your thirties, you must portray someone in his teens, *you will better serve the character* by using one of the conditions that manifest themselves in the body as a result of those years and its psychological effect on you than by illustrating a cliché of that age. Many of the infirmities that develop in the aging process are due to heart or respiratory illness or to various forms of arthritis and circulatory problems, which result in such things as shortness of breath, dizziness, or faulty balance, stiff or swollen limbs and joints, aching backs and sore feet. An anxiety or protectiveness about the stricken area usually accompanies the condition. A fear of falling is not uncommon in the later years. You should now be able to apply the principles of the fifth exercise (re-creating the physical sensations) by particularizing *one* of these conditions, for instance, shortness of breath after a brisk run, tired feet after doing the rounds, an aching back after hours of typing, sore knees because of a fall, etc., **to use as a constant for the character.** The skillful application of makeup may complete the illusion for an audience and give you the needed faith that you are the appropriate age.

Aside from possessing a fit body, the physicalization of extreme youth often begins by making one aspect of clothing particular in order to determine its influence on body and soul. I'm sure you will remember how you once felt in garments that were either too large or too small, the ones you were supposed to grow into or those you had already outgrown: the futile attempts to lengthen the arms when sleeves reached the knuckles of the fingers, or those of hitching up the elbows and shoulders when the sleeves were so short they exposed bony wrists; the hemlines that had to be hiked up continually as they swooshed in an ungainly fashion around the calves, or yanked down a year later when they barely reached the top of knobby knees. I can still see the boys who pretended that their trouser cuffs had *not* been turned up, cuffs that, even so, brushed the laces of their shoes, or when the next year they had ridden up to reveal scrawny ankles, pretended they were long enough; the collars that were either so large they swallowed the neck or so tight that a newly developed Adam's apple bulged over them, and the blushes that flooded the face when someone noticed. Along with physical experimentation on one such suggestive area of clothing, set yourself the kind of high social expectations which young people are so anxious to live up to in regard to fashion, manners, and matters of intelligence. Remember that we emulated our role models and adult behavior, continually trying to prove our "maturity." We didn't *want* to feel *young;* we wanted to be accepted as older than our years. It is also easy to find transferrable circumstances in which we *still* behave naively, perhaps even rashly, responding on impulse, without considering the consequences of our behavior—which is such a mark of youth.

My statement about playing roles *close* to your own age is based on the conviction that "close" encompasses many years on either side of your actual age. Recently, a thirty-two-year-old actress complained that the forty-year-old character I'd assigned for scene study was too old for her. I laughingly assured her that by the time she, herself, arrived at such a ripe old age, she would not only look but feel exactly the same. I asked if she felt differently now than she had at nineteen or twenty, and she admitted that she did not. A minute later she also laughed when she realized that, from her present vantage, today's teenagers seemed like foolish children.

In other words, our notions about our own *and* other people's ages are often mistaken. At the very first meeting with someone, we usually place them in the wrong category. To test this theory, ask a friend about the actual ages of relatives or acquaintances whom you've met at least once, whose age you will already have assessed. You will most likely be off the mark, perhaps by as much as ten years. Once you recognize this tendency to misjudge, you will understand that the manifestation of age is a result of health and fitness, grooming, genes, and, *particularly*, of how old a person feels and presents himself to others under the given circumstances, and that no one can make accurate assumptions unless they are in on the facts. However, **you can use the discovery of the wide range of years you have at your disposal** when identifying with the age of your character. Note the effect of the age difference between yourself and the other characters on your interaction with them.

You may already be aware that the way in which you respond to someone you think is older or younger than you are is markedly different. Depending on numerous other things, you may defer consciously or otherwise to an older person with courtesy, admiration, or humility, or, if you dislike him, with a feigned respect for his years. You might challenge him in areas where you believe yourself to be his equal, even assuming seniority in areas where you have superior knowledge or experience. In contrast, you may treat someone younger than you with gentleness, benevolence, tolerance or, perhaps, with aloofness, disdain, or a grudging acceptance. In case you want to prove that you aren't "pulling rank," that the age difference doesn't matter, you might be his pal or play at being his age. In close friendships, whenever age truly makes no difference, you will feel and behave as though he were your peer.

The *other* person's response to *your* age may be even more influential in making you feel and behave either younger or older than your years. Miss Le Gallienne, with whom I worked more than fifty years ago, still makes me feel like an unruly child. I once developed rather motherly feelings for a charming young juvenile during the run of a play because of my conviction that he was in his early teens. I was "already" twenty-three, and it amused me that he had a crush on me. When I learned that he was really several years my senior, it discombobulated me to such an extent that I was never able to establish a proper friendship with him.

Such examples, when taken from your own life, are serviceable substitutes for a variety of occasions: for a similar relationship in a play; when you want intuitive sensations and behavior suitable for a character considerably younger or older than your actual years; or when the *real* age difference between yourself and the other *actor* is inappropriate. In each instance, you bring about what you need by endowing the *partner* with the desired age difference.

Determining the relative positioning between your character and those of the others in the play in regard to WHO LEADS AND WHO FOLLOWS is a subject to which I attach great importance because of its influence on human interaction. In its most positive sense, leadership implies guidance in areas in which the leader has more experience and knowledge, or a higher degree of maturity, intelligence, or just plain common sense than the others, when full responsibility is taken for the guidance, and when it is freely offered to a willing follower. In the course of an ordinary interchange, on a less lofty plain, this positioning can change as swiftly as the topic of conversation. Here is a simple example that may make you chuckle: When, during a social evening at home, the subject turns to philosophy, my husband leads and I follow. If it switches to current politics, I lead and he follows. If, however, Saul Bellow is in the room, we both become followers. When matters of the theatre come up, we are equals, even when we disagree, and the rest of the company may follow unless it includes someone like Mike Nichols or Jessica Tandy or possibly a colleague from abroad expressing his views on the state of the European theatre.

But, let me return to the higher stakes in a play and the broader aspects that make it **essential to find the appropriate leader-follower relationships and the ways in which they shift from one scene to the next** in order to unearth the logic of our character's actions, to bring about GIVE AND TAKE.

When the conflict is between *opponents,* the positioning is usually clear. When this is not the case, it may be more difficult to determine. For instance, in *Death of a Salesman,* Hap's hero worship of his older brother, Biff, obviously makes him into the follower. However, in the bedroom scene, Biff is filled with insecurities and anxieties and appears to be giving Hap the upper hand. If you look more deeply into this relationship, you will find that, even when Hap boasts about his own comparative security and success, he remains the awed kid brother who **tries to prove** his newly attained maturity in hopes of being considered an equal. Until the two actresses in Lanford Wilson's charming one-act play, *Ludlow Fair,* realize that Agnes is the leader, the scene will present problems. At first glance, they usually assume that because Rachel is the prettier one, the more sought after, and seems to be giving the orders, she is leading the dumpy, buxom Agnes, who always has a cold (because of her "susceptibility to drafts") and thinks her life is a big bore. But it is the latter's humor and ability to cope realistically that determines her leadership. Rachel **seeks her approval** and **relies on** Agnes's wit and common sense to help her out of her dilemma. The two performers are amazed when, after making this readjustment in the relationship, the scene begins to fly.

Whenever I assign the scene in the recreation room between Gately and Sylvio from James McLure's *Pvt. Wars,* the actors make a similar mistake. They almost always decide that Sylvio is the leader because he sets the scene, acting out his fantasy of a lonely priest picking up a girl in a bar, persuading Gately to play the part of the girl. Sylvio seems to be dictating the terms, and Gately, in the play as a whole, is described as an innocent. The actors fail to see that under these particular circumstances, Gately has the upper hand, lacks respect for Sylvio, and is really "putting him on" when he joins in the game, while Sylvio is *unsuccessfully* **trying to establish a superior prowess,** to prove that he knows more about life and sex. When the scene is reworked from this perspective, the actors are rewarded by the discovery that what had seemed like a rather contrived and hokey scene has become a logical and hilariously truthful one.

Other determining factors in leader-follower positioning are, of course, those **within the family, in love and sex, and in the work situation, as well as differences in social status, economics, and education.** Whenever leadership is earned and of benefit to a willing follower, human beings are free to grow and develop. When it is abused, used as a position of rank, for power and domination, and when the follower is forced into submission and obedience, he is enslaved.

Democracy, which is based on the premise that all men are created equal, is in ever-present danger. A *title* designating a specific position should be representative of achievement in a given field and remain in effect as long as responsible service is given. But when the title is viewed either by its holder *or* by someone touched by it as being synonymous with rank, power, and domination, it is a sign of an emerging class system, in which a difference in human worth is made between the privileged and the underprivileged, the educated and the illiterate, the sexes, the races, and the various ethnic groups—in other words, it becomes evidence of social corruption.

Today, not just in politics but in every walk of life, in the worlds of academia, art, science, medicine, and law, in commerce—from superconglomerates down to the smallest store, even in not-for-profit organizations—there is a growing tendency to establish individual kingdoms in which titles become designations of rank rather than of true service. Whether the title is president, cabinet member, dean, professor, student, doctor, nurse, junior executive, salesperson, waiter, janitor, producer, director, or actor, it should be a badge of merit for a responsibly executed service. Instead, it is used more and more as a tool to lord it over others, as a rank to be obsequiously catered to or slavishly knuckled under to. Then the difference in status and behavior is slight between president and king, between members of Congress and dukes or barons, lords and ladies, or, at the other end of the spectrum, between domestics, laborers, poor farmers, and peasants or vassals.

Statements that in our democracy it is easier to climb the social

ladder, to break class barriers, to beat the system than in an established monarchy like England should be frighteningly familiar to
you. True or not, such statements are manifestations of something
rotten in the state of Denmark. Perhaps even more recognizable will
be the power plays and exercises in one-upmanship that are based
purely on egotism, prevalent not just in the battle of the sexes but in
all walks of life in a self-serving society. *Who's Afraid of Virginia
Woolf?* is a sharp reflection of this.

I am dealing with these matters not for the purpose of writing a
moral or political thesis, but to help you evaluate and relate them to
all the fine plays in which they exist, usually as a criticism of a
particular society and a *challenge* to it. Once you acknowledge elements of these conditions *in your own experience*, you will be able to
use them as parallels to the social positioning that exists in meaningful
contemporary comedies and dramas, as well as in the classics and the
European plays in which rank is such a crucial conditioning force.

You will find *genuine* sources for a character's relation to royalty
and serfdom, to superiors and subordinates, instead of being mired in
one-dimensional character illustrations. From your new perspective,
you may find a reality even for such fairy-tale characters as those in
Molnár's *The Swan*. And think with what faith and delight you will
be able to imagine yourself as someone like Eliza Doolittle bridging
the gap between a slum in the 1900s in London (or one in today's
Bronx) and an elegant Victorian drawing room (or in Jackie O's
living room) with the help of "your" mentor, Professor Henry Hig-
gins.

When we identify with *any* character, what qualifies our responses
and interaction with those who lead or follow is, of course, a matter
of individual character, of faith in human rights, of personal strengths
and weaknesses, of ambition or laissez-faire, of a sense of security or
a feelin of failure. And, the more you understand about yourself, the
better you will be able to apply your understanding creatively to the
interpretation of your character's relationships in the play.

As a final fillip, let me add that we shouldn't forget that, as artists,
our responsibility lies in hopes of bettering and enlightening the human condition, and that, "The fault is not in our stars, but in ourselves, that we are underlings."

* * *

After the relative positioning of the opponents has been determined—who the protagonist and antagonist of the author's theme are—difficulties frequently arise for the actor whose role is that of THE ANTAGONIST. It is, of course, far easier to identify with the good guy, the one whom the author has made certain the audience will sympathize with and root for. The answer to the problem does *not* rest in *retaining objectivity* about the antagonist's provocative behavior by laying on villainy with a heavy, illustrative hand (which so many formalistic actors enjoy doing), *nor* in softening the behavior, thereby eliminating or weakening the dramatic conflict. To become a genuine opponent, we have to take a different path: We must find *justification* for the actions, no matter how evil they appear, in order to find *subjective* identification with the antagonist (just as we do in our personal lives when we behave badly).

As I have stated before, the actor must know that he is as capable of ignoble actions as everyone else. He is capable of betrayal (which is, to me, probably the worst of them). And, in varying degrees, he can be vengeful, cruel, selfish, manipulative, and abusive, and manifest most of the other negative aspects of human behavior. In regard to the previous section, for example, if you believe yourself to be blameless in participating in a ranking system, examine your personal relationships with producers, agents, stars, supporting actors, and bit players, with colleagues who can boast of professional experience, and with those you're sure will never make it. Consider how you differentiate between those who appear Off-Off-Broadway, Off-Broadway, and on Broadway, regardless of an assessment of their talent or the quality of their work, even while you protest that such things are irrelevant. And, if you still have reservations about your own culpability, remember that the gentlest and meekest among you has at one time or another exercised power and pulled rank, if only over a sibling. I don't mean to imply that it shouldn't be a lifelong task to better oneself, to correct one's failings from the very worst of them down to the smallest expression of vanity, pride, or arrogance. But **to correct our faults, we must know them, and, once we know them, we can *also* call on them for identification with those inherent in the role.**

No matter how monstrously human beings behave, they will try to justify what they do. Most of history's tyrants fiercely backed up their actions with a "noble" cause, and, from their perspective, their *victims* were the evildoers or impediments to the realization of that cause. In order to fulfill our obligation to the play, as antagonists we must apply the same principle, **finding justification for the character's actions, strengthening our needs until they *supersede* the wishes of our opponents.** We have to *forget* all the sympathetic information the playwright has given us about the protagonist or, at least, know more about our own wishes while giving ourselves substantial reasons for them. In other words, we must **particularize the relationship to our opponents from the viewpoint of our character.**

When playing Eugene Gant's mother in *Look Homeward, Angel,* for example, a woman who tyrannically harasses and enchains her son, kicks out the girl he loves, and remains otherwise totally insensitive to his needs, the actress must block out her knowledge of Eugene's problems and fortify her own. She can readily justify her dependence on his help in the backbreaking work of maintaining the boarding house, needing to support him to keep a roof over his head. The girl he loves is considerably older than he, comes from the big city, and will probably hurt him by using him as a passing diversion, etc.

Similarly, the performer working on the mother of the blind young man in *Butterflies Are Free,* as the antagonist to his fight for independence, should remind herself that his blindness has prevented him from managing without her help in the past and that his previous girlfriend had almost broken his heart. In her case the motive for interference in his life springs from a genuine love for him.

To give human dimension even to archetypal villains like Iago or Richard III, to arrive at something deeper and more enlightening in the characters than the predictable fare so often offered up, the actor must find the character's *cause*. In Iago's case, it is the terrible injustice he believes has been done him when being bypassed for the promotion that was to be the logical reward for loyal service to Othello which gives him his need for vengeance. And Richard's manipulative destruction of everyone in his path on the way to the crown has its roots in rage against the fates that have so hideously deformed him and at the world's refusal to acknowledge his "rightful" position as ruling monarch.

Regardless of our position as antagonist or protagonist, GUILT can be a powerful conditioner in our interaction with others. It is a feeling as prevalent as that of any other in the human psyche. The awareness that we have committed a hurtful act of omission or an abusive, cruel, selfish, or insensitive one usually occurs *after* the fact—as its effect on the recipient moves in on us. Then guilt sets in. If we take responsibility for such an act, we apologize or try to make up for it in other ways. In a play there is little difficulty in identifying with such an event. However, whenever we dislike admitting to a fault (a not uncommon occurrence), an instinctive and subtler manifestation of guilt takes place, one which we must learn to recognize so that we can put it to use for all the characters who respond similarly. We might become defensive and insist that our hurtful actions were provoked. We may even come up with justifications that are unreasonable and illogical because of our refusal to take the blame. We sometimes overcompensate for bad behavior by extending ourselves graciously to the very person we have abused with a pretense that nothing is wrong. We try to forget about it. Occasionally we even look for *approval* of abusive actions. The latter usually occurs when the person we are dealing with, rather than being the target of our attack, is being used as a confidant or sounding board for airing the incident as we try to ease a bad conscience. We want to be told that we were in the right or, at least, not so terribly wrong.

There is an amusing example of this in Neil Simon's *Barefoot in the Park,* in the scene between Corie and Paul when they return from the dinner party. Although Corie is young, imaginative, and selfish, she is not stupid. She *knows* the evening was a disaster and that she was mostly to blame for it. An actress working on the scene is frequently misled by the beginning, when Corie seems to sum up the events of the dinner with such pleasure and exuberance. She must learn to discern that Corie's actions spring from a desire to delude herself, to deny her feelings of guilt; that she wants her husband to play along in this game, to win his assurance that everything was fine. When he refuses, instead confirming her guilt, she instigates a showdown, counterattacking with accusations of his being a stuffed shirt, justifying herself as a fun-loving, adventurous innocent, until she boxes herself into a corner from which the only way out is the pronouncement that they are mismatched and that divorce is the only answer. When the presentation of the scene is based on this understanding, every man and woman who views it, no matter what their age, will laugh with *self-recognition* and empathy for such immature, idiotic behavior.

On the subject of provoking a showdown (something that occurs in more plays than can be counted), I'm sure you will remember times when you were aware of behaving unreasonably and obnoxiously right *in the middle* of a confrontation, but were unable to stop yourself, slugging ahead until you won or lost. A classic example of self-justification for a guilty life can be found in *Mrs. Warren's Profession*, at the end of the second act, when Vivie, having discovered the nature of that profession, confronts her mother. Mrs. Warren's tirade in defense of her life as a procuress of young prostitutes, her desperate attempts to make the daughter accept it, is almost epic in its proportions. Shaw, of course, makes a pretty solid case for her!

My final point having to do with human relations in general applies to the stages of the DEVELOPMENT OF RELATIONSHIPS and its relevance to the play. It begins with the premise that **a relationship to someone starts at the moment when we first hear about him,** which might be long before an actual meeting with him (in life—or before the curtain goes up on stage). Based on what we have been told, we speculate about what he is like and how he looks and behaves, often making definitive judgments of whether or not he meets with our approval, whether he should be looked up to or ignored, etc.

As an illustration, I play a trick on my students, asking who will volunteer to deliver a script to my agent, Sophie Katz, after class. I inform them that the office is on Forty-third Street between Broadway and Eighth Avenue and give them permission, when they meet her, to mention that they study with me and to see if she would consider submitting them for parts. After confessing that I have invented the name, the address, and the errand, I ask them to describe how they had visualized and assessed Sophie Katz and what they had planned while they still believed that the situation had genuine possibilities. To one of them Sophie will be in her sixties, gray-haired, plump, and jovial, wearing a blousy print dress. Dreaming about a possible job opportunity, he will have already planned to impress her with a charming deference. To another actor, she is gaunt, dark, middle-aged, and forbidding in her mannish shirt and tweed suit; he had speculated on making a frontal attack in order to make his mark before being dismissed or thrown out. Everyone also always gives a detailed description of the office they had envisioned, usually based on previous visits to that neighborhood when doing the rounds.

On the numerous occasions when I *have* sent an eager messenger on such an errand to my real agent (who doesn't fit into either of the above categories any more than would "Sophie Katz," if she existed), he, of course, also makes assumptions about what she will be like. He visualizes the office on the Upper West Side and makes plans for worming his way into her good graces. From the moment the door is opened, his plans will change as he confronts a secretary instead of an agent and enters the foyer of an elegant apartment on the Upper West Side rather than a gloomy Times Square office. If and when he has the opportunity to be ushered into the presence of the agent, *the next stage of a developing relationship begins.* This entails an immediate adjustment to the difference between his expectations and the actual person he is now encountering. The adjustment necessitates a change in his behavior to conform to these differences.

Hopefully, you will become observant about such matters in your daily life. Take a lesson from something as trivial as sizing up the butchers while waiting in line at a new meat market. You will quickly decide on your favorite one and how to maneuver him into giving you the best cuts. You will most likely be mistaken, but by the time you leave, after discussing little but the weather and the meat with him, you will think yourself able to write his biography—where he comes from, how old he is, whether he is married or single, how he treats his wife and children, etc.

To return to the play *A Streetcar Named Desire,* you may now understand how much Blanche must have already imagined and assumed about Stanley *before* arriving in New Orleans based on the likelihood of letters from Stella at the time of their marriage and afterward. Think how Blanche will reevaluate her assumptions about him with each new thing she learns about him in the first scene (added to her new perceptions about the Kowalskis' living conditions). Her vision of him and plans of approach are in continual flux and will be a determining factor in the surprise at their first actual meeting.

A first confrontation can take many forms. One of them, which occurs frequently and not only in the classics, can pose enormous problems for the modern actor: How does he motivate the heightened reality of an encounter that results in something as extraordinary as love at first sight? Before their meeting at the ball, although Romeo has heard about Juliet and knows what she represents in society, he must be struck as if by lightning when confronted by her actual presence. When Alison comes unannounced into the Mayor's hall in Christopher Fry's *The Lady's Not for Burning*, the clerk, Richard, must blurt out, "Is God sending a flame to nest in my flax?" And later in the same play, as Jennet runs in, fleeing from the witch-hunters at her heels, Thomas must call out "Oh God! She's young!" as he, too, begins to fall in love. In the flashback scene between Julien and Colombe in Jean Anouilh's *Mademoiselle Colombe*, within a few minutes of their meeting, they must be in each other's arms. You may not be able to find a similarly powerful experience to transfer from your own life to that in the play, but to a lesser degree you will surely have been bowled over by someone at first sight and, after catching your breath, muttered "Wow!" This doesn't mean that you had *no* prior frame of reference to the person at stake. On the contrary, **your response is based on an already existing dream of an ideally imagined person** who suddenly becomes a reality, the embodiment of your dream of perfection. Therefore, in order to find substance for such a moment, you must specify the nature of a personal ideal, whether it has been inspired by a poem, a painting, a picture-book fantasy, or a likeness to a childhood idol. This ideal can then be transferred imaginatively to the love object to bring about the awestruck response at the moment of the confrontation on stage.

Once the readjustment to the first moment of a meeting has been made, **the development of any new relationship and the nature of the interaction between the two people is conditioned by a series of changing expectations and assessments.** The frame of reference for such intuitive, often subconscious, hastily made evaluations hinges on what we have already heard about him and how this contradicts or coincides with what we now discover about his profession, age range, and social and educational background. We form further opinions by instinctively sizing up his appearance and demeanor, and, of course, by the ways in which he relates and responds to *us*. We usually open up to those who fit our concept of an interesting, friendly person and pull back in wariness from someone who does not. (I formed an instant dislike for each of the men I eventually married, during our first meeting. Within a week, my assessments of them had reversed and I was in love.) Dramatic literature abounds with scenes of budding relationships. When exploring one of them, remember that it is what you *don't* know and mistakenly *think* you know about the other character that will make for the discoveries that animate the interaction and heighten the event. Of course, an **established relationship,** an ongoing one, **is based,** among other things, **on an affirmed knowledge and the familiarity of responses to each other** as well as to responses that occur during a shared event. Surprises will still occur—usually when the other's responses *don't* conform to the accustomed expectation.

Armed with some of the important elements that are at work in human relationships, we can now incorporate whatever applies to our character's relationships in the play. We will **make considerations about them during the homework and test their influence during rehearsals.** We will now **explore each of "our" relationships with respect to newness or familiarity, pertinent age differences, and the relative positioning of protagonist and antagonist, of leader and follower, and the possibility of rank.**

I have reserved the most fundamental aspect of relationships for last because it needs the least amount of explanation. It concerns the *feelings* we have about someone that take hold and sometimes control us against our better judgment. We must **examine what it is in the other characters that "we" love, hate, or are indifferent to, like, dislike, pity, adore, disdain, admire, envy, are obsessed by,** etc.

It is almost impossible to study a role without experiencing the beginnings of such emotions. As I have said before, when they spring from your own (reader's) point of view *about* the character, they should be disregarded as misleading or, at least, recognized as such. If, instead, they arise as imaginative germs *from an identification with the character,* they may be considered pure gold. In any case, emotions have their roots in the characters' objectives, in their main drives, and in **what they want from others,** which is the premise of the section that follows, the exploration of "What do 'I' want?"

The homework involved in all aspects of our relationship to the other characters, including our feelings about them, should now be self-evident, always remembering that whatever stays *only* in our head is not merely useless but will become burdensome. **Our explorations and considerations must be brought to rehearsals to be tested and put into practice.** This process entails making a detailed particularization of the *partners* to see what about and in them serves the relationship directly. Whenever something about your partner's actual persona is physically or psychologically at variance with his character, something he may be unable to provide in the present or in later rehearsals (such as the appropriate age), you will endow him with it by use of transferences until he becomes the "hot object" you need for the creation of truthfully animated interaction between the two of you.

The most important thing to keep in mind when exploring and testing "your" relationship to others during rehearsals (or during a performance, for that matter), is to remain wide open and vulnerable to your partners. From the perspective of your character, be receptive to *everything they do,* to each action sent to you. Be alert even to the flicker of an eye, the furrowing of a brow, the slightest hesitation, the nuance of an inflection or a tone of voice, their lightest touch. Then your lover will only have to *look* at you or take your hand to make you flush with pleasure; when he proposes, your heart will pound; when your boss threatens, your palms will sweat; when challenged, your blood will race. *Never* take a partner for granted or use him as a convenient or necessary prop to bolster your own performance. An analogy can be made between the stage and the tennis court: The strokes that are practiced against a wall may be executed brilliantly but serve little purpose until they are tested in a delivery across the net to an opponent, when the player *knows* that his next shot is dependent on how it will be sent back, on how he will *receive* it—during a singles *or* a doubles match. Our fellow actors must be treated as worthy partners, not as ball boys. Then we may reach the ideal state of becoming members of what is often loosely referred to as "a fine ensemble."

4. WHAT DO "I" WANT?

As long as we are alive, we want something. We have conscious, instinctive, and subconscious needs, wishes, desires, aims, goals, or objectives that originate in the body or the soul. And our lives are spent in pursuit of gratifying these wishes. Once we understand that **the sources of an individual's needs and desires lie in the nature of his upbringing and the society that has helped to shape his character,** it becomes clear that the initial exploration of "Who 'I' am" must be continued by an investigation of "What 'I' want." And rather than relying solely on intuitively found answers, this subject can be approached from several different standpoints that provide a more solid and dependable structure for the scoring of our role. The first one has already been undertaken during the analysis of the play itself.

Following the precepts of Chapter 22, you will have determined **what the play wants** thematically, its main objective, the inherent conflict, and the adversaries involved in it. You will have aligned your character on the side of the protagonist or antagonist. Obviously, if you are for or against something, you must *want* something, and it is what "you" want, in the broadest sense, that constitutes **the character's main objective,** the guiding force that propels "you" through the life of the play. While evaluating the play, you will have defined **what the character wants in *general terms* of his world, of his work, and of the people in his life.** These needs or objectives are rarely mysterious and need deeper exploration at this stage only if they remain dry facts or are difficult to identify with. For instance, if I come to the conclusion that Saint Joan's main objective is **to save France in the service of God,** I couldn't dispute it but, because I personally have a horror of nationalism and am an agnostic at heart, it would leave me cold. I might catch fire, on the other hand, if I substantiated this goal by substituting a desire **to save the theatre in the service of art.** More difficult for me would be Medea's need **to avenge herself for Jason's betrayal,** a need so profound that she is willing to sacrifice her children to prove it. Revenge is alien to me, but if I dig deep I could draw on several events when I, too, was shamefully betrayed and unjustly abandoned, when out of my agony

278

I stirred up *fantasies* of a vengeance horrible enough to become synonymous with Medea's objective.

There are two further categories of objectives which should now be explored. After determining "your" MAIN OBJECTIVE IN THE PLAY, making sure that what follows will be in tune with it, you will hunt for "your" MAIN OBJECTIVE IN EACH SCENE, based on the content, the events, the given circumstances, and "your" relationship to the other characters in the scene. Finally, you will search for "your" IMMEDIATE OBJECTIVES, what it is "you" want from one moment to the next, hinging on the progression of events. To refer back to the example of Blanche DuBois in Chapter 5, in which we assumed that in the life of the play the spine of her character is the need **to find beauty, gentility, tenderness, and protection,** we may discover that her motivating objective in the first scene is **the desire to find a haven** from the storm that has thrown her, not only out of her home and position, but out of the town in which she was raised. To this urgent need we can link each of her immediate objectives: Before entering the apartment, she already has the desire **to present herself as a gentlewoman** to the lowly inhabitants of the neighborhood; during her moments alone, she wants **to refresh herself, to make herself ready for the struggle, to prove herself worthy of acceptance** in her sister's home. Blanche's desire **to reestablish a loving position of authority over her sister** sets in with Stella's entrance. All of the above relates to her need for a haven, as should her ensuing objectives, which will also arise from the developing conflicts in the scene. It is important to note that **an immediate objective stays in effect from the moment of its inception until the wish has been fulfilled or has failed, at which point it will be replaced by another one.**

If any of the above seems complicated, let me make a simpler comparison which might be applied to the objectives of any character in any play: Suppose you are on a journey and have a burning desire to get to the top of a mountain. You are on foot in the valley below and have come to a river that needs to be crossed. Just *wishing* for that, no matter how intensely, will not get you there. You will have to consider all possible means of achieving your wish: swimming, wading, walking on the rocks, using a boat, or finding a bridge. Whichever choice is the most logical under the circumstances will entail its own objectives. If you decide to swim, you will need to discard cumbersome clothes, to fight the rushing currents, to test your endurance. If you wade, you will want to carry your shoes and to deal with the muddy or pebbly river bottom. If you leap from one slippery rock to the next, you will need to keep your balance to protect yourself from falling in. If you decide on the abandoned, leaky boat on the shore, you will have to find the oars or a substitute for them, bail out the water en route to keep from sinking, or, if you choose the bridge, you will have to find it first. The bridge might be the last resort after having tried several (or all) of these means of transport, each of which had failed to fulfill your objective.

If an objective is valid, it will stimulate not only your feelings but the will to do something about it, imaginatively suggesting many possible actions. The definition of the character's actions is, of course, your ultimate goal. Remember to phrase the objectives with an active verb rather than a qualifying noun. (I want **to find beauty**, or, I want to **make things beautiful,** *not,* I want beauty.) It should be clear that *considerations* of the character's overall objectives as well as his main objectives in each scene should be a part of the initial homework. However, the *immediate* objectives can only be discovered and explored during the actual rehearsals, as they arise in the form of *responses* to time, place, the environs, and the *interaction with your partners.*

If any of these aspects of determining "your" needs, wishes, or objectives are new to you, let me assure you that as soon as you put them into practice, they will prove so helpful to the score of the role that it will become second nature to look for them. Don't be pedantic about the definitions; don't mechanize the procedure or feel you must write everything down. Your selections should stimulate your senses and your imagination. They have become such an intuitive part of my own work that I stop to analyze an immediate objective during a rehearsal *only* when I realize that my actions are dry, empty, and unsubstantiated by a true cause or motive.

There is a big difference between what we **want to do** and what we **have to do.** Something that must be done or is supposed to be done is frequently something we *don't* **want to do.** When, in the play, a "don't want" is a logical fact, always ask what it is you really want *instead* of it. If you are so shy or frightened that you *don't* want to look into someone's eyes, you may discover that, instead, you would rather examine the pattern of the carpet. Many times when I knew I *had to* work on this book, I *really* wanted to do a puzzle or watch a TV special. Sometimes I have guiltily given in to the desire. At other times, just to salve my conscience, I have dashed off a few pages before deciding that as a result of an unproductive state of mind, **I needed to relax** with a jigsaw puzzle. Often, I have simply wanted to delay getting down to work, feeling that I first **needed** to tidy the desk, arrange the papers, sharpen each pencil, check the correction fluid, straighten the paper clips, fetch a Pepsi—until I have run out of excuses and knuckled down to the actual task. How I scrub the kitchen when **I revel in it** is totally different from when I furiously want **to take out my resentment** on each spot of grease because I am **supposed to** clean it. In other words, a genuine desire leads to specific action, whereas a negatively posed "must," without an alternative, leads to an inactive, burdensome emotion. The thing you do *not* want may very well be the obstacle you need to overcome in the pursuit of the objective, which will be the subject of the following section, step five.

We have arrived at the final aspect of defining the objectives, differentiating between the character's CONSCIOUS and SUBCONSCIOUS needs. It is not as difficult to understand as it is to put *subjectively* into action. The **conscious objectives of most human beings are aligned with their self-image and sense of morality. Subconscious desires may override or bury the conscious ones. Then, relinquishing the moral censor, we are driven into ignoble behavior, which we try to justify at any cost.** Based on an understanding of yourself, it should not be hard to determine a character's *conscious* objectives. When they are *subconscious*, even though you will soon learn to recognize them as such, you may well wonder how to make them active without remaining objective about them, without standing apart from the character to judge, "look what he's doing." In the previous section, when exploring the relationships, I gave a number of examples that dealt with this matter as it pertains to guilt. One of them was Corie's subconscious need to provoke a showdown with Paul.* I suggested

---

* See page 272.

drawing on events when you, too, wanted to gain approval for hurtful actions, ignoring your better self in the process.

However, when we approach the problem of subconscious needs in a deeper, more complex character, this is not as easy to solve. Let me use *A Month in the Country* for clarification. Written by Turgenev, a precursor of Chekhov, it is one of my favorite plays, and you should study and relish it in any event. There is a devastating scene between its heroine, Natalya Petrovna, and her young ward, Vera, that perfectly illustrates the problem. Natalya is a sensitive, educated woman who has made a marriage of convenience with a kind and wealthy landowner. They have a son who is looked after by servants, and, most recently, by a handsome young tutor from Moscow. Natalya has little to do but amuse herself with daily social routines and the attentions of an ardent admirer. Without consciously admitting to it, she falls feverishly in love for the first time in her life with the tutor. When she discovers that Vera may be infatuated with the tutor and that he may be infatuated with her, she confronts the girl and tries to pawn her off in marriage to an elderly, ugly, rich neighbor. Her desperate but subconscious need is to get Vera out of the way. Her conscious objective is to provide a secure life for her and make sure that the poor little orphan will be well taken care of. Someone who consciously sets about ruining the life of a dependent and helpless person is a monster. Someone who does it subconsciously, out of feelings of vulnerable and personal deprivation, is culpable of a profound human frailty. Later, when Natalya becomes aware of what she's done and that she has broken the girl's heart, she, too, is in despair.

When I first worked on the role, I was baffled about the subtlety of Natalya's chimeric behavior in this scene. As a reader, I felt that the gentility with which she manipulates Vera, victimizes her, apologizes, teases, bullies, pulls rank, coaxes and wheedles her, seemed to be in turn ruthless, funny, awkward, sly, very funny, yet ultimately heartbreaking—a revelation of the passion she herself doesn't understand and is unable to rationalize. Although Natalya is the heroine of the piece, I solved my dilemma in this scene by approaching it as though she would be the antagonist. I gave myself a noble cause to justify each action. I particularized Vera with new eyes as a rival, allowing my needs to supersede an awareness of hers. Of course I had to ensure that the tutor was such a hot object for me that the very mention of his name and recall of his image made my flesh tingle and my heart pound. Then I made myself vulnerable to Vera's extreme youth, innocence, and beauty to further stimulate my jealousy. I particularized her as an upstart, someone beholden to me and ungrateful for my concern about her, giving myself cause to pull rank, to remind her of my sponsorship and kindness to her. Whenever I became too aware of wounding her, I was forced into making light of my behavior or into self-deluding, defensive actions.

I'm not sure whether I tested the following way of working on Natalya or on Martha in *Who's Afraid of Virginia Woolf?* and although I don't recommend it as a rule, when all else fails you might try this alternate way of substantiating a subconscious objective. In early rehearsals, first deal *openly* with the hidden objective, act on every impulse it suggests—whether it be to lash out, belittle, deceive, to aggrandize yourself, to get even, or to execute any other action that will get you what you nakedly want. Then, try honestly to forget it and pursue only what you consciously think you want, in line with the character's moral self-image. The former should, ideally, strongly influence the latter and put the two differing needs into balance.

In conclusion, I hope you have understood that the search for the character's objectives and an identification with them is an essential part of the score of the role.

We have yet to examine that which stands in the way of what we want, the obstacle, which, in an effort to overcome it, will intensify our needs and wishes.

5. WHAT'S IN "MY" WAY?

We already know that CONFLICT is the essence of drama in both comedy and tragedy. Anything worthy of presentation reflects a **human struggle to overcome problems** posed by fate, the world, or society, the particular circumstances and the other people in the life of an individual. The very word *problem* implies the presence of an *obstacle*. The actor should know that by grappling with whatever is *in the way of* what his character wants, with the **obstacle to "his" wishes,** he heightens and intensifies them (remembering that what is easily available is, perversely, rarely as desirable as something difficult to attain). He should know that in the *absence* of a specific problem, there is little to engage one in forward moving action. In most plays the conflicts are so apparent that it is unnecessary to go on a hunt for them. However, their most influential aspects must be explored and particularized, and, when necessary, transferences for them should be made.

In line with the first four steps, you will **determine the obstacles as they relate to the character's overall needs, the main objectives in each scene, and whatever stands in the way of the immediate objectives.** (You will explore them in greater depth whenever they seem elusive or are not self-evident.) For example, the obstacles to Blanche DuBois' overall objective of finding beauty, kindness, and protection can be drawn from the social upheavals in her world, from poverty, and from her sensitivity to brutality. In the first scene, in her search for a haven and for acceptance, her lurid past and fear of its exposure, the nature of the apartment and the absence of a separate room for her are all powerful obstacles. From the moment of her appearance on the street of the Latin Quarter, she faces *problems* of uncertainty about the address, fatigue from the journey, the heat of the day, and the terrifying creatures who accost her on the way. Once in the apartment, almost everything in it becomes an obstacle to readying herself for Stella, a need which, out of panic, she actually verbalizes: "I've got to keep hold of myself!"

Let me again stress that you shouldn't intellectualize or be pedantic about defining "What's in 'my' way?" Considerations for the obstacles will become an instinctive part of your homework and rehearsals. Stop to analyze and make mental or written notes about them *only* when you feel an obstacle is lacking or elusive, that your will is low, or that it is *too* easy to get what you want. Avoid what many contemporary actors seem to enjoy doing: In an effort to be at ease or comfortable, as they put it, they ignore even the most obvious obstacles and, by thus removing the dramatic tension of the scene, end up with irrelevant, naturalistic behavior. Few playwrights provide "comfortable" situations for their characters.

If you had not already understood the importance and function of obstacles or are still uncertain about ways of determining them, let me say in summation that they are an inherent part of everything you *do* on stage—and that they are involved in the exploration of each of the previous four steps. They can be drawn from things in the character's past, from specific character traits, from the events in the play, from the environs, the circumstances, the furnishings and the tangible objects, from the relationships and certain aspects of them such as age differences, and, finally, from their juxtaposition to all three kinds of objectives.

Suppose you are preparing an exercise in which your objective is to get ready for an important date. Your task is to finish your grooming, gather up your coat and bag and depart when the caller is announced. If *nothing* is wrong or in the way, you will most likely get bored while rehearsing and be trapped into a naturalistic presentation during which your main desire will be to feel comfortable and "at ease" on stage. If, on the other hand, your date is a distinguished, elderly gentleman who hates to be kept waiting and has made reservations at a posh restaurant, if you are ravenous because you had skipped lunch, had rushed home twenty minutes later than planned from a frantic work day, if your best blouse has a grease spot, the apartment is so overheated that your makeup streaks while applying it, if the mirror is fogged up, the lipstick cap sticks, your roommate is napping in the next room, one of your antique earrings is missing, etc., etc.—you will certainly know what *to do,* becoming involved both physically and psychologically in the "struggle" to get ready.

When asked "Does there *always* have to be an obstacle?" I reply emphatically, "In the theatre, yes!" To drive my point home, I cite the time when a director asked me to jump up and down to express a moment of joy in a particular scene. I obliged him but felt self-consciously foolish executing this action. Then I decided that *gravity* was the obstacle, preventing me from getting as high into the air as I wanted. I pushed upward toward the unreachable sky and was immediately flooded by a feeling of elation.

6. WHAT DO "I" *DO* TO GET WHAT "I" WANT?

This question is posed as the *final* one in the score of the role *only* because relevant and *conclusive* answers are dependent on the exploration of the previously overlapping phases of work. Of course, **you**

will already have been in action on the hunt for your character's past when you improvised on imagined events such as dressing for an occasion, readying yourself for a meal, for a party, or for bed. Alone and in rehearsals with your partners, you will have *actively* tested the influence *on your behavior* of time, place, the environment, the furnishings, the previous and given circumstances, and those that pertain to your relationships. You will have struggled with the obstacles and tried many ways of fulfilling your wishes. Hopefully, you have understood that whatever is imagined, mentally considered, or thought through should provide stimuli for the body and the soul and **the desire to do something** about it—and that private theorizing or communal intellectual discussions which do *not* do so are fruitless. By now, you should have absorbed something I have stressed in almost every chapter: that you will be engaged in *actions* from the time of your earliest homework until the final work on the score which deals with the selection of the most relevant and revealing of "your" actions, those that will propel "you" through the life of the play.

The true test of your artistry will rest on your *selections* as well as **on the *aliveness* with which you *execute* the character's actions.**

To act means to do. The dictionary says so. Fine actors have learned that this is true. Genius actors have always known it in their bones. And yet, even after many years of training and experience, some actors continue to muddy their behavior and the words, glide over the prescribed actions, and ride through the scenes on the back of their thoughts and feelings. They believe that *emotion* is all; that thoughts, feelings, attitudes, moods, and states of being can be expressed in the absence of actions. Some of them echo the dictum of old pros that "acting is really *re*acting." They confuse cleverly devised "pieces of business" and naturalistic mannerisms with genuine occupation. And the formalists compose a score of illustrative, external actions, which they then execute with forced energy, mechanically, as if by rote. If these complaints sound familiar, if you have heard me repeat them, perhaps for the tenth time, it is because their causes remain so blatantly and rampantly in evidence. *Real* actions, *animated actions* are what I ultimately ask for in my own work, in that of my colleagues, and in that of my students.

If you are still in doubt about the meaning of a real action, reread

Chapter 8, Animation, keeping in mind that **to animate** *means* "to enliven, to put into action." The entire chapter is devoted to this matter. In it I have tried to demonstrate not only what activates the body and the words we speak but also the process of thinking and listening, that **actions are either physical, verbal, psychological, or a combination of all three; they must travel toward a target in order to** *interact* **with the physical, verbal, and psychological actions of others. And what is** *done to you* **by someone or something causes your** *responses,* **your sensations, and your feelings, about which you will want** *to do* **the next thing.**

I have stated that an action must be designated by an active *verb.* If "I want to convince you" to come over to my side of an argument, I might achieve my objective if I try **to persuade** or **to bully, to coax,** or **to implore** you to do so. Rather than asking, "What do I do to get what I want?" it is also possible to ask, "**How** (by what means) do I get what I want?" and find answers such as, "**by persuading, by bullying, by coaxing, or by imploring.**" I personally prefer the use of the verb.

Whichever one of the above approaches you employ, **beware of their** *qualifying adjectives* **which must** *never* **be a part of your considerations.** They are the *result* of the care with which you particularize and make meaningful each person, object, and detail of the circumstances with which you come in contact while in action. Always remember that you cannot get what you want by "gladly," "sadly," "angrily," "smilingly," or "furiously"! Take my previous advice: Cross out such descriptive adverbs in your script, preferably at the first reading. Cross them out until they become illegible, or, if you use a printed version that shouldn't be marked up, omit them when retyping it. All adjectives and adverbs are dangerously influential in predetermining interpretations, interfering with a truthful investigation of the character's needs, responses, and behavior. They will trap you into attitudes rather than allowing for clean actions, and, in my book, "attitudinizing" is a cardinal acting sin. Think of the endless printed versions of plays based on their London or Broadway productions that even include the designer's and stage manager's floor plans, the "blocking" for each scene, and detailed, adverbial descriptions of the behavior and reactions of the original performers. They are open invitations to copy externally that which has already been done and are of benefit only to the noncreative aspects of the community and amateur theatrical ventures that exist throughout the country. Shakespeare trusted and challenged both directors and actors when his only descriptive hints were those of THEY ENTER and EXEUNT.

Actions must be defined in conjunction with steps four and five in the broadest sense, as they relate to the fulfillment of the character's overall objectives and the struggle with the overall obstacles, as they relate to the main objectives in each scene, what "you" do to attain them and how "you" try to overcome the main obstacles; and, of course, as they are influenced by immediate objectives and obstacles from moment to moment.

Remember that you don't have to do the dishes or clean house like a chicken with its head cut off to prove you are in action. You can challenge or wound someone with a *stare* as actively as you would with the stab of a dagger or the thrust of cruel words. **You are truly in action when you are engaged by it, engrossed in it, alert to its target, to the discovery of its consequence, whether it matches your expectations, whether it will succeed or fail.** There is *no room* in a real action for homework, for weighing how it feels, watching how you're doing it, listening to how it sounds, or considering its effect on the audience. You must send and receive while caught up in the imaginatively stimulated circumstances of the play.

The **selection of actions** of which I have spoken, the final work on the score for your role, is dependent on a thorough investigation of the first five steps and the ways in which you have given reality and substance to their various elements in order to bring the character into existence. What you *do* will reveal the body and soul of the new "you." Heed the old adage: "Tell me what a man does and I will tell you who he is." A farmer who comes inside after digging and plowing, who washes up and cleans his fingernails before sitting down to supper, is a different man from the one who sits right down to eat when coming in from the field.

Plato says TO BE IS TO DO. I keep this always in mind when working on a role. I must hunt for everything that will give me knowledge and faith in who "I" am; then I will discover what "I" do. I reserve Socrates' maxim, TO DO IS TO BE, for my performance, knowing that what "I" do is proof of who "I" am.

EPILOGUE

In the early hours of November 5, 1990, my husband, Herbert Berghof, died. For the better part of my life he was my beloved comrade and colleague, a fast friend, always ready to offer compassionate support and help. Unfailingly he clarified the purpose of every venture I might undertake—such as this book. One of the things that flashed through my mind on that traumatic November morning was that, during the past four years, he had read every word of it, argued many points, dissuaded me from dogmatic pronouncements and challenged muddy generalizations, steering me ever back onto a path of pure intent—just as he had done in other phases of our life together. It seemed almost providential that, since these last pages still lay ahead of me, they should become as much a reflection and summary of his principles as of mine.

Echoes of Socrates' and Plato's philosophies, *To do is to be* and *To be is to do*, are to be found throughout history, as in the *Discourses* of Epictetus: "First say to yourself what you would be; and then do what you have to do"; or in Emerson's *Conduct of Life:* "As we are so we do." They are guideposts not only for acting, but for a very way of life. And, since humanism is at the root of our craft, if we honestly and seriously encompass it in our work, a crucial social offering will be in the making. Fine acting is never empty of this purpose.

The good will and noble intentions of the *un*skilled are useless.

Unfortunately, they are as prevalent as is the stagnant state of mediocrity in today's commercial theatre. You will by now understand that the acquisition of superb acting skills is a never-ending labor of love. If your desire is to be a true artist, know that this is a private matter which can be proven only to *yourself* through your efforts to become one. You cannot simply label yourself as such. Only by setting an example, by functioning at our best, can we be of influence in making the theatre a better place. When success or failure is measured solely by one's personal sense of growth, the humiliations to which the actor is so often subjected become inconsequential. The *struggle* to attain perfection is what matters. It includes maintaining innocence (as opposed to cynicism), curiosity (as opposed to smugness), a willingness to question and to search for new answers, the readiness to take risks and the daring to fail. And, if enough of us really mean it, we can join in a *communal* effort to make acting a truly noble profession.

Let me end with the words Herbert pinned on his wall, the words of his mentor, Max Reinhardt:

> I believe in the immortality of the theatre. It is the most joyous hideaway for all those who have secretly put their childhood in their pocket and gone off and away with it to play on to the end of their days.

FOR THE TEACHER

For years I have been bombarded with legitimate questions from teachers who were using my earlier book, *Respect for Acting*, as a practical text for their students, who remained confused about certain areas of the techniques, the exercises, and the applicability of both to the role. I hope I have provided them with the answers in *A Challenge for the Actor*. Of course you will interpret the material in your own way, but, in this book, some of you may find more to *disagree* with, since it is far less general and not at all as "convenient" as the first. It has been my *goal* to leave little room for *mis*interpretation because many teachers (and actors) retain a secret longing for formalistic expression and have tried in the past to bend my meaning to fit—even to justify—their desire. Or they stand with one foot on each side of the fence, failing to see that this muddies *both* issues. Within the full context of *A Challenge* this should no longer be possible.

You will have seen that what I have proposed is based almost entirely on my own discoveries as a functioning actress, on various attempts to solve the problems that confronted me throughout the years when working in private, in rehearsals, and in performance. When I point out an error to students, giving them a reason for it, sometimes including their thoughts at the moment of making it, they seem to wonder if I am a mind reader. "How did you *know* that that was what I was thinking?" It is because, hundreds of times, I have had the same thought when making the identical error for the same reason. In fact, there are few technical gaffes of which I have *not* been guilty. Similarly, I have made countless mistakes as a *teacher* which I now want to share as things to correct or to guard against.

Don't abuse your title, don't pull rank or sit on a throne. I have always heeded my husband's warning that **the teacher's chair is a dangerous one.** It can inflate the ego, make for feelings of omnipotence and a belief that one knows everything. It can lead to a development of coteries, of pseudo-cultism. I always try to remember that my students are my colleagues or potential ones. Don't fall prey to their admiration. Set them on their own feet. Don't allow them to become dependent on you.

And **stay out of their personal lives.** Long ago, while performing for six months in Chicago, I was asked to conduct several classes. When the time came to move on with the tour, I was appalled, not so much by the numbers of students who asked to meet me in private, but by the nature of their complaint: their sobs that they didn't know what they were going to do without me. I felt like a sinner, having failed to give them the solid ground and the tools with which to develop on their own. By changing only *one* tactic, I never faced this problem again. Before, when they used to come to me prior to, during, or after a class with *personal* problems about their love lives, their parents, their finances, jobs, or careers, I had always involved myself sympathetically and offered friendly or motherly advice. Since then, whenever such an occasion arises, I cut them short with a reminder that I am their *acting* adviser and that for help with any personal matter they must go to more appropriate sources—their friends or therapists.

Another aspect of freeing the students from overreliance on the teacher is to develop the *self-evaluation* of their work. I always ask them for it immediately after a presentation of a scene or exercise and *before* I have offered my own criticism. Self-evaluation is an important part of the actor's growth in any event. Since neither teacher nor director is likely to be present at the performances following an opening night, the actors will cease to improve in their parts unless they themselves have learned to recognize their flaws and how to correct them.

This self-criticism need not be brilliantly articulated. At first it will be primitive or even inaccurate. Gradually it will be accompanied by questions with a need for answers to such things as "I lost my faith,"

"I had no privacy," "I couldn't concentrate," "I started rushing," "I was pushing—indicating—anticipating," etc. Often this is followed by "Why?" or possibly by giving a mistaken reason for it. Students are well on their way, however, when they begin to recognize and acknowledge their problems. Only the actor who remains blind to his faults and thinks his presentation was "just great" is in real trouble.

Just as the actor must finally learn how to select the most relevant of his character's actions, so the teacher must be able to select **the most relevant criticism** as it pertains to the individual actor's problems. If you have a sharp eye and ear, it is almost *too* easy to inform the actor about *everything* that was wrong with a presentation. Don't overwhelm him with *all* that he may have failed to incorporate in his score and *all* of his technical errors. This only creates feelings of abject failure and, burdened with too much information, he will not know where to begin or on what to concentrate when he reworks the material.

Criticism based on a concise, pertinent selection of the areas that deal with the particular actor's individual problems should lead him to a positive approach, to making step-by-step progress. Learning how to provide it is probably the most difficult aspect of teaching and remains something I steadily try to improve. If you agree that too much information about what was wrong with a presentaion can have adverse results, you will understand that criticism offered by the *observing* students piled on top of the teacher's evaluation can be devastating to the recipient. I allow it on rare occasions *only* when the judgment is put to *me* (rather than to the performer) and in the form of a question relating directly to a problem of the student offering the criticism. Then the performer will not feel attacked from all sides. Anyone who has ever been on stage should know how vulnerable we are, how exposed we feel at such moments. It should also be unnecessary to add that cruel, derisive, or denigrating attacks have *nothing* to do with constructive criticism.

While on the subject of vulnerability, I ask you to make use of my advice to the actor who misuses emotional recall by trying to tap a shattering past experience, one which he had previously kept hidden, even from himself.* Steer him clear of such dangerous territory. I

* See page 89.

have observed classes in which teachers, without scientific or clinical qualifications, have actually tried to break down a student's psychological defenses by *forcing* him to delve into traumatic experiences such as the death of a parent—all in the name of "emotional exercising." This can easily lead to hysteria or a *new* trauma—now experienced in a classroom. In any event, **it serves no artistic purpose.**

Another common error is **to quarrel with an actor's interpretation** of a role, or, if he has none, to give him one. If you believe that your own is definitive, or the only one, you are not only wrong, but you will stultify the actor's imagination and rob him of creative freedom. Of course, a student should be held to the logic of the playwright's prescriptions and his given circumstances. He must not be allowed to develop habits of bending these to his own will or of conveniently or lazily ignoring them. As long as you lead the actors into their own identification with the author's world, their interpretations will evolve into ones which might even surprise, enlighten, or teach *you* a thing or two.

In my early teaching years, before I understood this, I not only forced my interpretations on the actors but actually *directed* them in the scenes they had prepared, including giving them their physical positioning and line readings. I was pretty good at it, too, so that when I had finished, the actors usually felt secure, even successful upon following my instructions. It took months to realize that I hadn't really taught them *anything,* that they approached each new scene with the identical awkwardness or ineptitude with which they'd begun in the first class. Even worse, they became "hooked" on the "fix" such candy provided, looking dependently on me as their supplier. It was a bitter lesson, one I have never forgotten.

In my many years as a guest teacher of master classes, whatever that means, at colleges, drama schools, and regional theatres, I have observed numerous things I feel should be improved on, some of which are not just the responsibility of a faculty member but of the dean or director of the institution.

I am often appalled by **the conditions of the space provided for my classes** (usually identical to those under which the actors are asked to function with their resident instructor). They will consist of a bare stage, or worse, an empty dance studio, its walls lined by full-length mirrors and dance barres, or a classroom cluttered with desks that face a narrow platform, or with a few feet cleared to make room for a bench, a table, and a few chairs. When the teacher tells me that they have been working on scenes and my exercises in these places, I assure them that it had to have been *impossible*. To me it is comparable to a claim that you have taught painting without paper, canvas, easels, paints, or brushes. Or that you have conducted cooking lessons without bowls, pots, knives, spoons, chopping blocks, and the ingredients of recipes.

Here, then, are my urgent suggestions for the *prerequisites* of an actor's space, for a studio, workshop, atelier, stage, or classroom. **Whatever it may be, it should serve as a laboratory.** There should be basic furniture such as a couch or settee, an armchair, benches, table and chairs, a coffee table, a bed or cot, or both. (I use a platform of double-bed height and width, with a mattress that can also be used on the floor. The bare platform can serve other purposes.) There should also be a desk, a bureau with drawers, one or two standing shelves, and small tables of differing heights. Such furnishings can be borrowed or purchased from the Salvation Army. If you can't swipe a discarded refrigerator, stove, and sink from the street before the garbage collector picks them up, then substitute a cabinet for the fridge, use a table or bureau for the stove, and put a basin and dish rack on a table to create a sink. Put heavy furniture on casters for easy mobility. You will need three movable, standing wooden frames, one including a workable door, one for a room divider, and, ideally, one with a workable window frame. The back of the room should have prop shelves containing such basics as a lamp or two, a telephone, pillows, a blanket, books and magazines, and a telephone directory, some pots and pans, dishes, flatware, a coffeepot, an alarm clock, perhaps an ironing board, and so forth.

It is up to the individual actor to bring the personal items he may need for a particular scene or exercise, those which he knows are not supplied by the studio, such as special items of clothing, a sheet or pillowcase, cosmetics, a toothbrush or a razor, a particular book or a letter or a vase, etc.—important things on which his selected actions may depend.

A backstage area from which to enter and exit can be created by hanging a simple burlap curtain on a rod with rings so it can be drawn back and forth to divide the prop area from the playing area. Preferably, the curtain should consist of several panels. Or you might use folding screens instead.

Once you have found or created a place that fulfills these requirements, the actors are free to cook on all four burners. Make yourself and the other faculty members, even your students, responsible for establishing such basic conditions. If your institution is poor, a leaky roof, insufficient heat, or a beat-up floor are inconsequential, and hand-me-down wobbly furniture or props can be repaired and made to function. Once the actors become familiar with the workplace and the objects in it, they will quickly learn how to re-create their own rooms in it or to establish a valid setting for their scenes.

Obviously, there should be a seating area for the observing students.

By working within the framework of all the realities implicit in these furnishings, students may eventually arrive at the point of eliminating what is *not* necessary, at *selective* reality, finally developing the heightened realities with which they will one day be able to imaginatively enliven an *empty* space.

Based on my observation of the training offered by other teachers, I have found that classes dealing with improvisations and exercises, even when brilliantly taught, are too often conducted as ends in themselves. The principles they should instill, the reflexes they should establish in the actor for such things as spontaneous give-and-take, the development of a sensory physical life, the strengthening of focused concentration, expansion of the imagination, etc., are too often forgotten when it comes time to work on a play—almost as if the work were a separate, unrelated entity. I look for and expect students to incorporate the purpose of each and every one of my exercises in their scene work in the course of their progress and remind them of it whenever they have failed to do so.

I am fully aware that a university's obligation is to provide budding artists with a rounded humanistic education, and that, in the drama department, this includes classic dramatic literature. *Of course* they should be made to study these plays until they understand, not just their relevance to the time in which they were written, but to their own society and their own lives. On the other hand, asking them to *perform* in them before they are technically, physically, verbally, or

psychologically ready to fulfill them will have most of the dire presentational consequences of which I have spoken throughout this
book. I *implore* you to let the actors work on, practice, and perform
material which echoes the familiar world around them, whose content stimulates their minds and souls, that has a meaning for them
that they will *want* to express. Stick to the plays in which they can
explore truthful human behavior to develop their inner and outer
techniques. Later, when they have absorbed these techniques, they
will be ready to put them to use in the classics. If the intent of a drama
department is to prepare the students for the acting *profession*, it does
them a terrible disservice to cast them as Romeo, Juliet, or the Nurse,
as Hamlet, Gertrude, or Polonius, Hedda Gabler, John Gabriel
Borkman, Saint Joan, or the Dauphin or—King Lear! You will force
them back into amateur techniques and cripple their instruments. The
more often they play such parts in productions, the more they turn
into "rehabilitation cases." Even worse, great roles will have been
ruined for them if the opportunity should arise to play these parts in
the future, because each false move and intonation they had made will
be etched in their memories and stuck in their bones. If your dean or
director *insists* on classical productions, at least stay with less demanding plays such as *The Two Gentlemen of Verona.*

Almost as an afterthought, I offer you a suggestion, one which I
cannot back up practically because I have never seen it attempted. In
fact, it refutes my previous convictions about **training for teenagers
and for the very young.** In the past, when parents or teachers have
asked my advice about appropriate classes for talented youngsters, I
based my answer on the belief that their *acting* classes should be
limited to improvisations and exercises, that in addition they should
be guided by work in the *related* performing arts of dance and music;
that they can develop their bodies and kinetic sensibilities through
modern dance or ballet, learning the necessity for discipline along the
way. Noncontact sports are also valuable. Their voices and a good ear
can be trained in singing classes and choral groups and, when they
themselves are sufficiently motivated, they can take speech classes.
All of this I still believe.

My reasons for discouraging their participation in scene study or in
performances or in *any* class that emphasizes performing have always

been based on the damage that can be done. During their formative years, young people are so impressionable, so ready to imitate, so prone to picking up affectations and acquiring mannerisms, so self-conscious, and *so* unready to come to grips with their own psyches, let alone with that of characters in plays, that they are easily trapped into illustrations, external forms, and a desire to show off for an audience, their teacher, or their fellow students—*particularly* when they are gifted. Rather than building reflex habits of truthful behavior and animated interaction, while observed, the opposite becomes ingrained. (Only a handful of professional child actors have survived to make it in the theatre as adults!)

Recently, while reworking the proposals for my exercises, it suddenly occurred to me how useful they might be for teenagers, even for younger children. Such things as destination, entrances and exits, establishing a fourth side, making physical endowments, finding the sensory aspects of conditioning forces, creating the outdoors, even an exploration of historical imagination could become a positive adventure for them—everything drawn from their personal experiences. And learning how to establish aliveness **within the magic circle** of the imaginative world they have created when **presenting the work** to their teacher and classmates might instill the same principles that apply to the techniques of mature adults. And if discipline can be established for youngsters in a ballet class, I don't see why an acting class should always be conducted as though it were a game! These budding ideas are shared with you humbly, without any knowledge of their results.

Let me make one final observation. Don't allow applause in the workroom. The actors must always keep in mind that they are not there to perform for a paying audience or to impress the teacher or their colleagues—but to learn a noble craft.

INDEX

ABOUT THE AUTHOR

Uta Hagen was born in Germany, then she moved to the United States, where her father was head of the Art History Department at the University of Wisconsin in Madison. Her first role was as Ophelia in Eva Le Gallienne's production of *Hamlet*. She then played the role of Nina in the Lunts' production of *The Sea Gull*. She has also appeared in *Key Largo, A Streetcar Named Desire, The Country Girl, Saint Joan*, and *Who's Afraid of Virginia Woolf?* She has recently appeared on "American Playhouse" for PBS, and among her recent films is *Reversal of Fortune*. She was married for more than forty years to Herbert Berghof, the internationally known director, actor, and teacher. Uta Hagen lives in New York City.